Dressing Up

DRESSING UP

Menswear in the Age of Social Media

Joshua M. Bluteau

berghahn
NEW YORK • OXFORD
www.berghahnbooks.com

First published in 2022 by
Berghahn Books
www.berghahnbooks.com

Library of Congress Cataloging-in-Publication Data

Names: Bluteau, Joshua M., author.
Title: Dressing up : menswear in the age of social media / Joshua M. Bluteau.
Description: New York : Berghahn Books, 2022. | Includes bibliographical references and
  index.
Identifiers: LCCN 2021028788 (print) | LCCN 2021028789 (ebook) |
  ISBN 9781800732766 (hardback) | ISBN 9781800732773 (ebook)
Subjects: LCSH: Men's clothing—Social aspects. | Social media—Influence. | Fashion
  merchandising. | Masculinity.
Classification: LCC GT1710 .B58 2022 (print) | LCC GT1710 (ebook) |
  DDC 391/.1—dc23
LC record available at https://lccn.loc.gov/2021028788
LC ebook record available at https://lccn.loc.gov/2021028789

British Library Cataloguing in Publication Data

A catalogue record for this book is available from the British Library

ISBN 978-1-80073-276-6 hardback
ISBN 978-1-80073-277-3 ebook

For André, Patricia, Raynette and Roy

CONTENTS

ILLUSTRATIONS

PREFACE

It is hard to be unimpressed by the miracle of tailoring: how a set of figures read off a measuring tape and translated into a paper pattern, becomes something that almost lives – a second skin in which to feel supremely comfortable.
—Nick Foulkes, 'The Bespoke Experience', 2016

The anthropology of clothing and adornment is a disparate field which has received irregular attention. Indeed, the first authoritative anthology on the subject has only just been published as I prepare the final manuscript for this book (Luvaas and Eicher 2019). However even here, this compendium of prior and current anthropological thought on the subject fails to address menswear, avant-garde fashion or the implications of social media on anthropological understandings of dress and fashion in any depth. Cole has long noted the lack of academic work concerning menswear (Cole 2000: 1–9; see also Cole and Lambert 2021). Hansen (2004: 369–70) confirms this omission, suggesting that dress has long been seen as merely symbolic or semiotic in a larger theoretical analysis, while Luvaas and Eicher (2019: 3) concur, suggesting that while fashion is 'fine when it is a part of what we study', it can be met with condescension when 'it is the focus of our study'. It is this gap which this book fills, demonstrating how, far from being an oddity, the anthropology of dress, fashion, clothing and adornment is vital to the understanding of a raft of broad thematic tropes, including self-making, individuality, (in) visibility and the digital landscape.

The fieldwork for this book began in the latter months of 2015 and initially ran for two years. Since that time the world has changed and as the final proofs of this manuscript are prepared the world is still in the grips of the Coronavirus pandemic. This has brought an entirely different lens to two of the key themes of this book – dressing up and the presentation of self online. With self-isolation and working from home these activities have taken on a new relevance, with the typical boundaries of home violated by the gaze of work colleagues and an increased focus on the presentation of one's self in the digital world being thrust unwittingly into the daily lives of many. Sartorially menswear has suffered casualisation in many areas, although many of the characters in this book have continued to present themselves online dressed beautifully in spite of, and in response to the unfolding situation. Post-pandemic, it is difficult to predict how life will return to normal both digitally and terrestrially, but this book is in the fortunate position of offering a window into the past, insights into the present and hope for the future in equal measure.

INTRODUCTION

Men Who Shop

> Although male heads of state wear suits at summit meetings, male job applicants wear them to interviews, and men accused of rape and murder wear them in court. . . the pants-jacket-shirt-and-tie costume, formal or informal, is often called boring or worse. . . but men's suits are neither post-modern nor minimalist, multicultural nor confessional – they are relentlessly modern, in the best classical sense.
>
> —Ann Hollander, *Sex and Suits*

This morning I woke from a dream filled slumber. I stirred, and the extraneous limbs that fell beyond the comforting protection of the blankets felt a soft, gently-cooling breeze meander its way in through the open window. Dave (the monstera gigantea) cautiously steadied himself in the new morning light like a drunk who thought he could get away with hiding the excesses of last night's revelry and the hackles on my neck responded to the ingress of new oxygen. Beyond the window the builders had arrived at the half-built skyscraper next door – a skeletal hand reaching into the clouds. The sonorous sounds of angle grinders on steel and scaffolding being dropped cut through the last vestige of sleep, letting the dream filled world I had been enjoying spool out of my head like letting go of a full, untied balloon. Try as I might, no amount of grasping in the gloom could bring back the dreams, once so vivid, that had whizzed across the room into intangible nothingness.

Swinging my legs out of bed I stood, felt the blood rush to my head, and sat down again defeated. Reeling slightly, I retrieved my iPhone from the bedside table and squinted as the black rectangle lit up with a slew of bright vivid colours, shocking my retinas into consciousness. This momentary orbital distress was quickly forgotten as I saw a series of affirming notifications laid out in neat rows. The image I had posted to Instagram the night before had amassed 74 likes while I slept, a new personal record. The digital version of myself had been abroad, seen in America, South Korea and a handful of European countries while the tousled haired offline me slept. I stood again, this time with more purpose, and moved toward the wardrobe. Getting dressed had once been a haphazard event but over the past two years I have thought more about clothes than I thought possible, with my wardrobe growing corpulent as a result.

I reached into the dark folds and felt around, gently passing my hand over the shoulders of the assembled jackets that waited patiently on the rail. Textures passed under my fingertips, coarse tweed, soft cotton, stiff denim, ridged corduroy and luxurious velvet. After lingering over a particular linen favourite I gave the subtly textured shoulder a nostalgic squeeze and then found it – sartorial salvation – right at the end of the rail: an unassuming black suit made of achingly soft moleskin that made me smile quite uncontrollably when my fingertips brushed over the short pile of the cloth. My concerns about what to wear that day were banished to the dark, like the dreams that preceded them.

Pulling the soft suit from its wooden hanger, I threw the jacket gently on the bed – it looked back at me mischievously, crumpled and demure – while I slid into the matching trousers, slim as a pair of skinny jeans. Pulling a shirt from the same tailor from a drawer, I slipped the soft fabric over my head and fastened the cuffs with black mother of pearl buttons that felt cool under my fingers. The slightly stretchy fabric (cotton with just a hint of Lycra) shimmered in the reflected light of the still glowing smartphone screen. One might almost have mistaken it for silk but it was even more comfortable next to the skin, a masterstroke of cloth selection. The Cuban collar sat flat against my chest, like a luxurious pyjama, and as I slid my arms into the unlined jacket I felt an instant comfort as the soft fabric enrobed me, banishing the chill from the cool morning air.

The jacket fitted like a second skin, somehow touching the whole of my torso, yet without clinging in any one place, simply hanging beautifully from the tips of my shoulders. As I cast my eyes down on to the subtle details of the cuffs, cloth and collar I remembered why it was one of my favourites. The cuffs were secured with a single button, larger that the three or four smaller buttons one would typically find on a suit jacket's cuff. There was a working buttonhole and where the sleeve ended at my wrist, the edge of the cuff was bound in obsidian-black silk grosgrain ribbon, with the hand stitches visible on the inside of the cuff.

Fastening the jacket at my natural waist, I stood in front of the floor length mirror and reflected on how my form was framed by the simplicity of the all black outfit. The jacket appeared to be a three roll two closure – a three-button front, where the top button is part of the lapel that rolls away, giving the elegance of a two-button cut with the versatility of a three. Yet as I popped the collar, thumbs brushing the black suede where usually there would be melton, I smiled back at myself as the hidden buttons under the lapel became visible and the option for a five-button closure and Nehru collar peeked out at me. Diverted by the playfulness of my plain black suit I absentmindedly pulled back the bedroom curtain and stared out at the autumnal city.

Unlike the majority of my suits, the one I was currently inhabiting was almost entirely unstructured. There was no shoulder padding, canvassing or lining (bar the sleeves). This form of soft tailoring is supremely comfort-able, but lacks the feeling of insulation and impregnability offered by heavi-er-weight tailoring. These qualities were not needed indoors, but as I stood by the window and the wind exercised a gaggle of troubled umbrellas below I realised a little more insulation would be needed before I ventured outdoors. Moving back to the wardrobe I rummaged for a coat and pulled out a suitably intemperate offering. This piece of tailoring was far more structured and as I slid my arms into the thick wool sleeves, this time over my jacket, the coat fell heavily over my frame, grazing the backs of my knees and weighing down on my shoulders with a gentle thump as it slid into place like a pair of paternal hands.

I ventured down onto the street, pausing at the threshold to take a number of photographs with my iPhone. These selfies would be reviewed later and posted to Instagram at my leisure; I made sure to include some variation displaying different facets of my outfit so that I could post multiple times, commenting on different aspects of this look. Ignoring the bemusement of several passers-by, I finally slid my phone into the inside pocket of my suit jacket where the tailor's label bearing a secret message was hidden: Spencer Hart sincerely hopes you get laid in this product.

What are you wearing? I have told you how I got dressed this morning but what about you? This is not a sordid enquiry or sarcastic insult but a genuine question – a question that has become even more important as an object of anthropological study with the advent of the increasingly globalised phenomenon of social media. There are many words in English for the objects we use to cover our bodies from dress, clothing and attire through to apparel, garments and costume and even slang like clobber, gear, togs and threads. Yet these terms do not linguistically define individual garments or details of garments; for this the lexicon is vast. From civvies and mufti to lounge suits and morning dress, spaces, events and class can be navigated through an understanding of the dressed body. So I reiterate the question. What are you wearing, right now? Or perhaps why are you wearing it? This may seem simple but is it? Throughout life we learn how to successfully navigate social spaces, and the right kind of costume that we must wear to be admitted and thrive in certain social spheres. Even those who defy convention do so with an awareness of these rules. Life is a performance, and whether you are a dedicated follower of fashion, or not, we all wear clothes that, no matter how hard we try, will to some extent define us.

Yet here we reach the rub. For some people, each morning's transformation from undress to dressed marks a set of carefully choreographed decisions vital to their self-making, yet for others it is a far less marked endeavour with clothes scattered on the floor being pulled on with little more than a weary shrug. This disparity between those who live to get dressed and those who get dressed to live, is central to a whole host of magazines, advertisements and other media, with the assertion that those who dress well will be more successful in their work life, social life and love life. Yet despite this all pervading narrative surrounding being well dressed, western menswear has for the most part evaded scholarship.

In this book I combine ethnographic accounts of meeting tailors and attending fashion shows with the purchasing and wearing of garments as methodology to rethink why we wear what we wear. The journey has been interesting and I have worn many strange and flamboyant combinations of clothes as I have travelled it, with outfits frequently garnering comment from strangers, ranging from the rude – 'why are you wearing that hat' – to the admiring – 'sir, that is the maddest jacket I've seen in a long time'. Dress which stands out serves to empower the wearer, as one can dictate one's visibility in space. Yet such a move can disempower in equal measure, leaving one at the mercy of the gaze.

It is this phenomenon which drew me to tailoring and the reason why tailored menswear dominates this book. The suit can equally empower and disempower depending on the context, wearer and suit in question. A suit can be invisible in a room full of suits or stand out if it is made of a vibrant fabric. Cost may have some impact on this, but then again it may not. What if a bespoke suit originally retailing at between two and three thousand pounds and handmade for a specific client is later sold for fifty pounds to someone else? This is the case for the Spencer Hart suit I describe in the opening vignette, that I acquired during my fieldwork from the online auction website eBay. Does this change how the wearer is perceived, and why do some men choose to spend such large sums of money on fairly unremarkable clothing, which only a few others will notice?

Further to these questions, this book also moves beyond the world of wardrobes, workshops and catwalks, into the digital world of Instagram where many of these tiny tailored details are photographed in high definition and posted for other users to enjoy. This book is the first to take Instagram, the image sharing social media platform, as a primary anthropological fieldsite, providing a timely commentary on our digitised modernity, but also allowing the online and offline worlds surrounding fashion and personal representation to be approached as a single cohesive field. Many of the themes of this book will be things you already intrinsically know, whether it's the instinctual revulsion at the thought of wearing hot pants to a funeral or the horror of turning up to a black tie event wearing a Hawaiian shirt. Have you ever been refused entry into a club for wearing the wrong kind of shoes, or felt overdressed at a party? This book may not answer these specific questions, but I hope it will give you a chance to reflect more broadly on what you are wearing and why. By the end of the book, I can guarantee one thing, you will never look at a man in a suit in the same way.

I hope that the same is true for selfies and Instagram posts. This book ventures into a digital world with a plethora of available images of every conceivable type to view at one's leisure – a 'post-scarcity' space (Slater 2000: 123). The sensation of using a platform such as Instagram is that there are infinite images to consume, a factor which irrespective of thematic genre radically changes the manner in which notions of self, identity and personhood are constructed. This is something worth considering when we look around ourselves, on the train or at a neighbouring café table, where hunched digital consumers endlessly scroll. This has become a familiar sight, and perhaps the repetitive nature of this scrolling speaks to the endless sensation of content, but also the dissatisfactory nature of digital communication. Miller notes that 'people do not regard sending an e-mail greeting card as satisfactory as being there when one's child blows out the candles. . . They do, however, understand that an animated and personalized egreeting card is much better than no card at all' (Miller 2003a: 17). The key idea here is that digital communication is a 'better class of substitute' (idem). However, my work on the digital platform Instagram differs subtly from this avenue of analysis as it does not directly replace a previous form of communication or technology. There are elements of other technologies that it incorporates such as photography, postcards, letters and the publication of images found in fashion magazines, but Instagram is not a direct substitution of anything, yet it is highly compulsive: but why is looking at other men's clothing so engaging?

Whether it's a beautifully tailored suit or an old pair of jeans, scuffed trainers or those shoes you can hardly walk in (but look fantastic when you sit down), the visible nature of dress is abundantly clear. However, by bridging the online and offline world, this issue becomes more complex. The notion of visibility and invisibility in the digital world is one which has been noted by Horst (2009: 107), who suggests that digital social media gives access to spaces which would otherwise be invisible, such as into one's bedroom. Yet

Instagram is more pernicious than this, with a lens that lives in our pockets and offers a view that often only one who had violated our personal space would be able to achieve. I concur with Horst (idem) that this implies a blurring of the boundaries identified by Goffman (1980) between public and private spaces, but I would go further than this to suggest that smartphones have established themselves in the lives of heavy users to such an extent that they become a cybernetic object of intimacy. For users who take their smartphone to the bathroom, place them on their bedside tables during moments of extreme intimacy, diarise their lives through them, and never let them run out of battery, there is not only an intimacy in the relationship crafted between phone and user – usually reserved for lovers or family – but a curiously perturbing agency exerted by that combination of screen, lens and speaker that is at best symbiotic and at its most sinister parasitic.

The lens that Instagram offers, teamed with the kind of user this book is concerned with, highlights the clothes we wear as aesthetic objects of desire. Yet this is not a universal way of engaging with the clothes that we wear. The term depth ontology (see Miller and Woodward 2012: 89–120) has been used to explore whether the clothes we wear are a true representation of who we are – a shallow or surface ontology – or whether the true nature of ourselves lies deeper within. Miller and Woodwood's (2012: 89) work on denim explores this idea, and they give blue jeans the moniker of the 'post-semiotic garment'. This concept is used to explore why people choose to wear intellectually invisible garments, as blue jeans are labelled, as well as the layers of meaning that can be read through one's decisions to shop in particular shops and wear specific garments. For these blue jean wearing participants of Miller and Woodward's (idem) work the thought of wearing semiotically loud garments engenders a palpable sense of concern, drawing on the fear that they will be judged as superficial by others for trying to define themselves through their dress. This book sits at the other end of the spectrum, as for my informants the invisible denim is treated with vehement repugnance and contempt. These individuals actively seek out unusual or flamboyant tailoring and these semiotically loud garments and their wearers allow for the often facile interpretation of western menswear to be explored. That is not to say that certain tailoring is post-semiotic. Indeed, an off the peg black suit worn at a funeral could be conceptualised in this way. Such a suit can render the wearer devoid of discussion as to their sartorial inclinations, instead presenting the world with a uniformed body ready to perform the tasks required without distraction. This is why the suit is ubiquitous, worn by heads of state and those on trial for murder (Hollander 1994: 3), yet a bespoke suit, or one made by one of the tailors I have worked with, are hugely semiotic objects, and far from being invisible become an indispensable part of an individual wearer's performance (see Bluteau 2021: 68).

The semiotics of dress and the complexities of visibility have long been established in menswear, yet often symbols can only be read by those who are part of the same network. This is the case for homosexual men who have historically dressed to make their sexual orientation invisible to others (Cole 2000: 59–69) and visible to each other (Cole 2013: 135–65). Such nuance has not been lost on designers, nor the way in which men present themselves, with historical garments and cues from subculture frequently re-emerging on catwalks and high streets. Yet for all of this reinterpretation there is still a deeply engrained suspicion of men who do not fit within the bounds of typical dress for the time. Even in the world of formalwear there are strict rules and well used adages that accompany wearers of certain objects that breach these guidelines. 'No brown in town' is a prime example, urging men not to wear brown coloured clothing such as tweeds in the city, though this phrase is now more often limited to an assault on those who wear brown shoes with lounge suits. Shoes have their own mythology, certain shapes are seen as staid, others daringly racy, and one friend during my fieldwork recalled a cautionary tale told by a fearsome housemistress while at school, urging her to beware of men with overly shined shoes – who would employ such footwear to see up her skirt. Whilst I have doubts about the practicalities of this, perhaps it speaks to a broader suspicion towards men overly invested in their appearance – an allusion again to depth ontology.

Yet for all this rhetoric about the rules of menswear and the numerous books, blogs and media outlets that reinforce such patterns, there is equally a growing presence advising how to break these rules, and how to break them correctly. This is naturally just an extension of the previous 'rules' and a relaxing of certain diktats, yet it is in this space that many of the Instagrammers I work with reside. Despite this sartorial evolution, it appears that many men actively police their dress to avoid being seen as not conforming to 'masculine norms' (Barry 2017). This is particularly noticeable for men who are inclined to dress in a more flamboyant or exuberant manner than their work colleagues who have been observed to choose 'dark jackets in lieu of colorful tops when . . . interviewing for a promotion' (idem). Approaching the layered nature of both physically and intellectually clothing the male body will form a thread that is drawn throughout this book, tying together the online and offline fieldsites by concentrating on the presentation of the self in this blended single field.

The fieldwork for this book employed a blended approach, with individual methods for both the terrestrial and digital aspects of my research being used to complement each other. This allowed me to develop a comprehensive methodology which provided me with the ability to move between terrestrial and digital fieldsites without treating them as distinct separate entities, assisted by supplementing my research diary with a large number of digital images. My fieldwork is not truly multi-sited or even fully multi-local, but the blend of terrestrial and digital methodologies employed calls for an acknowledgment of this book as a study with a quasi multi-local approach, perhaps best described as multi-dimensional. As a result of this I developed a blended methodology termed immersive cohabitation (see Bluteau 2019) that prioritised producing digital content as a means of cohabiting in the digital space.

It is worth noting at this point that I use the terms digital and terrestrial in this book as a means of labelling the online and offline worlds in which I conducted my fieldwork. The term digital is used over other possibilities such as virtual as it is used by both my informants and other digital anthropologists, while the choice of the term terrestrial is carefully chosen and specific to the context of my research. It conveys being temporally and geographically bounded, contrasting the digital, but does not imply the same disconnect inherent in the terms online and offline. It became apparent very quickly that this was not a useful way of engaging with a post-digital field where the online and offline worlds were so deeply enmeshed into each other that it was impossible to separate the two. Consequently, I developed a blended approach, combining terrestrial and digital research, both given equal prominence, to mirror the world in which I situated my research, one where the presence of my informants in the digital world was impossible to ignore.

At the start of my fieldwork I began by approaching tailors, initially by email and later in person; this led me to engage with a small number of tailors who were happy to talk to me. I repeatedly visited their shops, observed them at work and conducted informal interviews throughout the course of my fieldwork, typically with notes being written up afterwards. The tailors that allowed me access were Mark Powell, Joshua Kane, and Gieves and Hawkes. In addition to this I also spent time visiting shops, acquainting myself with areas of London and purchasing garments which I would later wear during the course of my research. This included incorporating notions of walking through the city (Lee and Ingold 2006; Yi'En 2014), taking photographs as a complementary form of narrative to the traditional field diary (Irving 2010) and dressing in a similar style to my informants (Coffey 1993, 1999). Furthermore, I managed to obtain invitations to a number of fashion shows from the tailors Joshua Kane and Sir Tom Baker which I attended.

As I began fieldwork in the terrestrial world, I set up an Instagram account to begin complementary digital fieldwork. This Instagram account, set up under the name @anthrodandy, enabled me to view the digital content being produced by the tailors I met in person, but it also afforded me access to a wider network of other tailors, manufacturers and retailers. At this point I identified myself as a researcher in my Instagram bio and made the ethical decision to only engage with open access accounts. As I delved deeper into the digital world, I began to discover clients of tailors, who became visible through the interactions that take place in Instagram; I followed them too. This practice of following those whom I believed had links, either in the terrestrial world or shared interests in tailoring and sartorial matters, eventually led me to a network of interconnected individual accounts where I conducted my primary digital fieldwork. Initially, this amounted to a kind of digital participant observation – using my smartphone screen as a portal into this digital world – but it quickly became clear that in order to gain a fuller insight I needed to move beyond this and work as an observing participant (see Holy 1988; Wacquant 2004; Luvaas 2016).

I began to produce content which I posted on my Instagram account. This was inspired by, and to a certain degree imitated, the images that I had observed from the accounts that I was following. I set a goal of posting one image every day, a goal which I did not meet in the early days of my digital research as often I could not think what to post – or what the network would find interesting. However, as the number of hours I spent online increased, I attempted to produce regular unique content as often as I could, and in the later stages of my digital fieldwork I sometimes posted multiple images in the same day. This process of conceiving, capturing and posting images on a regular basis formed a key facet of my methodology. In the early stages of my fieldwork, I observed that many of the tailors I followed were prodigious users of social media, regularly updating their followers as to their stock levels, current outfit, and what they were doing that day, often posting multiple images in any given day, practically every day. These included photos of their shops, new items of tailoring they were working on, and, most frequently, images of their current outfit, a trend that accounted for the majority of published images in the digital network I worked with.

As a reaction to this realisation, I began posting images of myself in various outfits to Instagram. This became crucial to my methodology, as through this digital fieldwork I did not merely observe my participants, but actively engaged in the same processes that they undertook on a daily basis. I completed twelve months of terrestrial fieldwork, returning on a small number of occasions over the following year to attend fashion shows. In contrast, I completed twenty-four months of digital fieldwork, published 850 images, and continued working online once I had returned from my terrestrial fieldsite and begun the process of writing this book. Given the length of time it had taken to establish myself in the digital world, with most of the connections and insight only coming after the first year of interaction, this extension to my digital fieldwork was invaluable.

One Sunday morning, early in my fieldwork, I was perched on the narrow bench, pressed to the shop front at what would become one of my favourite coffee shops – the Flat White. Typically, Berwick Street in London's Soho is thronged with bustling stalls but on Sundays the market is closed and the street takes on both a visual and olfactory calmness. Despite being devoid of the customary sumptuous scents of the street food vendors from Afghanistan, the Caribbean, Spain and others, the overwhelming aroma of freshly ground coffee surrounded me in a cloud of caffeinated air every time the shop door opened. One of the joys of conducting fieldwork in London is the people watching, and the excellent coffee. This was a particularly fine cup. Served in a short glass, perhaps three or four inches tall, with a knurled fluted pattern pressed into the glass where my fingertips nestled comfortably. This double espresso was unlike anything I had tasted before. The dark brown, almost black liquid had a creamy coloured head and as it touched my lips and the hot black liquid ran through the crema into my mouth, I tasted coffee as it should be for the first time. Acid first, fresh lemon zest cut through the bitterness of the potent drink. A burst of toasted almonds and then just a hint of burnt sugar slowly fading to warmth made up of the intense flavour of coffee. Finally, as the slightly oily residue from that first mouthful left a coating on the inside of my mouth, I took a breath, and the city air mixed with the last vestige of that mouthful – analogous to that earthy headiness that one gets from trudging through autumnal leaf litter.

I had been perched on the rickety bench for about fifteen minutes sipping gently at the aforementioned beverage, watching tourists and locals go about their daily pursuits, when I saw him. Looking up from my glass I saw a figure walking up the street on the opposite pavement from where I sat. This tall and lanky gentleman, instantly stood out from the others meandering down the street. His gait was purposeful, long legs making easy progress, with a confident swagger. The lollop that began at his shoulders radiated through his strides and seemed to carve its own path through space. A shock of ginger-orange hair surmounted his frame with punkish spikes twitching in the breeze.

My eyes followed the man, entranced. He was wearing black skin-tight jeans over metallic red boots that had a severely pointed toe and cuban heel. Over this ensemble he wore a long black topcoat. Longer than a jacket with a cutaway front taking style cues from the morning coat and frock coat. Yet this garment was wilfully modern, a beautifully almost viciously tailored coat that was cut close to the body and featured a myriad of handcrafted details from top stitched lapels, a pointed rear collar, leather trim and metal skulls at the cuffs. Before I could take any more in he had walked on, and the details had begun to blur. I watched him until he disappeared out of sight and then realised – I knew who it was. Reaching into my pocket I pulled out my phone and searched for an article I had recently read about London's best bespoke tailors who were not situated on Savile Row. The 'Savile Rogues', described by the article, featured the man I had just seen – Sir Tom Baker. I finished my coffee and went to find his shop.

Throughout London there exist many small tailor's shops, and if you are lucky enough to walk past them you can see all sorts of items on display, from traditional window displays to the more avant-garde and even ceremonial military uniforms. On London's famous street of establishment tailors, Savile Row, mannequins are typically festooned with tweed jackets, evening suits and seasonal accessories. These range from the accoutrements of society events to seasonal offerings such as quilted smoking jackets and cream linen suits. A walk from Savile Row in Mayfair to one of London's other districts, such as Soho or Shoreditch, would lead you to similar tailor's shops. However, if you looked through the gleaming plate-glass windows a little more closely you might get the sense that these shops cater to a slightly different client, one equally concerned with quality and production, but looking for something a little different. In Soho, Mark Powell's shop is full of three-piece gangster inspired, modernist and neo-Edwardian suits in a variety of hues, ranging from sober greys to bright purples. A little deeper into Soho's winding alleys there is Sir Tom Baker, whose shopfront bay window is topped with a huge silver skull and typically features suits in garish fabrics, including sequins and lamé, sometimes deconstructed, or distressed with a shotgun blast. Walking into this dark shop you will find punk inspired accessories and long black fur-collared coats, and if you were to take a peek inside one of his jackets you might find the words FUCK OFF stitched in large letters into the lining. A little further from Savile Row is the nouveau-cool Shoreditch, home of tailor Joshua Kane, a relative newcomer to the world of bespoke tailoring but one who is rapidly making his presence known. Gazing through the windows at the front of Joshua Kane's shop is akin to a looking into a brightly lit wonderland; handcrafted umbrellas hang from the ceiling, and rails of exotic prints and wildly pigmented woven fabrics, tailored into tight fitting short-cut jackets or dramatic long overcoats, hang on rails and clothe the mannequins that stand in the window wearing signature wide-brimmed hats and mirrored sunglasses. Despite the riot of colour and pattern this shop still maintains an achingly calm coolness, and somehow manages to evoke a minimalistic aesthetic, despite the exuberant fabrics on display.

Before beginning fieldwork in London I lived briefly in Oxford. During that period I was in the habit of working in a coffee shop – part of a large chain – that looked out over the market square called Gloucester Green. This location afforded me both the Wi-Fi that was required for pre-fieldwork scoping, but also ample opportunity to begin thinking about how and why people dress. One day, I sat outside in a waft of roll up cigarette smoke, drinking (what I now know to be a disappointing) espresso. Little Green Bag by the George Baker Selection, distorted by old speakers but nevertheless unmistakable, drifted through the still air from the vintage record stall. The market was in full flow as a lunchtime rush of tourists and office workers weaved in and out of each other searching for trinkets and sustenance. In the distance the butcher's refrigerated van and the greengrocer's stall vied for attention. 'Strawberries . . . pound a bowl . . . buy two get one free . . . three for three quid', boomed the greengrocer, who despite the illogical arithmetic managed to drown out the butcher's deals. Behind me the deep rumble of a diesel engine heralded the arrival of buses that each disgorged a new phalanx of tourists who trundled past where I was sat. Their wheeled suitcases trailed behind them, adding to the hubbub, and overhead pigeons swooped ever lower settling near the market bins to pick through discarded detritus for lunch. As I sipped at my coffee the wind picked up and I could nose, for the briefest moment, the whiff of freshly spread manure, doubtless from one of the college gardens.

The dress of the market goers is the one thing that keeps me staring out at the passing footfall, and the aspect that truly piques my interest is how unremarkable it is. Most of the people who pass me are in blue jeans with the rest of their garments made up of shades of black, blue and grey. There is the occasional flash of colour but they are few and far between. If you were to view the crowd from afar it would be akin to looking at a bolt of Donegal tweed – predominantly grey/blue with the occasional coloured fleck. Then, two men walked past, one dressed in leopard print tights, tiny denim shorts, fur boots and a leather jacket, while the other, significantly taller wore a long purple dress, to match his long hair. These two individuals might easily have been viewed by onlookers as cross-dressers, but I instinctively took their personal styles as more ambiguous and androgynous than this. There was the faintest flicker of interest from the other café-goers before they relapsed into indifference and returned to their coffees, cigarettes and conversations.

This observation fed the kernel of an idea that I had been ruminating over for some time. How do we think about men who look different? This notion of difference could be men who dress to defy social convention or those who intentionally craft their identity through the clothes they wear. In this book this is mostly explored through tailored menswear and bespoke suits, but I also want to consider a broader question of where men go to seek out clothes (of any sort) that they use to make themselves look a particular way – both online and offline.

A considerable part of this crafting of identity through dress (see Wulff 1988: 162–64), is not only the clothes themselves, but also the retail space in which such clothes are purchased. Such spaces can be highly performative and in this book we will visit an eclectic mix of retail spaces from the avant-garde Dover Street Market, to the consultation rooms of bespoke tailors. In some ways these spaces are far removed, but the performance inherent in such spaces makes them closer together than the normality of the majority of high-street retail (see Miller 1998 and Miller et al. 1998). The atelier is a performative space that is able to craft certain types of individual, by offering more than simply garments for sale. By offering an experience too, the specific shop is elevated and it resonates on a spectrum of desirability and authenticity for its customers.

The intentionality of individual customers finding unusual spaces to shop exemplifies the purchase of performance, that can be purchased alongside a material object. Such a purchase can be the aesthetics of a shop, the age of a garment or even a fashion show. All of these are performances which become attached to the garment which is finally purchased. These acquired performances, attached to and purchased alongside the basic garment, add to the native narrative of authenticity, raising the garment above comparable objects and giving it the allure of being special. This allure commands a higher price but is crucial in the creation of certain types of individual through their dress.

As we accompany one another through this book, you will encounter a number of individuals – which is only right as the question about what it means to be individual looms large throughout. Individuality is therefore conceived as a native category – how my informants think of themselves – where the individual is an autonomous actor beyond the restrictions of society (Dumont 1986). In this sense, my informants' individuality is not 'innate but learned' (Morris 1991: 263), crafted through the habitual digital and terrestrial actions that they undertake. These actions are performative (following Goffman 1980: 245), but can be altered for differing situations allowing my informants to present different individual selves in the digital and terrestrial worlds. These selves are able to adapt to the changing digital and terrestrial landscapes in which they exist, yet inevitably are moulded by the society in which they live, becoming 'collective constructs . . . reflecting social position' (Berger 1970: 375).

This juxtaposed nature of individuality allows for my contention that the individuals I worked with performed in a way that made them both different from those they regarded as normally (or badly) dressed members of society, yet alike those in the digital network they inhabited. In the words of Battaglia, 'the placedness of the subject is important', as is 'the dispersed habitation of the self in various forms' (Battaglia 1995: 3). Essentially, the performance of self in different spaces is bound to differ, however once there are multiple habitual spaces where selves perform across both the digital and terrestrial spectrum this becomes less clearly defined. Crucially, we must consider what 'effect this has on . . . sites of self-encounter' (idem), and bear in mind the dangers of self-loss and self-corruption when living and working across boundaryless interconnected interdimensional spaces.

Chapter 1

LET'S GO SHOPPING

It is difficult to live in Europe or North America and not be struck by the ubiq-
uity of the notion of authenticity . . . in the society at large.
                        —Thomas Fillitz and A. Jamie Saris, *Debating Authenticity*

London is a vast warren of wide avenues and ancient side streets. Dover Street
and Savile Row lie a stone's throw from each other, less than ten minutes'
walk for a hand-stitched brogue or Japanese sneaker (see Kawamura 2016),
but within these streets exist different worlds, albeit inhabited by a similar
clientele: the highly affluent and sartorially inclined. My first visit to Dover
Street Market, or DSM as it is known – the concept store created by Rei
Kawakubo of Comme des Garçons in 2004 – was in February 2016; it was a
place I had read about but never found time to visit. I took the underground
to Green Park, walked for a brief stretch up wide and bustling Piccadilly,
crammed with buses and tourists, past the iconic lights of the Ritz hotel and
into Dover Street. The experience of turning off one of the wide and heavily
laden boulevards of London, down a side street, is always one of relief as the
noise level drops and a measure of calm envelops you. In this most expensive
and exclusive part of London, Mayfair, stepping down a side street is akin to
leaving a motor racing circuit and entering a thickly carpeted and beautifully
upholstered library. The street instantly quietens, the crowd thins, the streets
close in and one can almost feel one's pupils dilate as you are cocooned in
a warm and cosy concrete embrace. Even the air tastes sweeter down these
side streets, devoid of the pollutant heavy taint laid down by buses and taxis.

Within moments of turning down Dover Street I passed a bright red Ferrari, with the top down, parked directly outside a private member's club, The Arts Club; a uniformed and top hatted doorman stood sentinel wearing the cultivated look of bored efficiency. A little further along Dover Street there was a Christian Louboutin shoe shop, whose window was devoid of the usual iconic stilettos. Instead, gold spike encrusted high-top trainers hung like Christmas baubles glinting with menacing sparkle in the dappled sunlight.

I spied an unusual looking glass fronted shop a little ahead, covered in black geometric shapes with the letters D S M emblazoned across the front of the glass. I crossed the street, and was suddenly struck with a sense of foreboding. As I approached I could see through the glass into the shop beyond, but 'shop' was something of a misnomer because all I could see was a concrete room with a lift on the far side, a series of enormous angled mirrors growing out of the floor like a geological phenomenon, and in the corner a shack that looked as if it had been picked up from a beach-front bar in Tahiti. This shack, made from paint streaked corrugated metal and thatched in straw, contained a member of staff dressed in black. The single suggestion that this was a shop at all consisted of a few t-shirts placed reverentially on the counter of the shack. I pushed through the glass doors.

The atrium of the shop was indeed as it had appeared from the outside: sparse, concrete, brutalistic, mirrored and intimidating, more detention centre than high-end shopping experience. There were stairs next to the lift at the back of the room that had been obscured from the outside by a mirror, but no signs. I was unsure where to go when several other customers emerged from a small concrete arch on the right-hand side of the atrium that led to a different room. They seemed to know what they were doing, so as they called the lift and waited for the car to arrive, I walked through the arch and into the next room. The contrast was stark. Whereas the first room had been minimalistic to the point of intimidation, this next room was akin to entering a jungle: an organic maze of clothes rails, some hanging from the ceiling, others dangling from semi-constructed scaffolding units. Unlike the traditional shop where everything is arranged in neat rows this was anarchic, clothes stood in corners, hung at different heights, some were grouped together but with no obvious purpose or shared identity. Brands, genders and genres of clothing were intermingled with glass cases full of jewellery and perhaps most disturbingly of all, and the first thing one saw upon entering this room, a set of five or so sabre tooth tiger skulls in a glass case gazing defiantly at prospective customers from their hollow eyes. In the centre of the room was another beach shack, again staffed by an almost lifeless employee, dressed in black.

I wandered through this labyrinthine warren trying to get my bearings, to little avail. It was as though a high-end clothes shop had collided at some force with a hyper-modern art gallery and then an alien being who had never visited either had tried, unsuccessfully, to rearrange the broken furniture and put the two spaces back together. The clothing that was held captive in this menagerie was alternative to say the least. Some could be termed wearable, but a great deal of it less so. I held up what I initially took to be a black suit by Comme Des Garçons, and whilst it was a black suit in essence it was of a cut I had never seen before. The two sides of the front of the jacket hung at different lengths and the sleeves were cropped and vented so that the arm would emerge from the sleeve at the elbow and the rest of the deconstructed sleeve would hang below that like a pseudo (Cambridge MA style) academic gown sleeve. I may not have painted a very compelling image of this piece but let me assure you it was beautiful. Beautiful it may have been but cheap it was not: the jacket alone retailed at over a thousand pounds. Another black suit by the same brand was a typical black suit bar the horizontal slit between the two-button closure straight across the front of the jacket, making the centre of the front of the jacket gape like a huge mouth, surrounded by delicate metallic embroidery.

Having exhausted the ground floor, I moved back towards the concrete atrium. Just before passing back through the arch there was a sign listing the floors and the designers represented on each floor; it was very long, and almost indecipherable. I decided to explore without the 'map', so I passed back through the arch and headed upstairs. The stairs were narrow, cast from polished concrete and wound endlessly and uniformly upward, giving no indication as to what floor you were on, or what that floor contained. To access each floor, you had to pass through a white door (identical on each landing) and into a small white room where there were toilets and then through a further white door to access the floor, it all felt rather like an air-lock, through which you had to pass before entering a strange alien planet. All the floors I visited had a different character and were decorated in varying styles; some were composed of raw brickwork and paint splattered concrete floors with scaffold constructed skeletons from which hung the garments for sale, others had floors of polished metal tiles and mirrored cabinets which held precious articles for sale. One floor was more disparate, having various areas of hyper-modern or antique furniture, some carpeted luxuriously, others with bare boards or concrete flooring, more of a collaged room, reminiscent in some ways of an antique emporium housed in one large space but made up of differing vendors' little enclaves. For all this disparity, however, one thing held the floors together as a coherent unit: the staff. Each floor had an almost identical beach hut kiosk which functioned as the till and residence for the staff; black clothed and mostly silent apart from when gliding noiselessly to the elbow of prospective customers and informing them in a calm but purposeful manner: 'We don't allow photographs to be taken . . . because of the designs . . . I'm sorry'.

It was as though one had entered into the realm of the avant-garde surreal, where these monastic librarians acted as guardian and steward of this private realm. This was an experience reminiscent of Belarde-Lewis' (2013) comments on the issues surrounding photography of sacred objects in anthropological museums, and in the case of DSM, the shop assistants were clearly making an assertion as to the power and importance of the objects that they sell by prohibiting photography. One could almost feel their eyes beating a tattoo on the back of your head as they dared you to break any of the unwritten rules of this sacrosanct space, or attempt to buy an item beyond your means. However, in all the time I was in DSM no one approached me, asked if they could assist or if I was looking for anything in particular, even a friendly smile directed towards a member of staff was barely returned; it was as though they were working to a script, a preordained aloofness towards those who had dared to come into their gallery just to look. It is hard to know without having witnessed it whether this attitude changes for those who can afford to spend large sums within this concrete temple.

The above account is from my first visit to DSM when I was dressed rather casually. It is worth noting that during later visits to DSM, wearing rather more expensive and avant-garde outfits (more in keeping with the style of items which are sold at DSM), the staff were engaging and friendly. It is interesting to consider that while informants of the anthropologist mimicking and appropriating western forms of dress (in more geographical traditional fieldsites) have been discussed in detail by those such as Ferguson (2002) and Gable (2002), there is little written about anthropologists modifying their own dress to gain access to the fieldsite. An exception to this would be the work of Coffey (1999: 65), who describes trying to dress 'like an accountant' while completing the research for her PhD (Coffey 1993).

Throughout the process of my fieldwork I situated myself within a network of individuals (both terrestrially and digitally) who crafted their performed identities through the clothes that they wore. It became apparent during this fieldwork that garments and objects used to clothe the body were very carefully chosen and even the smallest details could change aspects of the performed identity of the wearer – for example, whether one chose to wear a suit jacket with a buttonhole on the lapel or not, whether it was machine stitched or hand-sewn, and whether this buttonhole was the traditional Savile Row style, the more modern keyhole style or the exotically exquisite, and laboriously produced, Milanese style (see Crompton 2015: 87). Each of these choices tells you something about the aesthetics of the wearer, if of course, you can be certain that the wearer has made an active choice on such matters and has not simply let himself be dressed by his tailor: an entirely different sort of performance. Butler (1990) suggests that gender is something which we perform. Dress, therefore, is a highly visible aspect of this performance, so to have a tailor decide or advise on what you should wear is to place one's notion of self and gender in the hands of another. There are however a set of signs within the world of menswear and tailoring which could be used by the dresser to create a particular type of image and gendered self. It is these details I will concentrate on, and conceptualise as a performance carried out by the garment itself: a performance which still exists when the garment is stripped from the body and hung on a hanger, but which when combined with the body performs alongside the performance of the individual in order to craft a complex performance of self. These performed details are all examples which would be thought of as natively authentic, somehow better (to my informants) than garments without them. To explore this, I will now return to my opening vignette in Dover Street Market, and take you to one of the top floors where a designer called Paul Harnden is stocked.

On the most disparate of the floors, there was an area in one corner, carpeted in a thick red shag pile with a couple of pieces of antique furniture on one side and a tall sturdy wrought iron clothing rail on the other, forming a cosy corner. The clothes in this tiny section captivated me from across the room. At first I thought they were vintage, and was intrigued that DSM were selling second-hand vintage clothes alongside their avant-garde designs, but then as I grew closer I realised that they were not vintage, yet displayed the most extraordinary cut, cloth and patina (see Csaba and Ger 2013). The designer in question was a brand called Paul Harnden Shoemaker and the clothes were strange but captivating. The rail held several garments, and all the garments in this small collection shared a similar aesthetic, one which initially prompted me to question whether these clothes had been pulled out of a river after several years of languishing at the bottom in the silt. One garment particularly, a heavy dappled brown patinated suit, at least in the sense that it was trousers and a jacket in matching cloth, was particularly engaging. It was cut to evoke a vintage military style, with wide legged and high-waisted trousers, and a long coat-length jacket that buttoned up to the neck and was devoid of any of the traditional formalised features of a suit jacket but was more coherent with the styling cues of military tunics from the second half of the nineteenth century. I later learned that Paul Harnden takes a lot of inspiration for his clothes from American Civil War era dress; this garment was a fine example of such style inspiration.

Although the cut of this Paul Harnden suit was interesting, it was the cloth itself that was the most engaging thing about this ensemble. It did not fall gracefully from the hanger under its own weight as most clothes do, rather it resembled mummified leather though to the touch felt like lightly waxed cotton, lined with heavy grey linen. The colour of the outer material was not uniform, but instead bore all the hallmarks of a museum quality garment that had been aged by time and usage to create a complex spider's web of colours, stains and patches of wear within a muted spectrum. It was remarkable, but what was even more interesting was that I had never heard of Paul Harnden before, which given the general thrust of my research was surprising. After some later research it transpired that Paul Harnden Shoemakers as a brand had a rather enigmatic quality. The designer Paul Harnden is Canadian but lives and works in Britain, somewhere on the coast, refuses interviews, doesn't conduct fashion shows and only supplies his clothes to a handful of shops. Further to these unusual working practices in terms of advertising and business management, this brand also reputedly operates highly secret production methods for the small number of objects it produces. Cloth is custom woven in British mills to specific colour palettes and shoes are allegedly buried in the ground for up to a year before retail to age the leather and acquire such a unique distressed patina. McCracken (1998: 32) suggests that through the process of gaining a patina, objects also develop an identity. This is a crucial idea for understanding how texture, patina and age are associated with my informant's belief that such objects are more natively authentic. While it is very difficult to garner any information at all about this designer, the internet mainly offering speculation or gushing blog posts about purchasing one lusted-after garment (see Mead 2013), the *Financial Times* online does mention him:

> Sometimes, in fashion, wear and tear is the best accessory. . . For many niche brands, this is partly about distancing themselves from the mainstream. . . Not to be confused with fads for distressed-denim and faux aged leather that appear every few fashion cycles, the current move toward the 'new aged' has more to do with the fact that spending four figures on a jacket in a quality hide is an investment and for men, in particular, its gradual softening and scuffing suggests a life well lived and a certain insouciance.
>
> The allure of the 'old' is not limited to leather. A handful of contemporary designers have pioneered a similar approach to other textiles. For example, Homme Plus suits by Comme Des Garçons are often made in boiled wool or polyester . . . it's not the instant ageing of All Saints or Levis. What might be perceived as imperfections are highly desirable – the result of fabrication sourced from a few family run mills left in business. (O'Flaherty 2012)

In this excerpt O'Flaherty (idem) attempts to differentiate between artisan and instant ageing, arguing that the latter is a vulgar little brother of intention to the high art of using methods that leave natural imperfections. There is certainly a difference between the intentional and the random acts of aging, as discussed by Dilley (2004: 803–7). This distinction is concerned with garments developing a narrative of their own, only available to garments which are able to offer a history and their own sense of identity to a potential purchaser. This makes the garment more natively authentic, and as such offers the same notions of authenticity to the individuals who choose such garments to craft their own self (see Kondo 2009; see also Coffey 1999 and Woodward 2005). This would be comparable to the work of the tailor Sir Tom Baker, particularly in terms of deconstruction and gunshot garments: a signature design of Sir Tom Baker, where tailored garments are distressed with shot-gun blasts and sold full of holes. O'Flaherty goes on to elaborate on the destructive habits of certain designers:

> The shop assistants in Rick Owens' stores wear their proprietor's black and 'dark dust' coloured T-shirts to work, often in tatters, and serve as an instruction manual for newcomers to the brand; Owens designs some of his raw edged items, such as sheer cotton T-shirts, to distress, artfully, over time. 'I see it as a restrained patina,' says Owens. 'Think of British gentlemen who used to give their new shoes to a valet to reduce the newness'.

> Brighton-based designer Paul Harnden creates tailoring . . . but has never produced a catwalk show. He refuses party invitations, interviews and online retail, selling exclusively at a few stores. . . Much of his work resembles wrinkled, rugged, American Civil War costume, with heavy cotton and twists of Victoriana . . . the majority of each collection sells out on arrival. (O'Flaherty 2012)

This is a prime example of garments displaying a patina of age and the process of production, and there are similar garments available in DSM more easily identifiable as tailoring. Indeed, on one of the middle floors I was drawn to a pair of suits from one of the many lines of Comme Des Garçons, a brand stalwart at DSM. These suits were beautifully fragile, one a rich fawn and the other a deep sage green, simply cut two-button and single-breasted in style but they were constructed from a material that I had never seen before, it looked like woven moss, light and soft to the touch but with a cotton-wool-esque quality that looked like it would disintegrate as soon as it was worn. Again, like almost everything in this dystopian retail monolith, these suits were prohibitively expensive. Such a clear difference in wealth between researcher and informants could be framed as studying up, however following Wulff (2015a: 157–59) who builds on the work of Hannerz (2010), to suggest 'studying sideways', my work is best described as somewhere between these two approaches, akin to studying diagonally. The experience of visiting DSM and experiencing clothes such as these led me to consider the juxtaposition of the tailor and the designer as producers of suits, as well as notions of 'wearability' and whether certain garments can be classed as adornment and not clothing. Furthermore, it prompted a greater discussion on one of the nuanced and ongoing questions of this book; how does clothing as art fit into a world of performance and spectacle? Clothing that is considered as art is a divisive issue and one which is beyond the scope of this book. However, many of my informants use the term 'art' to describe clothes which they consider to be particularly fine or beautiful. Perhaps art is therefore a synonym for the highest form of the native authentic. In addition, one of the key aspects of this study is to examine what the suit is, what it can be and how a broad spectrum of designs can all be classified as the same type of garment, as well as an analysis of how this is important for a western view of masculinity. Building on the work of Simpson (2014), notions of modern western masculinity must be reassessed. Simpson (idem) argues that there is a type of modern man for whom their own selves are an object of self-love; however, I suggest (following Connell 2005; see also Kimmel 1996; Beynon 2002; Connell and Messerschmidt 2005) that there is no longer one single form of masculinity and that we must conceptualise modern western masculinity as post-particular: beyond a specific or particular set of ideals. This allows notions of dress such as Moore's (2018) suggestion that some men dress 'fabulously' as an attempt to define themselves to fit alongside the work of Miller and Woodward (2007, 2010, 2012) who report that many of their informants have a desire to dress invisibly.

Like many things discussed in this chapter, performance is not something abstract and ethereal but rather a commodity for purchase. This could be a new suit made from vintage cloth, designer distressed ripped jeans or a truly old garment. In any case the purchaser is able to buy time woven into the cloth and in wearing said garment is performing their identity along with the garment: a process which allows both the garment and the individual to be perceived as being natively authentic. These details can range from whether the buttonholes are hand-sewn or not through to where the cloth for the garments was woven, and how the garment was constructed and by whom. In this case I have specifically been discussing artificial aging and the display of a historical narrative, which is performed by the clothes as a commodity available for purchase in addition to the commodity of the garment itself. Further to the garment itself performing *authentic* attributes which are purchased alongside the garment, the actual production of the garment can be a form of performance which is enacted and can be procured.

Spotting Authenticity

Modern consumer society in late capitalism is intimately entwined with debates about authenticity, not just with products, whose validity needs somehow to be authorised – from organic food to art (that is, the sense of authentic origins) – but also with respect to certain sorts of experiences and ways of being-in-the-world (that is, in the sense of the authentic correspondence of content). (Fillitz and Saris 2013: 1)

Fillitz and Saris (2013: 1) assert that 'the modern deployment of authenticity
. . . presupposes that there is a downmarket variety of what is on offer'. This is
certainly the case in terms of menswear that I saw during my fieldwork, where
an ostensibly similar suit could range from less than one hundred pounds off
the peg in a high-street shop to in excess of five thousand pounds for one made
bespoke by a Savile Row tailor. Fillitz and Saris concur with this phenomenon,
stating that 'cost is one of the ways of avoiding this [downmarket] part of the
market, but connoisseurship is even more necessary' (idem). It is this connoisseurship which forms the basis for the less tangible aspect of the authentic
described by Callahan and Adams (2016: 219) – one must be a cognoscente,
equipped not only with the funds to purchase from the higher end of the market, but also an understanding of the highly complex nuance of, in the case
of clothing, quality, detail, style, etiquette and taste. This is where the native
concept of the authentic becomes useful as it encompasses an understanding of
materials, quality, production, longevity and fit as well as the more ephemeral
notion of style and the obvious arbiter of difference posited by Fillitz and Saris
(2013: 1): cost. An understanding of these categories is vital for those wishing
to perform as individuals within the world of my fieldsite.

Beyond the disembodied authenticity of clothing itself it is also of merit to
consider the authenticity of the individual: the one who wears these clothes.
This is a complex and convoluted issue, perhaps best conceived by thinking of
the notion of being 'true to oneself', and in the case of my research findings,
participants being true to themselves and being (an) individual are synonymous. Dilley tells us that this might be called 'expressive or existential authenticity' and that it 'refers to the problem of how we live authentically by "being
true to oneself"' (2013: 192). He supports this theory with 'Sartre's idea that
an inauthentic act is one that betrays one's responsibility for behaving in a
manner that is true to oneself, that is to act in bad faith' (idem). This idea is
the crux of how I conceptualise authenticity in terms of the individual, yet
within this book, authenticity is used broadly as a concept for analysis ranging from the cost and connoisseurship associated with the production, display
and wearing of clothing, to a discussion on the nature of the individual.

> This obligation is not different from that which is imposed on all tradesmen.
> Their condition is wholly one of ceremony . . . there is the dance of the grocer,
> of the tailor, of the auctioneer, by which they endeavour to persuade the cli-
> entele that they are nothing but a grocer, an auctioneer, a tailor. A grocer who
> dreams is offensive to the buyer, because such a grocer is not wholly a grocer.
> Society demands that he limit himself to his function as a grocer. . . (Sartre
> 1993: 167)

Sartre (idem) tells us that society demands we limit ourselves to our 'function'
within society. This is inseparable from the performance which we present

to society in our everyday lives, a crucial part of remaining authentic to our function. This includes the way we dress, speak and conduct ourselves; to present oneself in a way that surpasses your function is, Sartre tells us, 'offensive' (idem). This suggests that should the presentation of one's personal ceremony, with regard to their societal function, become too far removed from the societally approved norm, then other members of that society will cease to engage with you. They will cease to believe or trust in the function you claim to be able to provide.

It is the validity of this idea that I explore here. My fieldwork has led me to observe and appreciate the dance of the tailor, indeed this is a function which more than any other it is imperative that one dress and act the part, since one is buying not only clothes from them, but also, by association, style. However, it is here that Sartre's contention as to the strictness with which we must adhere to our societal function begins to unravel. It is the customers of the tailor, who wish to dress in the style of the tailor, which problematise Sartre's contention, and as such I wish to consider that which Sartre considers offensive: the grocer who dares to dream (idem).

The customers of the tailor – these dreaming grocers – purchase garments for their transformational properties, but there are many other attributes that are made available to customers beyond simply the performative notion of dressing up that is for sale. Time itself is commodified and made available for purchase as part of certain clothes and accessories. There are elements of this process which fetishise the commodity of time, through an obsessive interest in production, and the life of garments. This can be divided further into various strands including the time-rich process of production, artificially distressing garments, garments designed to age quickly, and those which display a desirable manufactured heritage of wear. All of these strands can enhance the native notion of authenticity. Furthermore, small details of clothing can offer a performance enmeshed within the garment, creating an object for purchase which is more complex than a simply functional garment. Yet beyond this, even the production of a garment can be conceptualised as a form of performance. This means that much like the garment's performance of authentic details and history, the performance of production can also be offered for purchase alongside specific garments.

The Visibility of Production

To get a comparison to the shopping experience of DSM I left the concrete atrium and headed towards Savile Row – the home of London's finest and most established tailors. After a short walk down Grafton Street and Clifford Street, both quietly imposing Mayfair backwaters, you arrive at the midpoint of Savile Row, the heart of the tailoring establishment. A hush seems to descend within the confines of 'The Row', as though you are walking on hallowed ground. Few cars venture down this street, further adding to the quiet. There are a scant number of people walking along the pavement but those that are wear beautiful handmade suits, and their leather soled shoes, echo gently against the buildings as they move smartly to their next engagement.

As I turned onto Savile Row and wandered along it, tailor blended into tailor, some famous names, and others that I had never heard of. At some, plate glass windows show off their designs and characteristic style, whereas at others one can barely see in and a bell has to be rung for admittance. One similarity that links a great many of these tailors though is the visual accessibility of the production. Leaning over the railing in front of the shops one can peer into the basements where more often than not the suits are created. Walking along the row one might catch a glimpse of an apprentice basting a lapel in an almost monastic repetition of tiny stitches, or a master cutter putting shears to cloth on an enormous table.

The visibility of this production, intentionally situated within buildings along Savile Row where it can be glimpsed, whilst still maintaining an aura of guarded mystique, led me to draw comparisons with the work of Dilley (2004). Dilley describes the 'production and sale of craft objects in Senegal' including descriptions of both where one can 'observe the processes of production' and cases where 'the point of production was separated from the point of consumption' (Dilley 2004: 798-806). In the latter example the objects are artificially aged so that they may be presented to unwary purchasers as genuine 'African "antiques" and objets d'art', a process which could be compared with some of the items I described in DSM designed to give the illusion that they have greater age and history than they really do (ibid.: 798). This juxtaposition between forms of production which are visible and those which are invisible is the crux of this article, a feature which Dilley uses to unpack an argument theoretically based on Baudrillardian hyperreality to suggest that 'a hyperreal world of consumption is predicated upon making production invisible' (ibid.: 808). If this is the case, then we are able to 'argue for a hyperreal world of the free-floating commodity sign' (idem).

Dilley recalls Miller's statement that 'consumption has become the vanguard of history', an idea that suggests production is no longer as important as consumption (Miller 1995a: 1, in Dilley 2004: 798). However, I concur with Dilley's suggestion that 'production has not become invisible because production itself has become unimportant' – though in the vast majority of the fashion world production is typically invisible – but this merely changes the relationship and issues regarding ethical issues of production as still engaged with by consumers (Dilley 2004: 809). Miller's argument that consumption is an area of people's lives which they 'struggle towards control over' in an attempt to establish 'the definition of themselves and their values' is a valid one, yet it does not negate the validity and importance of production; indeed, for many of those I conducted research with, production was as much a part of the allure of consumption as the act of consuming itself (Miller 1995b: 277).

The visibility of production on Savile Row is connected to the value of the garments being produced, not only monetarily but also socially and aesthetically. It is interesting to note that while the workshops may be on partial display there are shops on the Row which one cannot see into from the street and must ring a bell for access. This is a clear symbolic hierarchical differentiation between the prized production and less lauded consumption. It also highlights that while anyone can appreciate and consume the quality of the production, very few can afford to own the finished garment. The handmade nature of these garments, drafted from a paper pattern designed from the measurements of a specific person, to their precise specifications and completed entirely by hand, is the joy of such garments and the reason why the production is made visible. Interestingly, while tailors Gieves and Hawkes, whom I visited, are happy to take people into their workshops, my guide told me that they almost never have anyone with a bespoke commission coming to see the tailors at work.

Gieves and Hawkes – Into the Basement

Descending the stairs from the shop floor, plush carpet gave way to bare concrete under my feet, and muffled footsteps began to echo gently. As I pushed through a decidedly industrial looking door I was greeted with an Aladdin's cave of suits. The basement of Gieves and Hawkes, below their main shop on the corner of Savile Row, houses the workshops where all their bespoke garments are totally handmade. The sound that greeted my ears was not the aggressive chatter of sewing machines and mechanisation but rather the quiet murmur of occasional conversation, the soft rustling of fabric, the hiss of steam irons, and the gentle swish of the workers' quiet efficiency. The basement comprised several rooms all well-lit by white overhead lights, neat and well-ordered yet with a hint of creative organic chaos, as though when someone new arrived they were simply given a work station in any available corner. Racks of half-made suits hung from a variety of rails in various stages of completion, and the still air was fragrant with the gentle smell of machine oil, the aerated dust from a thousand offcuts of fabric and the damp musk that emanated from the application of a steam iron to pure wool fabric: a strangely organic mixture of damp sheep and well-oiled efficacy, yet comforting and cosy. The basements did not have the feel of a hostile factory but more a creative artist's studio, albeit with fabric being the media.

As I was shown around by my guide, Joseph, I was surprised by how few people were working in this department but also how specialised each of their tasks were. There was a room with a huge table where two or three people worked to draft the heavy brown paper patterns that each bespoke client requires (they just stick on a new bit if the client changes shape, Joseph told me) and cut the cloth to match, using as little as they can get away with. This is a much harder task with a big pattern where each piece must match up. In another tiny glass fronted room which looked like a repurposed ticket booth from a provincial village theatre, sat a man who was solely responsible for alterations which came in from clients after garments had been collected. Then in another larger room, fewer than a dozen other people worked. There was one apprentice, who had already been there for several years and was still closely supervised by the senior coat maker. Another man was solely responsible for steaming the canvas and horsehair internal construction within the suit jackets to create a perfect three-dimensional shape to match the body of the client, a task that Joseph referred to with an unreserved reverence. There are parallels with this process in the work of Wulff (2002: 76) who describes the lengths ballet dancers will go to in an attempt to mould their shoes to the shape of their feet. This was more than cutting and stitching flat pieces of fabric to make a jacket, this was the true art of bespoke. There is a comparison to draw here with the work of Csaba and Ger on carpets. They describe 'how different actors account for the quality and value of oriental carpets' and how 'the evaluative practices of the actors reflect a field that values age and tradition, rather than novelty and creativity' (Csaba and Ger 2013: 260). This is similar to the notion of native authenticity held by my research subjects, where intellectual knowledge of production and visual assessment of patina combine to give a sartorial object greater status. There were more specialised tasks too; at the back of the room sat a young woman whose role was embroidery and the hand finishing of gold details that were required on bespoke military uniforms. I watched her constructing the most beautiful circular gold detailing on a navel epaulette from a straight piece of heavy gold ribbon (akin to thick aluminium kitchen foil) by repeatedly folding the thick metal of the woven gold thread that made up the ribbon dozens of times for this singular circular detail and hand stitching it in place: a task that involved an almost unfathomable level of precision and patience. While she did this she chatted away in a very jolly way saying that she didn't mind the monotony of it unless they had a big order of them to fulfil. She told the story of them having to do hundreds when the Prince of Tonga recently ordered for his entire wedding retinue new military uniforms from Gieves and Hawkes, with substantial amounts of gold embroidery. Samples from this order hung as a reminder in the corner of the room, gold glinting against heavy green wool.

The woman who was working on embroidery seemed one of the youngest staff in the basement, though it was hard to tell; the rest varied in age substantially but all had a casual air to their presentation. I had almost imagined them all to be beautifully dressed old and slightly dusty men, and though some wore suits they were not what one might describe as sharp: they were there to work, a ramshackle bunch of below stairs artisans, scruffy, dishevelled, chalk-stained or casual. There wasn't a specific look here and you would pass them in the street without a second glance, yet here in the basement of Number One Savile Row, they worked together to make some of the finest clothes money could buy.

It is from ethnographic encounters such as this that my ideas surrounding the native concept of authenticity and the nature of the individual started to form, with a special focus on the production, marketing and acquisition of small run and one-off bespoke garments. Individuality emerged as the primary theme which will be negotiated and discussed throughout my work, but it is the importance of production which really captured my imagination after this particular ethnographic encounter. Savile Row is an obvious starting point for a discussion of production due to its visibility and legendary quality. However, the quality and artisanal flair of the small group of tailors I encountered was on a completely different level to that which one might imagine from a scant glimpse of their work through the workshop windows that face the street. Production is not merely the creation of the garment, as well as the quality and longevity that this process may or may not entail, but it evokes something additional. One is able to purchase heritage, an association with illustrious former clients, design, individuality and, perhaps least tangible of all, style. These are all attributes that a garment is able to perform, making itself and its wearer more natively authentic.

This notion of authenticity used by the participants of my research is widespread and difficult to define, as it flexes to suit circumstance and object. It is related to depth ontology (Miller 2010), but also more objective concepts of quality and production as mentioned above. It essentially functions as a hegemonic tool for ranking garments and therefore their wearers, yet I am cautious to not grant it an ontological status beyond the discourse of my informants. Those with the skills to read these sartorial symbols can participate in wordless interaction, identify the sartorial character and allegiance of the wearer or acknowledge that, however removed, there is a shared interest and knowledge between certain individuals.

The Digital Visibility of Production

The visibility of production of tailored clothing is continued beyond the physical realm of visible workshops on Savile Row and into the digital world of social media (there are links here to the work of Rocamora 2016). Practically every bespoke tailor from Savile Row and beyond will show images or video on their social media of either the sewing and cutting of their bespoke suits or the part-made suits being fitted to clients. Often images of both sorts are a regular feature. In this way production is made visible even for tailors who do not have workshops which can be easily seen or accessed – crucial when trying to be thought of as natively authentic.

This highlights the sign-value of suiting as a commodity. Baudrillard tells us that beyond the utility or exchange-value of a commodity there is a sign-value which places one object in relation to another sign; this is typically related to socially stratified prestige and status (Baudrillard 1981, 1998). In terms of tailoring, this sign-value has a complex relationship with production. Ostensibly production is detached from a piece of tailoring's sign-value; however, in some cases the sign-value is dependent entirely upon the production. For example, the social cachet of a hand-made bespoke suit would typically be greater than one bought from a supermarket. It is in cases like this that the native notion of authenticity and sign-value could be conceived as belonging to the same hierarchical structure.

There are, however, additional layers of complexity to this discussion; the physical act of production is visible to the consumer on the street from certain Savile Row premises. This performance of production is as much of a product available for consumption as the garments themselves. Even if you choose not to consume this performed production you can still be cognisant of its existence. This provenance is a crucial part of the finished garment; however, such provenance is now no longer limited to the physical world since digital platforms such as Instagram allow us to see inside the workshops and fitting rooms of tailors. This radically changes how one can consume such production; whether this is watching a video of a tailor stitching, a client being fitted or a new fabric being cut. Such a form of consumption is notionally physically detached from the geographical and temporal reality of the tailor at work, however the experience offers the feeling of greater connection since the images and video give a closer look than it would be possible to obtain looking into a Savile Row workshop from the street – an experience more akin to the visit I made when I walked through the workshop of Gieves and Hawkes.

This 'proximity' to the tailor and their work which a digital lens can offer gives an immense feeling of connection and exclusivity despite the open access nature of the content. This visibility of production has allowed production itself to enter the world of hyperreality. Such production, offered as tempting morsels to a hungry digital consumer, can be binged upon, consuming the same content repeatedly in a way that could not be achieved in a physical reality. This visual bingeing can be a one-way digital stream or can manifest itself in a comparable way to Frankland's (2009) description of bulimic consumption, with images consumed and then intellectually regurgitated with a similar but altered form of content being produced. If we consider avantgarde and bespoke menswear as an 'other', in contrast to the mainstream products of the fashion industry, then much like Frankland's description of tourist encounters with pygmies in Uganda, those concerned with consuming 'otherness' will continue to do so as 'long as we can believe in the authenticity of the experiential encounter' and as 'long as we feel that we are getting something above and beyond the normalcy' that one experiences in the safe spaces of the mainstream fashion industry (Frankland 2009: 95). This search for the authentic is a good explanation for the resurgence of interest in vintage clothing over recent years. Indeed, there are many Instagram users who are part of the network I worked with but are more interested in vintage clothing and dressing in historical styles. This normalcy in terms of the fashion industry is the world examined in depth by Miller and Woodward in their work on blue jeans, a garment so unremarkable and normal that they term it 'postsemiotic' (Miller and Woodward 2012: 89). The images from tailors (in both a physical and digital world) are consumed and the looks inspired by these images are reproduced by others within the digital network, and physical reality, as imitations of those they view. As Frankland tells us, 'the vertical and progressive circularity of the bulimic consumption of strangeness, has locked them within an endless loop of hyperreality' (Frankland 2009: 113). In the same way, Debord suggests that within a society at the mercy of the spectacle there is at the same time 'a faithful mirror . . . held up to the production of things and a distorting objectification of the producers' (Debord 2012: 16). This highlights the way in which the mass of produced and consumed images within digital media can manipulate and even fetishise the manner in which we consume the production of garments, and the lives of the producers themselves. This is reflected in the ever more frequent use of digital media and the images that members of networks post in response, homage and imitation of those they follow. The outcome of this hyperreality for Sartre's dreaming grocer is the same as for Frankland's tourists desperately in search of the authentic 'other'. The 'other' is no longer an *other* but instead has become an 'embodiment of our own fears and desires'; this is the case for those desperately seeking unusual clothing to craft their identity (Frankland 2009: 114). This fear of the normal and desire to acquire otherness through dress is inherent to the circularity of identity, modernity and hyperreality. Jouhki (2017: 96) discusses the hyperreal nature of the men depicted in adverts for online poker websites, displaying exaggerated masculine characteristics and the trappings of 'masculine fantasies'. Jouhki suggests that the 'hyperreal male is a lucid and powerful compensatory model' designed to appeal to young males 'who acknowledge that being "a gamer" might . . . go against traditional images of masculinity' (idem). Similar ideas of hyperreal images could be unpacked in relation to the world of men's fashion, an interest in which is not typically associated with hyper-masculine characteristics, despite the type of imagery which is usually employed in the advertising. In contrast, the plethora of digital images on Instagram which show men who are interested in fashion and sartorial matters may begin to alter notions of masculinity, expressed by Cole (2000: 2) whereby an 'interest in dress is frivolous, and . . . feminine'.

The nature of production is an enormously important part of garments being identified as different or 'other' within the fashion industry. This digital consumption of production allows for garments to garner a provenance without the act of production being physically visible. However, this glut of visibility in the digital space also allows for an equal measure of invisibility. The nature of the digital image means that manipulation of either the image itself or the angle from which it is taken allows the taker and poster of the image to craft the production which they want their followers to consume. Sontag (2008: 11) notes that 'taking photographs has set up a chronic voyeuristic relation to the world'; this has certainly become the case for the images posted on social media. However, she also suggests that this relationship 'levels the meaning of all events', which I suggest is better conceptualised as raising all events to the level of the hyperreal (idem). This means that while it may appear that production is highly visible in the digital space it is hard to confirm how truthfully accurate this visibility is. As such there is also a substantial presence of invisibility in this digital world. This is comparable to Dilley (2019) where he describes how photographs can be cropped before publication to alter how they would be interpreted by the consumer. However, the visibility and invisibility of production are not confined to the digital content of garment makers. Other users may deceive, with regard to the production values of the items that they are wearing in one of their uploaded images, in an attempt to manipulate the sign-value of that object and by association the image they are presenting for feedback. This can be done through clever photography or simply by stating that an item is from a particular brand or has, for example, been handmade, when it has not been.

Dilley tells us that 'by making production invisible and by considering only consumer desire, Baudrillard . . . [is] able to argue for a hyperreal world of the free-floating commodity sign' (Dilley 2004: 808). I want to examine this statement a little more closely in relation to my work in the digital world. The sign-value of the garments displayed within digital images, in the Instagram network which I have worked in, are entangled with the notion of the image itself as a form of Foucauldian discourse, which is regulated by the approval of the network as a collective. As such the commodity sign is not as free-floating as Baudrillard would have us believe since the digital network regulates the images, treating them as a form of discourse and passing collective judgment on them, through likes and follows. The network has the notion or notions of the perfect image and the perfect garment, and while these notions may not ever be realised, they situate images and their associated contents on a sliding scale of implied value. This naturally affects Baudrillard's ideas that signs are entirely free-floating. It should also be noted that Baudrillard (1993: 93) suggests that 'fashion itself' is a sign. He goes on to tell us that the 'semiurgy of fashion rebels against the functionalism of the economic sphere' (idem). Essentially, in fashion, new meanings are constantly being created as new signs are constantly being created, an occurrence which is detached from traditional notions of objects and clothing being simply function items. However, Baudrillard also describes fashion as a 'universal form' (ibid.: 92) and one which 'exists only within the framework of modernity . . . in a schema of rupture, progress and innovation' (ibid.: 89). It is hard to know whether he is writing with regard to male or female fashion or a synthesis; however, male bespoke tailoring in the UK, which I have studied, does not exist only in the framework of modernity, but has huge historical precedence (see Nixon 1996; Edwards 1997; Breward 1999) and its sign-value is substantially dependent upon its position within a historical narrative. However, I do not want to suggest that signs are fixed, rather that they are free-floating but affected by *ocean currents*, free to float as they please at times, and other times forced to change order by the circumstances around them. For example, the sign ceases to be free-floating when it is clear what an image is, contains or represents and this clarity is shared by all those who view it; however, if some of those who view and interact with the image and its contents are not aware of the brand, the production or any of the associated provenance or cachet, then the sign-value begins to float again. Likewise, the use of hashtags can alter the buoyancy of these signs, bringing their attention to a wider audience, with creative disguise or hyperbolic description.

Digital networks prevent the signs from being free-floating, and a closed network may be able to stratify these signs in a very fixed way. However, the network I worked with was permeable to those spanning other networks and those with shared interests but different views. For example, Instagram users such as @westwoodcowboy and @stylescoundrel would place the designs of Vivienne Westwood hierarchically above a bespoke Savile Row suit, and users such as this prevent the signs from becoming fixed by the network. Despite this, you trust that the members of the network have the knowledge to empower the correct discourse, and validate the correct images. This mutual admiration society has the power then to validate images and the associated users which gives the illusion that signs are fixed even when they are, in fact, still free-floating albeit at the mercy of currents.

In the two years of digital research I conducted the most striking factor was that while the consumption of Instagram posts themselves is rampant, their actual production is one of the most invisible forms of production. This highlights the performative nature of the digital world, which has become so hyperreal that the digital performance has begun to mask physical reality.

Post-colonial Narrative?

On the corner of Clifford Street and Savile Row, the first two tailor's shops that I saw on my walk were Ozwald Boateng and Richard James. Boateng's shop appears at street level as a vast glass box inserted into the original façade; the interior is all black, floor, ceiling, walls, furniture, like a hyper-modern 5-star hotel lobby which has taken an austere devil worshiping teenager's bedroom as design inspiration. The only light and colour within this dark box (despite all the glass) are the suits on display. In the windows stood a minimalistic display of dark fabric modern cut suits on mannequins and a few accessories and shirts in glass topped, lit display cases, the sort you would find in jewellers on Old Bond Street. At the back of the black box were six or so suit jackets, identical in style (modern, peaked lapel, double-breasted) but each in a different bright colour, and beautifully lit so that it looked like piece of modern art exploiting the colour spectrum. Displays such as this could easily have made the shop feel camp (used here in the manner that Isherwood 1954: 125 does) or at the very least fun, but instead it retained a clinical, almost sinister aesthetic, enhanced rather than reduced by the few items of clothing on display.

The only life in this dark space was a single tailor. A black gentleman in a black suit sat in a black leather armchair in the corner of the sparse room, casually browsing his black iPhone. It struck me, intentionally or not, as a powerful statement about non-white identity in the heart of the predominantly white male bastion of Savile Row with all its collective history, and it is important to note that Boateng was the first black tailor to open a shop on the row. The link between dress, power and colonialism is a clear one on Savile Row. When I visited Gieves and Hawkes at Number One Savile Row, the archival items they had on display evoked their military heritage with pith helmets and Victorian military tunics forming part of the décor but also advertising their place in the history of a colonial past that they helped to dress. There is a similarity between the objects on show at Gieves and Hawkes and the work of Macdonald (2002) on folk museums in Britain. The objects on display at Gieves and Hawkes are not purely ceremonial; many would have been regularly used, suggesting, as Macdonald (ibid.: 89) does, 'the fetishization of past everyday life'. One particular design of the pith helmet, the Wolseley pattern, was patented by Hawkes and the display of such items brings to mind not only typical colonial photographs and images, but also Rouche's Les Maîtres Fous where pith helmets are worn by the subjects of the film mimicking their colonial aggressors (Tise-Isoré 2014: 80; Rouche 1955). This notion of mimicry is explored further in an example given by Cummings (2017) where she describes a Samoan bonnet presented to Queen Victoria. This bonnet uses local Samoan materials such as tortoiseshell but is to a European design, a fact which Cummings uses to unpack a concept she terms 'inbetweenness', due to the bonnet being produced at the 'interface of two cultures' (ibid.: 200). The combination of mimicry, hybrid design and inbetweenness allows us to consider this bonnet, according to Cummings, as an artefact with its own agency, the ability to alter traditional power relations and create new 'forms of cultural meaning' (idem). This idea is useful for considering the recent phenomenon in the wider fashion industry of indigenous communities accusing designers of plagiarism or cultural appropriation for copying aspects of their dress without permission (Larsson 2015).

Furthermore, before the tailors were on the site of Number One Savile Row it was the headquarters of the Royal Geographical Society, which in itself has an additional legacy of exploration linked to colonial expansion. The Gieves and Hawkes book which I was shown at the time of my visit, subtitled 'the invention of the English Gentleman', gives a narrative which explores the military dress, royal commissions and historical garments of the tailoring house in great detail (Tise-Isoré 2014). Indeed, the Savile Row shop still keeps the uniforms of the Honourable Corps of Gentlemen at Arms, the English sovereign's personal ceremonial bodyguard, in an upstairs room. The symbolic power of this link with the British crown explains why the tailor was seen as a legitimate target for the IRA when they bombed the Gieves premises on Old Bond Street in 1974. Tailors with this pedigree for dressing powerful individuals and links to colonial history have mostly modernised in recent years but their link to their colonial past is not only clear but cherished as an important part of their heritage and crucially a demonstrable portfolio of their tailoring experience.

Examples of military and civilian uniform being used as modes for power are found throughout history. Callaway records numerous examples of the colonial officers dressing for dinner either in dinner jackets or military evening dress as a means of displaying social and moral superiority over their colonial subjects (Callaway 1992: 234–35). The various trappings of formal dress are analysed, from the intricacies of medal ribbons to legal wigs and the cassocks of bishops, before the conclusion is drawn that 'these costumes with their symbolic traditions draped the male in mantles of social prestige' (ibid.: 238). These mantles could be considered as a Baudrillardian sign, but it is interesting to note that Callaway highlights Laver's view that many decorations stem from an aesthetic of masculine exaggeration; 'it gives him a head-dress which exaggerates his height; it puts a stripe on his trousers to exaggerate his apparent length of leg; it gives him epaulettes to exaggerate the width of his shoulders' (Laver 1969: 73, in Callaway 1992: 238). Elements of this exaggeration, such as a stripe on the trouser and padded shoulders, are still found in much of men's formal evening attire. Callaway (1992: 240) goes on to recall the steps taken by a young Lord Curzon in advance of a meeting with the Amir of Afghanistan. These included a trip to a theatrical outfitter in London to hire himself an 'enormous pair of gold epaulettes' and a number of medals which he was not entitled to (Rose 1969: 268). Curzon clearly hoped this exaggerated militaristic style would impress upon the Amir his colonial superiority.

Back on Savile Row, opposite Ozwald Boateng, on the other corner of Clifford Street, was Richard James. This looked more like a traditional clothes shop, bright, well lit and full of objects. The suits in the window were of a traditional cut but made of patterned cloth more reminiscent of a surfer's Hawaiian board shorts than a bespoke Savile Row suit. A sight that raised an instant and unconscious smile, they were silly certainly but joyous nonetheless. There are of course numerous other shops along Savile Row; however, I wanted to highlight the aesthetic nature of the window displays of these two shops that gaze out onto *The Row* and at each other. They have similarities in the use of colour in their suits but the way in which this is displayed is profoundly different. It is important to consider the nature of the shops and the way in which they display their aesthetic to the customer before they even step through the doors. This, for customers who do have their clothes made, is a crucial part of identity: identifying with a particular aesthetic, and entering into a space where they feel at 'home'. This notion of identifying with a particular aesthetic goes further too, encompassing a wider discussion of concepts of masculinity and national identity. This is discussed by Roberts (2017) who highlights a specific form of extreme masculinity present in Russia, with everyone from the president to fashion designers working to influence and alter notions of normal masculinity, and how one's masculine self should appear. This is a broad example of how one's environment can alter where one may feel at 'home' shopping, and which particular aesthetics may appeal.

This is the crux of the relationship between shop, tailor, customer and the formation of identity. The aesthetics of the space, the tailor, the service, the items on display and the finished product must appeal to and empower the wearer, so that they are purchasing something beyond merely the garment itself: they are buying an experience and they are buying power, both of which would be attributes termed natively authentic. This is the basis of the formation of an individual through dressing in high-end artisanal menswear. One purchases not just the garment, but the associated performances that come with the garment too. Whether these are the visible production, the aesthetics of the shop, the strangeness of the other garments the shop sells, or the artificial age of the garment, each of these performances is part of the purchase and empowers both cloth and wearer. Another performance the purchaser can buy in to are fashion shows and you can attend some of these with me in the next chapter.

Chapter 2

FASHION WEEK

I never used to like the word 'authentic' as applied to menswear . . . Companies with heritage were easy to define: they didn't necessarily make better products, but you knew how long they'd been doing so . . . it seemed to be assumed that a craftsman making things by hand in their shed was more authentic than something larger. But that doesn't really make sense, logically or linguistically . . . Heritage has been overemphasised. Frankly, some old companies make terrible products and are stuck in the past . . . The fact it is done by hand doesn't necessarily make it better. Some craftsmen set out on their own before they're ready, and deliver a poor product. And some things are just better made by machine.
—Simon Crompton, 'What Is Authenticity'

The venue was unmissable. Opposite Old Spitalfields Market stood a church, raised from street level behind spiked iron railings. A considerable number of stone steps and four gargantuan white columns fronted the building, through which you had to pass to reach the main door. Less a church than an acropolis, it was architecturally early eighteenth-century English Baroque, but looked part rural American religious monolith, part Greek temple. If the architecture itself was not impressive enough, the exterior of the venue had been lit neon blue, a stark bright-burning beacon against the early January dusk-laden sky. Part temple, part spaceship from another world, it was unmissable.

I had asked my mother to join me for the show and we approached the gate in the railings, at the time specified, to present ourselves to the two large men in black overcoats who stood sentinel. They enquired whether we were VIP's, 'sadly not' I said, and they informed us politely that the doors would not be opening to us for another thirty minutes. We went for a walk. Spital-fields is a busy and bustling place, even on a cold and gloomy Friday evening in January. We walked across the road from the neon church and into the market itself, which although the stalls had packed up for the day was still busy with numerous restaurants and bars. A busy and vibrant atmosphere invaded every inch of the vast iron beamed structure that houses the market. A melange of scents, dinner being cooked from a plethora of different cuisines, drifted through the electric lit darkening night air. It felt like an exciting and desirable place to be. As we began to head back towards the venue we walked past Joshua Kane's shop, which is on the outside edge of the market; it was closed, but well lit, with vibrant black and white clothing and accessories in the window. Houndstooth suits (#TheBrummell), matching coats (#TheFawcett) and enormously oversized monochromatic striped scarfs (#TheHollie and its larger sibling #TheShaw) dominated alongside sunglasses (#TheWardenclyffe), hats (#TheGostick) and umbrellas (#TheJeremiah). This window display clearly made a powerful impact on me as I would later come to own many of the items in this window. The display featured 'looks' from a previous show entitled Exploration Fawcett, and drew inspiration from the legendary explorer Percy Fawcett. I would come to wear an outfit very similar to those I saw in the window when, a year later, I attended the Joshua Kane AW17 Journey show. However, standing on that cold pavement in January 2016, looking into the bright shop, I could not imagine owning such treasures as those worn by the beautiful black-wood mannequins that stood in the window gazing out from behind mirrored sunglasses: part exotic aviary and part art installation.

As we approached the venue again we could see that a long queue had formed, snaking along the railing at the front of the church. We joined it, and were instantly enveloped in fragrant cigarette smoke – not the acrid fumes that one might find on any London high street, but more akin to a waft of European tobacco one might catch a faint hint of in Paris' artist quarter. The queue was long, and as we waited it got longer, while the cloud of smoke and vapour grew, and perfumed artificial scents mixed with the fug of smouldering tobacco.

The people queuing around us were an eclectic mix in both age and style, although the predominant group seemed to be the mid-twenties to mid-thirties hipster. Beautifully manicured beards, rolled up trousers, exposed ankles and expensively extensive full sleeve tattoos, swirled all around us.

'I'm working on my new knitwear collection at the moment' came a voice from in front of us.

'Well if you need any help darling just ask and I'll do anything I can' an acquaintance who had stopped to chat opined, before floating away from us.

'[name not heard] isn't here' a voice came from behind us.
'Have you seen [name not heard]' another voice replied.

The queue began to edge forward slowly and we came closer to the gap in the spiked railings that separated us from the venue; a certain degree of anxiety fluttered in the pit of my stomach. Whether this was excitement, the unknown nature of this being the first show I'd attended or a strange worry about not being granted entry, I'm not sure. Then, shocking me out of this thought, the queue surged forward, suddenly flooding through the narrow gap in the railings. It transpired that, whether because it was already rapidly approaching 8 o'clock, or for another reason, they had stopped checking people off the guest list and were now just letting anyone queuing through. We walked through the gates and were handed Joshua Kane branded paper wristbands; we had arrived.

Houndsditch

Among the most prominent (and performative) terrestrial events from my fieldwork were the fashion shows that I attended. They involve aspects of performance, encompass the notion of spectacle, and are associated with the native concept of authenticity, as well as acting as a hub for digital activity, and a site for the convergence of press interest and customers of a particular brand. The first shows I attended were part of the January 2016 London Men's Fashion week, which is known as London Collections Men (LCM). LCM is a reasonably new venture, having only been running biannually since the summer of 2012. It is held in addition to the traditional London Fashion Week, and showcases menswear from predominantly British designers and tailors. Unlike many other, and considerably larger Savile Row tailoring houses that exhibit at LCM, such as Gieves and Hawkes, Hardy Amies and Richard James, the shows I attended were not part of the official calendar and as such were much more easily accessed. In order to attend the likes of the Gieves and Hawkes show, you need to be a designer, photographer, work for an editorial magazine or be an accredited blogger. Initially, I had toyed with the idea of applying as a blogger but then I read the small print that stated the requirements to be considered for an application, which were extreme, and for me unfeasible. One needed more than 10,000 visitors to your blog each month and over 10,000 followers on your social media pages, a fact which highlights how prolific one has to be online to exist in this world.

Once we had ascended the stone steps and passed through the vast white columns that flanked the entrance, we walked through the west door of the church and entered what felt like the inner sanctum of this temple to aesthetics. The interior of the venue had substantial white columns, smaller brothers of those flanking the entrance, which stretched the length of the nave supporting the ceiling and the balconies that wrapped around the edge of the building. The centre of the nave was full height beneath a richly ornate flat ceiling. Golden chandeliers flickered, suspended in mid-air by heavy chains that fell from the heavens, and in the centre of all the English late baroque bombastic pomp was the catwalk itself, inscribed with the initials of Joshua Kane. It would have felt rather more like a traditional Christian space of worship had the entire interior of the venue not been bathed in blue neon light to match the exterior, giving it the aura that it had somehow descended from another world: a baroque spaceship perhaps, or a church from the future. At the far end of the nave, where the rood screen would have traditionally been situated, the space had been once again filled with wrought iron gates, again emblazoned with the gilded initials *JK*. Whether an intentional symbolic choice or not, this very much separated the clients, customers and press from the high altar of tailoring that resided beyond within the chancel, and of course the sanctum sanctorum, Joshua Kane himself. Yet for all this surrogate symbolism the bones of the Christian space of worship were still in place, and racks of candles and a font were pushed into a corner behind where we were stood. These were only small things but to my mind further delineated this building as a sacred space, no matter to whom you were proffering devotion.

The initial email invitation had claimed that there would be 600 attendees, but social media closer to the show increased this estimate to 1000. The venue was certainly full, six to eight rows of chairs lined each side of the catwalk with two or three rows of people standing behind. As the venue began to fill even the balconies played host to stragglers' attempts to gain a better view. In addition to the throng of onlookers that packed the building, film cameras on long boom arms carved tentative arcs in the neon gloom at the end of the catwalk, warming up for the big event itself, like the legs of a giant athletic arachnid. Below, countless eyes of numerous camera lenses winked from the restless photographers, itching to devour the suits that would walk towards them.

In addition to the gaping maw of media that lingered at the end of the catwalk, additional photographers roamed throughout the venue, dressed in black t-shirts; part of the Joshua Kane team. These free roaming agents of image capture pushed indiscriminately through the venue and the crowd for the duration of the show to get to different angles and capture the photographs they required.

We made our way to the left-hand side of the church and found a good spot next to a pillar with a good view over the heads of the people seated in front of us. The rows of seats were almost all full by this point, although some, situated behind pillars with no view, had been left empty. On all of the chairs

Illustration 2.1. An image taken by the author at the Joshua Kane Houndsditch fashion show, showing the interior of the venue. The image is heavily edited in keeping with the experimental style of the author in the early days of digital fieldworking. This image was posted to the author's Instagram account on 8 January 2016. © Joshua M. Bluteau.

in the venue sat a double-sided piece of A4 paper with what were the equivalent of the 'programme notes' you would get at a classical music concert, and while I was not allocated a seat, a pair of empty seats behind the pillar where we were standing allowed me to acquire one. It described the inspiration for the catwalk as coming from a historical event, the siege of Sidney Street in 1911: an East-End shoot-out between the police, led by Winston Churchill, and a band of armed robbers.

At first, I had thought that the name #HOUNDSDITCH was a portmanteau of the words houndstooth (a fabric which is a Joshua Kane signature) and Shoreditch (the location of his shop), but upon reading the 'programme' it became apparent that it was the name of a local street. However, it seemed that I was alone in actually reading this piece of paper so after a quick skim I slid it into an inside pocket of my jacket and began to do what everybody else seemed to be doing, which was looking at each other.

The atmosphere within the venue was fascinating, and a very clear social hierarchy was present within the ticketing structure, with those being granted an exclusive and elusive seat on the front row being highest up this hierarchical scale. Whether it went deeper than this and there was a most desirable place to be seated on the front row or not, I could not fathom. It was a strange sensation to know that the people seated on the front row were all extremely powerful and influential in this world, but I didn't recognise any of them. A gentleman on one end of the front row, facing me, seated at the furthest end of the catwalk where the models would turn, was particularly curious to watch. Not unlike Joshua Kane himself or a young Johnny Depp in appearance, he had shoulder length straight black hair, a small goatee beard and a waxed curled moustache that poked from the shadow cast by his enormous and oversized black hat, somewhere between a Stetson and a Fedora. He wore a beautiful slim fitting black overcoat and sat virtually motionless for a considerable period of time as the building filled. At one point, he stood and removed his coat revealing an equally beautiful fitted black suit that hugged his diminutive frame. As he held out the coat another man emerged from the shadows behind him to take it for him. He sat and inclined his head to the blond gentleman seated on his right who proceeded to engage him in conversation.

A moment later a kerfuffle unfolded just behind us: 'so . . . is somebody sitting in our seats?' A man I recognised as a star of the reality television series 'Made In Chelsea', and social media presence, with in excess of 427,000 Twitter followers, appeared behind us. He had walked as a model in a previous Joshua Kane catwalk show, had just arrived and it transpired very quickly that he did not have a seat. Dressed head to foot in a Joshua Kane navy blue suit and white polka dot shirt, with a gold crucifix dangling from his left ear, blond quaffed hair and with a girlfriend sporting a Joshua Kane red and gold military style jacket in tow, he flounced past us several times with security bustling around him desperately trying to find them seats. They moved away from us, security now carrying extra chairs and trying to find a space for them. A little later we saw them again across the catwalk being shoe-horned into the front row. Quite how this was accomplished when a moment before the front row had been full I do not know, but it was. This gentleman was not, it seemed, a shrinking violet, and as he ensconced himself in the front row he flung his arms around a fellow member of the front row who nestled a large camera in their lap, and who courteously returned the embrace. This incident particularly intrigued me, not only because it is the sort of behaviour that one might expect in a comedy pastiche of a fashion show, but rather more so because it felt as though it represented the attitude of the entire room. There seemed to be an intense sense of anxiety barely contained within the substantial walls of this behemoth of a building. Miller and Woodward (2007) discuss the relationship between anxiety and picking an outfit to wear, but here it was more palpable than this: anxiety of being forgotten perhaps, in the 'Made in Chelsea' star's case, the anxiety of the Joshua Kane team hoping people liked the collection, and there was more too. In waiting for the models to appear, an inflamed form of anxiety began to take hold, as the audience waited for potential new outfits their future selves may use to craft their identity. Whether it was this, a desire to be seen at the venue, where you sat in the pecking order, or some other motivation, anxiety hung thickly in the room like incense, finding its way into every corner; it was infectious.

These observations all occurred whilst waiting for the show to start, although really the show started the moment we walked through the doors. It seems to be a cliché that fashion shows always start late, but in the case of this show it was true. We waited for nearly forty-five minutes inside the venue and in that time the atmosphere grew exponentially more tense. It would not be hyperbolic to say that in the moments before the show started the atmosphere in the venue was akin to a seething mass of anxious expectation, or a bubbling cauldron of anticipation.

Eventually, at very nearly half past eight, the lights dimmed, and the first notes of music emerged from the huge speakers that were dotted on stands throughout the venue. A single solo vocalist began to sing in the semi darkness of the church, a plaintive, soaring, melancholy, heavily ornamented melody, that reminded me of a call to prayer. After this introduction, a solo guitar joined the voice in a flamenco fingerpicked style. The song grew and grew, adding more instruments until it had morphed into a fully developed rock sound with howling vocals. It was at this point that two models dressed in long coats, with mirrored red-lens sunglasses concealing their eyes appeared behind the gates at the far end of the illuminated catwalk, and opened them, before disappearing again. The show had begun. When the lights went down, and the music started, the feeling of anticipation and anxiety in the venue did not relax. In fact, the atmosphere still felt palpable, the air still and torpid with a visceral collective holding of breath. When the gates opened, there was a noticeable surge forward, with those sitting leaning forward for a better view and those standing crowding in behind. Only once the first model started to walk did the dam break and the tension dissolve into the warm darkness as the crowd became absorbed with the show and their attempts to capture it on 'film'. It was almost as if the crowd had been waiting to feast on the images that were going to be presented to them and as they waited got progressively hungrier until they were on the brink of starvation from visual atrophy.

This moment when the models first walked out on to the catwalk made me consider the transformation the models had made by moving from backstage onto the catwalk, and how the control of this had created such an atmosphere of tension and desire in the audience. However, Joshua Kane is very keen to let his audience into this space, albeit in a carefully controlled and well-crafted manner. Exclusive backstage photos will appear on social media before and after the show, a fact which highlights the power of the one who is able to control access to this liminality. Wulff (1998: 104–5) wonderfully describes theatre wings and backstage spaces, highlighting how controlling this liminal space can form part of a performance in itself. This is reminiscent of Goffman's (1971: 231) work on the control of backstage space, and comparable to Joshua Kane's use of images posted to social media, allowing a carefully curated glimpse of the backstage space to become visible to his digital audience. The images which are chosen to be shared craft a specific view into the liminal for the eager audience to see, which, while ostensibly behind-the-scenes, are as well prepared as any of the runway looks.

Houndsditch lasted nearly half an hour and consisted of thirty-four different 'looks' or outfits that were shown on the catwalk: a substantial number, especially as the Joshua Kane house is a small one. Social media indicated that it had taken six months to put the show together with approximately half the garments being made by Joshua Kane himself. The style of the garments was very much in keeping with previous work from Joshua Kane. The suits, and of course this being a tailor it was mainly suits, were in the distinctive Joshua Kane cut. #TheBrummell, slim two-button suit, with notched lapels and a 6-inch drop waist, and a matching low-scoop double-breasted six-button waistcoat with lapels, and #TheGeorge, which to my eye was the same cut but with a shawl lapel, dominated. These were joined by a 6+2-button double-breasted suit, that was new to his catwalks, as well as coats that were similar to the #TheFawcett coat of previous seasons in cut, but with fur panelling and a new style leather and fur bomber jacket; these were accompanied by hats (#TheGostick black with white band), sunglasses (ox-blood #TheWardenclyffe), gloves (new oversized mitten style in red and black oversized houndstooth) and headphones (a secret collaboration with Bang and Olufsen).

It was the fabric choices that moved this season forward conceptually, and bound the show together in a collection. A burgundy or ox-blood theme seemed to run through the collection, with almost all the looks having at least a flash of this colour somewhere. This was typified by the first look we saw, an ox-blood three-piece double-breasted suit with ox-blood #TheTailor shoes, matching socks, ox-blood #TheWardenclyffe sunglasses and ox-blood fur-trimmed Bang and Olufsen headphones. The collaboration with Bang and Olufsen is particularly interesting considering Krause-Jensen's (2013: 146) work with the electronics brand, and his investigation of 'good design', especially when the functionalist post-Bauhaus aesthetic found in traditional Bang & Olufsen products had been embellished with red fur and gold spikes courtesy of Joshua Kane. This look was teamed with oversized mittens in a large red and black houndstooth in a brighter shade of contrasting red. This ox-blood hue was continued through long tailored coats and short leather bomber jackets (both with colour matched zip-off fur panels) as well as the leather trim on a new set of luggage that some models carried. Even when the wilder fabrics appeared, tartan-esque exploded checks, they had hints of ox-blood running through them. The complementing red of the over-sized houndstooth mittens was continued into scarves, jumpers and knitwear. Black and white returned to the runway for a number of looks as polka dots in shirts and ties, but nearly always teamed with at least a flash of ox-blood. There were a couple of exceptions to the ox-blood theme in the middle of the show where a procession of black and white outfits were shown, as though to highlight the light and shade of this collection. This then softened into gold as a number of wildly patterned gold jacquard dinner suits were shown, and the ox-blood returned, woven alongside the gold. The selection that followed was a little more demure, mainly black (and more wearable) versions of clothes that we had already seen plus a smattering of the ubiquitous Joshua Kane trademark houndstooth, though a smaller version of the fabric than previous collections. Throughout this show the neckwear was interesting; mostly black on black shirts to highlight the tailoring, it moved from standard black ties to black bow ties as the show progressed, perhaps highlighting the passage of time into evening wear. The only colours that had really been seen up to this point, bar black and white, were gold and ox-blood. As the final model walked it became apparent that we weren't going to see any more. The show finished with a number of metallic off-white pieces showcasing a print of three tailors that Joshua Kane had previously sold as a print on scarves, and is tattooed onto his forearm. Rosenblatt (1997) explores how tattooing in the USA has moved from the preserve of subculture and the lower class to having a renaissance and becoming accepted and desired by a wider portion of society. He goes on (ibid.: 306–307) to explore how tattoos are connected to notions of the self and are both 'public and private acts' part of a 'larger process of self exploration'. Whether this is the case or not for Joshua Kane it is hard to say, but by linking the designs he sells to the images inked onto his body he is consciously selling a part of himself as the brand alongside these goods, perhaps elevating his notion of self beyond a corporeally bounded one.

The way the crowd responded to the models was fascinating. It was like participating in some sort of experimental promenade theatre. As each model began his walk a sea of glowing rectangles rose and fell in an almost symbiotic unison as the massed crowd attempted to capture the 'look' on their smartphones. I have to admit that this was a practice that somewhat bemused me, but despite this I found myself caught up in this singular collective response displayed by the crowd and reached into my pocket to take some pictures of my own. I was using an Apple iPhone 5s, which whilst not cutting-edge is fairly modern, and as you can see from illustration 2.2, the best photo that I was able to capture from the show is distinctly poor in quality: blurred, streaky and overexposed. I suspect this image is similar to those achieved by the vast majority of the people taking photos on their smartphones, particularly the ones who were not seated on the front row. This led me to question whether the purpose of taking photos on one's smartphone was really about

Illustration 2.2. An image taken by the author at the Joshua Kane Houndsditch fashion show, showing a model wearing a red and white checked, shearling trimmed greatcoat and oversized houndstooth mittens. This snapshot is of poor quality, but the best that the author was able to capture from his position at the show. © Joshua M. Bluteau.

trying to document the event or not, especially when the professional quality images taken by Joshua Kane's team would soon be available online. It seems as though the crowd's attempts to take pictures was less about capturing high-quality images of the show but more associated with a tool for acquiring markers of memory, and proof that one had attended the event, both of which can be utilised as fuel for one's social media post or personal posterity.

Wagner (1995) suggests that television adverts are more desirable than the actual products displayed in them. If we conceptualise these adverts as hyperreal images then it is possible to suggest that the image of an object is more desirable than the actual object itself (see Baudrillard 2003: 41). There is an element of this happening above when the attendees at the fashion show take photos to capture not the garments themselves, but a hyperreal version of them, stored in the form of a digital image. In this case, the explanation for such poor-quality images being taken of the catwalk is that capturing the outfits in this hyperreal fashion (on digital film) is actually seen as more desirable, than simply viewing them in a non-hyperreal reality (with one's eyes). Furthermore, there is an element of Sontag's (2008: 11) suggestion here, that photos confer 'a kind of immortality' on an event. Perhaps the attendees simply wanted to immortalise their participation in the show or perhaps, following Miller and Sinanan (2017), digitally documenting the event actually enhanced the audience's experience.

If the way in which the crowd reacted to the models was interesting, the way the models behaved was even more so. The general demeanour was that of a pallid, death-like, gaunt automaton, although it must be noted that with most wearing sunglasses and some hats or scarfs too, there was often not a great deal to be seen of their faces. The way they moved was captivating, the suits being cut so slim that one would have expected a shuffle, but in fact, and without appearing to move their limbs excessively, they appeared to glide up and down the catwalk like suited marionettes at the will and whim of some grand puppet master.

At the end of the show, once all thirty-four 'looks' had been shown, there was a pause, the lights dimmed then came back up again on the catwalk and all of the models did one final walk, staying close together this time, and as they entered through the big black gates they began to applaud. As the first models returned to the catwalk there was an initial clamorous welcome followed by a small polite smattering of applause from the audience, although this soon faded to almost nothing, with an occasional eruption for a particular look or model. It seemed that instead of using their hands to applaud, a large percentage of the audience were occupied with their smartphones, taking numerous pictures of this final walk of the models. Bright white rectangles of glowing screen flashed and glimmered throughout the darkened crowd: digital fireflies in the gloom. I wondered at the time whether the models applauding as they walked was an attempt to coerce the audience into greater applause to no avail, but later on reflection I realised that they were not clapping themselves, but the clothes. It seemed that in the world of fashion the models that carry the clothes up and down the catwalk are little more than clothes hangers. Mannequins whose true self is of little consequence, they exist purely to provide the new skin the designer has crafted from thread and cloth with a shape giving body of sinew and flesh; they are ontologically shallow. I would almost say that they were there to give the clothes life but that may be unfair to the garments in question, which did not appear to need the models to steal the show. There was a clear message that the clothes were the stars of this show, or perhaps I should say the performers in the show, for the true star was, of course, Joshua Kane.

When the last model had stepped onto the runway for the final time, and it was obvious that the event was drawing to a close, a hush fell on the waiting crowd, like the silence in the eye of a storm or the noiseless claustrophobia of being hit by a wave and pushed underwater. Then he appeared, the elfin-featured tailor himself, wearing what was a relatively demure outfit by the standards of his models, bounded out from behind the gates and onto the catwalk, eyelinered eyes twinkling from behind his spectacles. The wave broke, and noise erupted: applause, whoops, screams, whistles. An avalanche of devotion and adulation spilled forth from the waiting crowd who visibly surged forward again, as they had at the start of the show to better catch a glimpse of their idol, resplendently clad in a black and white thin striped 6+2-button double-breasted jacket, slim black trousers and the distinctive Gostick wide brimmed hat in black with a thick white ribbon band. The material of the jacket was made of disjointed diagonal stripes creating a disorientating effect, as though staring at the static noise on an analogue television screen, and the audience loved it. Their collective response felt like so much more than the mere acknowledgement of enjoyment or approval of the garments that had just been paraded before the crowd, as models prostituted their tailored wares. Instead, this had a distinct sensation of the spiritual, as though some strange form of transubstantiation had occurred in that moment and this tailor had been transformed into a deity. This may sound like an exaggeration or some hyperbolic rhetoric, but this is not the case; however, the deity in question in this case exists in a neo-religious spectacular world where he is a producer of images: a very Debordian construct (Debord 2012).

The sense of deification or perhaps beatification was further highlighted by those in the audience who had dressed in homage to Joshua Kane. There were numerous members of the audience wearing items that were distinctively Joshua Kane. #TheGostick hats, houndstooth trousers, black and white striped jackets, #TheFawcett camel coats and polka dot suits all floated through the room. Some even went further and had clearly styled their appearance after their idol, sporting long hair, goatee beards and curled moustaches. However, this notion of paying homage at the feet of this tailor by modelling oneself in his own image was reinforced by the models, some of whom looked like carbon copies of Joshua Kane himself.

Joshua Kane raised a hand in acknowledgment at the end of the catwalk, turned, and began to walk, catching up with the last model and giving him a congratulatory pat on the back. They disappeared together through the black gates, which were then closed behind them by two coated models. The show was over, the lights came up and as one the massed crowd began to dissipate, with a rapidity that surprised me.

Sir Tom Baker

Much like the Joshua Kane show, the Sir Tom Baker show falls within LCM but seems to be part of an under-the-radar cadre that doesn't feature on the official programme. An invitation was extended to those interested through email, although unlike the Joshua Kane show where this was done more than a month in advance, the email from Tom Baker came only seven days before the show. Despite this, my response elicited a hand addressed envelope which came through the post bearing a pair of invitations.

On one side of the heavyweight A5 card invitation were details of the time and location of the show, and on the reverse a sepia stained greyscale photograph, showing a lined piece of notepaper with the following hand-written words, in a heavy, disjointed hand:

BE <u>CALM</u> AND I WON'T SHOOT.
GIVE Me ALL YOUR BILLS
EXCEPT 1's & 2's,
QUICKLY

An intriguing hint at a theme perhaps? Were we to expect a raft of 1940's inspired double-breasted pin-striped bank robber suits? Given my previous knowledge of the work of Tom Baker I thought it unlikely. This is a tailor who can make a sequined suit sinister and seems to specialise in making lamé aggressive, so for us to witness anything traditional in his show was, I thought, unlikely. Indeed, if that had been the case I would have probably been disappointed. Yet despite my prediction that we would not see a traditional take on the bank robber, perhaps a flavour of the romance associated with the bank robber in popular culture would permeate the show.

This time, instead of the more traditional suit I had chosen to wear for the Joshua Kane show, I had picked a rather more punk inspired outfit, which

I thought fitting for Tom Baker. I wore skinny black jeans, with a black asymmetrical three-button Vivienne Westwood suit jacket over an Allsaints pink scoop neck t-shirt which was invisible under the jacket. An Alexander McQueen super skinny black tie with a blue paint splatter and skull print motif was tied around my bare neck and a white linen pocket square peaked from the jacket's chest pocket. On my feet were silver Barajas boots from Archie Eyebrows with a two-and-a-half inch Cuban heel. A Jeffery-West belt featuring a buckle styled as a vampiric hand snaked around my waist, and on my head was a burgundy mountain hat from Vivienne Westwood. I finished the look with a number of chunky rings from the Great Frog, including one of their iconically punk eyeball rings, and a smudge of eyeliner.

With the invitations in the inside pocket of my jacket, and accompanied this time by my partner, we tubed across London to Oxford Street, and presented ourselves at the 100 Club at 7.30pm, to be told to pop back in fifteen minutes time. We went for coffee, and clearly weren't the only ones waiting for the show to start because at the next table was a woman drinking coffee with an invitation to the show on her table picking her way through a pile of spectacles. Twenty minutes later we returned, manoeuvred our way past the newly formed gaggle of smokers crowding the door, down a short corridor and then halfway down a set of stairs to the makeshift kiosk cum box office, the thud of bass heavy music already loud as it crept up the stairs from the basement below. Here a tall thin youngish gentleman dressed entirely in black but for a black and white spotted scarf draped neatly around his neck, a look which seemed to clash rather with the bright red clipboard he held, checked our invitations and asked for a name to check off the guest list. 'Joshua Bluteau', I said. He consulted the list, flicking over a few pages. 'Jones?' he enquired. 'No, Bluteau'. He began to check down the list of names beginning with a P: 'with a B', I said. He looked up and waved a weary hand down the stairs gesturing for us to go in.

The music got louder as we descended the stairs into the basement club, walking in the footsteps of iconic punk bands The Sex Pistols, The Clash and The Stranglers who had all played the dingy cellar. Tonight it was bathed in red light from theatre-style lighting hung from the ceiling, and already humming and alive with the noise of people having conversations over the invasive bass of the music. As we walked in on our immediate left was the catwalk, covered in an off-white temporary plastic sheet, the sort of thing you see on the floor in films before a carefully planned murder. On our right was the bar, already three deep, and people were milling around, settling into their seats and chatting within their couples or little groups. It was like descending into an authentic 1970's working men's club that just happened to be situated within the immortal realm of a punk-loving Devil. Hellish certainly, though not unpleasant, and the guests certainly looked comfortable; there was not a

Illustration 2.3. An image taken prior to Sir Tom Baker's AW16 catwalk show, showing the interior of the 100 Club. The image is heavily edited in keeping with the experimental style of the author's early digital fieldwork and was posted to Instagram on 11 January 2016. © Joshua M. Bluteau.

trace of the anxiety that plagued Joshua Kane's show, rather a convivial informality and cosiness within the dark corners out of the red glare of the plastic catwalk. Our tickets allowed us a second-row seat or standing in the third, where since there was a good view of the end of the catwalk from a nice spot next to a pillar we chose to stand.

At seventeen minutes past eight, suddenly, all the lights went out, casting the room into total darkness but for the ubiquitous fire exit signs that cast a greenish fug into the darkened room. Then in the dark and suddenly silent room, a heavily distorted voice, pre-empted with a crackle of static, spoke through the speakers:

Allow me to be frank at the commencement. You will not like me. The gentle-men will be envious and the ladies will be repelled. You will not like me now and you will like me a good deal less as we go on. Ladies, an announcement: I am up for it, all the time. That is not a boast or an opinion, it is bone hard medical fact. I put it round you know. And you will watch me putting it round and sigh for it. Don't. It is a deal of trouble for you and you are better off watching and drawing your conclusions from a distance than you would be if I got my tarse up your petticoats. Gentlemen. Do not despair, I am up for that as well. And the same warning applies. Still your cheesy erections till I have had my say. But later when you shag – and later you will shag, I shall expect it of you and I will know if you have let me down – I wish you to shag with my homuncular image rattling in your gonads. Feel how it was for me, how it is for me and ponder. Was that the same shudder he sensed? Did he know something more profound? Or is there some wall of wretchedness that we all batter with our heads at that shining, livelong moment. That is my prologue, nothing in rhyme, no protestations of modesty, you were not expecting that I hope. I am John Wilmot, second Earl of Rochester and I do not want you to like me.

With that the music started and the lights came up, illuminating the catwalk in white light, with a spotlight on the far wall, a model in a long black coat and round brimmed hat spread-eagled against the wall, back to the audience. The music played for a few bars and then the model turned, topless and heav-ily tattooed beneath his open coat, knee-length, with fur collar and leather cuffs. He began to walk, long legs in skinny jeans that had been roughly coated in red fabric paint. The show had begun.

The catwalk show was what anyone who is familiar with the work of Sir Tom Baker would expect, that is to say a traditional tailoring style heavily influenced by a punk heritage and imbued with a series of classic Sir Tom Baker idiosyncrasies: beautiful English silhouette jackets (high arm holes, fit-ted waist, double vent) in a range of non-traditional fabrics from over-coating weight wool to lamé and sequins, heavily detailed with pointed rear (western inspired) collars, heavy use of top stitch, covered buttons, interesting cuff details (the large turn-back with a three-button detail was particularly prev-alent, similar to that which you might find on a pirate's frockcoat), frequent leather panelling, fur collars and biker inspired metal studding. The coats that came down the catwalk were similarly detailed but very long, dramatic and almost cape-like or fitted frockcoats with two buttons to the rear of the jacket, like one might find on a tailcoat but with a chain connecting them.

The vast majority of the collection was black, albeit highlighted with dif-ferent fabrics and textures, such as leather panels and fur collars. A sparkle was brought to some jackets with studding or satin-covered buttons. Very few of the models wore a conventional shirt and tie under the jackets or coats. Instead, black t-shirts, either with large black and white prints of faces, one bearing Aleister Crowley, another Edger Allan Poe, some with holes torn, or others scoop neck but unadulterated. The association with the faces that appeared on the t-shirts is an aspirational link with historical figures the tailor feels an affinity with or draws inspiration from. This is synonymous with the naming of Joshua Kane's two original suit styles, the Brummel and the George, a nod to the regency dandy Beau Brummel and the Prince Regent. Jeffery-West, the bootmaker, who provided the shoes and boots for Sir Tom Baker's show, equally employ historical figures (both real and fictional) to name their lasts. All of these associations are an attempt to increase the native authenticity of the brand, by situating it in a wider historical narrative of sartorially inspiring individuals. Perhaps there is also an element of aligning oneself, both as a brand and a purchaser of that brand, with notions of 'eccentricity', and historical eccentric figures, something Marcus (1995) suggests is important for some in establishing a sense of self.

When there was colour, other than the shoes, it was in the jackets; dark blues, silver, dark green and burgundy all made an appearance, but all muted and in unusual fabric such as brocade, velvet, or in one particularly fine example a needle-cord that looked as though it had been distressed with a blowtorch. An additional detail that intrigued me was the partial heavily pleated kilt-like skirts of differing lengths that some models wore. For some looks this just extended from the back of the jacket like a reimagined tailcoat in a matching fabric. At other times, it hung at a longer length down one leg matching the jeans in colour (of course black), or was shorter and hung above the knee at the front giving a very skirt-like appearance. This is not to say that there was anything remotely feminised about the looks being presented by Sir Tom Baker. If anything, the skirting which was used added to the sense of aggression which was being projected by the models, with the billowing skirts adding a sense of drama to their swaggering walks.

The trousers the models wore were particularly interesting. Only one or two of the models that walked wore suit trousers. The rest wore black skinny jeans, some with large holes cut in them, others acid washed, shredded or with a panel of the jacket's material appliquéd down the seams of one or both legs like a pair of futuristic tuxedo trousers. There was another reoccurring theme where a pair of the jeans had an inset red stripe, five inches or so wide, that ran around the left knee, almost like a bandage motif.

The shoes provided by Jeffery-West, or rather I should say boots, because they were almost all boots bar a few pairs of velvet slippers, were a wild range of patent and metallic leathers in a variety of wonderfully lurid colours that matched gloriously with the sinister vibe of the clothing. Pointed and subtly heeled, this selection of footwear is again very much what one would expect from Jeffery-West, a company that features a cloven heel design to the heel of all their shoes as an homage to the devil. They also name their lasts after some of their heroes, a selection that includes numerous, and typically notorious, artists, musicians and actors. Perhaps most appropriately, their super-pointy heeled boot that was seen frequently on this catwalk is named Rochester.

The models were an interesting bunch. They were made up to look at though they had just had a fight backstage, with cuts on their faces, and were pale against the bright lights that illuminated them. Some had long dank hair, though most wore it short, choppy and spiked. One of the models wore his hair in a rather shocking shade of green. The hats, when they were worn, were original one-off commissions from Stephen Jones and were mostly asymmetrical or otherwise subtly subverted versions of traditional western men's headwear. In contrast to the Joshua Kane show, Sir Tom Baker's models were not merely hangers for the clothes, or shallow ontological mannequins to be clothed by the tailor. Rather, they were chosen and made up to embody the aesthetic and attitude of the tailor himself, more an ontologically deep extension of the tailor's personal attitude and aesthetic than a blank canvas for the clothes. This differentiation between deep and shallow ontology was stark between the two shows. In Joshua Kane's show the clothes were all that mattered; this is a shallow ontology, providing a blank 'canvas' for new customers to step inside. However, Sir Tom Baker's models displayed an attitude in addition to their clothes which spoke of a deeper ontology. In this case Tom Baker is not only selling empty clothes for a new customer to inhabit, but is selling an attitude, and sense of self too. This speaks to Miller's (2010: 16) work on depth ontology but also Battaglia's (1995: 5) comments on the relationship between a self and an audience. She suggests that 'audiences indulging others' self-images . . . are actively . . . committing their own self action' and this relates to an appreciation of authenticity of self-production (idem). In the case of these fashion shows the relationship between audience and tailor offers possibilities for models, clothing and audience members to share in a process of shared identity construction. This sense of individuality permeated the designs and suggested not only an aesthetic which a potential customer might buy in to, in order to craft their individual identity, but an attitude as well.

Sir Tom Baker's models moved with a considerably greater presence than those at Joshua Kane's show. They seemed to not care especially how fast they walked or the precise place to stop on the catwalk before turning, yet all this was accomplished with immense swagger. This was in stark contrast to the emotionless models in Joshua Kane's show who seemed to glide perfectly with total disengagement from the reality of their situation. Naturally, the clothes were still centre stage, but for Tom Baker they still need to be inhabited by a personality.

The music mirrored this anarchic individualistic feel; a DJ in the booth next to the catwalk lurched between different tracks, sometimes seamlessly

Illustration 2.4. An image taken during Sir Tom Baker's AW16 catwalk show, showing a model wearing a frockcoat featuring embellished pockets, chain link detailing and western inspired pointed rear collar. The image was posted to Instagram on 11 January 2016 by the author. © Joshua M. Bluteau.

and at other times with noticeable gaps. Punk, heavy metal, screamo and classical were all represented, all oppressively loud, helping to perpetuate the mood that had been created by the clothes.

Twenty minutes or so after it had begun it was all over. The models completed one final walk, closer together this time, like one huge tailored snake, before they assembled at the rear of the catwalk looking mean, as Tom Baker himself appeared, tall and thin, dressed in black jeans, black t-shirt and a beautiful black jacket, with interesting seams on the back of the sleeves that stuck out; naturally Jeffery-West boots shod his feet. He sheepishly lolloped to nearly the end of the catwalk, his shock of ginger hair iridescent under the lights, before giving half a wave and retreating back off stage. The models followed, the lights returned to their pre-show hell-red setting and the music returned to a background thud, which now seemed rather quiet. Once again, the venue burst into life as people stood and began to make their way to the exit, and the club started to empty.

Comparison of Depth Ontology

It was impossible not to draw comparisons between the two shows, from Joshua Kane and Sir Tom Baker, having seen them in such rapid succession. My initial observations framed this comparison as a simplistic duality of light and dark: a heavenly and hellish pageant of brightly lit church and red gloom-shrouded basement. However, later reflection led me to consider the two shows as displaying differing approaches to the nature in which model and outfit interacted, both in isolation and under the gaze of an audience (see Entwistle and Wissinger 2006, 2012; see also Evans 2013).

In the case of fashion shows from the likes of Joshua Kane, I suggest a shallow ontology is at work where the models wearing the clothes are ontologically non-existent. The clothes themselves have more personality and life than the models, and it is the clothes themselves which have a character to play. This is undoubtedly a calculated choice to make the clothes more accessible and commercial for potential purchasers, but it projected a strangely dehumanised atmosphere when watching the outfits and their human fillers glide along the catwalk.

In contrast, the models walking for Sir Tom Baker display a much greater depth of ontology, suggesting that their outfits are an extension of their personality: a personality displayed by their make-up and idiosyncratic modes of walking the runway. This punk-inspired aggressive individuality was the chosen character for this show, but much like a troupe of actors Sir Tom Baker's models performed their role alongside their costumes and were more than just the clothes hangers that glided around Joshua Kane's runway. This is not to say that one method of display is better or more effective. It seems that differing depths of ontology are utilised by designers to best sell their garments. Both methods achieve a heightening of desirability for the garments on show, either by allowing the audience to project their own personal desire for individuality into the garment worn by an ontologically invisible model, such as in Kane's show, or by models performing the individual attitude of the tailor in question, such as in Baker's show, creating a desire to belong to the gang of individuals. It must be noted however, that such a differing approach does not distance either tailor from their customers as both shows had audience members clad in their tailor's wares.

Whether it is ontologically empty tailored clothes ready and waiting for prospective individuals to step into, or the gang of individuals ready to let you join them if only you purchase the right clothes, the same end point is achieved by such fashion shows. The tailor's latest collection is displayed and its desirability is heightened as much as possible. However, the depth ontology of the models is only a small part of this concocted desirability, which is driven most palpably by the spectacle as a whole.

The Spectacle

Aspects of these fashion shows felt ritualistic, and there was a temptation to analyse them accordingly. However, engaging with these shows as spectacular events, situated within a world of spectacles, is more apposite (see Evans 2013). As such it is Debord's work which I will use as an optic through which to view these events from my fieldwork: 'the spectacle is self-generated, and it makes up its own rules: it is a specious form of the sacred' (Debord 2012: 20). This is fitting, since this notion that the spectacle replaces our need for the sacred without totally fulfilling its role is crucial to the reason why I have chosen to analyse the fashion shows I attended as spectacles and not rituals. There is a pseudo-religiosity in their atmosphere and structure but this, as Debord tells us, is all part of the spectacle. Debord argues that a shift has occurred and that reality has become fiction.

He begins his treatise on the spectacle with the following statement: 'THE WHOLE LIFE of those societies in which modern conditions of production prevail presents itself as an immense accumulation of spectacles. All that was once directly lived has become mere representation' (ibid.: 12). He is stating here the very essence of his theory, that we have reached a stage where it is impossible to differentiate reality from illusion, which he terms the spectacle.

'THE SPECTACLE IS NOT a collection of images; rather, it is a social relationship between people that is mediated by images' (idem). This is crucial, since for Debord the spectacle is not confined to singular spectacular events such as the fashion shows that I am presently discussing, or even the images created by such shows, but is better understood as 'weltanschauung' or the philosophical world view of a group, the group in this case being western society (ibid.: 13). The spectacle is so tightly woven through society that it is impossible to separate the two. However, these images are still important; they may not make up the spectacle in their own right but they are the tools of the spectacle, reality has become saturated by images and these images are so prolific that people craft themselves in the image of images, the result being that notions of production become increasingly unimportant as people are distanced from the products themselves, instead content to purchase the image of the product, fashion shows being a prime example of the display, commercialisation and fetishisation of the image. This notion of consuming the image works on two levels, both in a Baudrillardian sense of consuming a product not for its economic worth but for its sign-value, but also in an increasingly digital world where people often purchase items which they have only ever seen as digital images and never seen in physical reality until they arrive.

> the spectacle is both the outcome and the goal of the dominant mode of production. It is not something added to the real world – not a decorative element, so to speak. On the contrary, it is the very heart of society's real unreality. In all its specific manifestations – such as news or propaganda, advertising or the actual consumption of entertainment – the spectacle epitomised the prevailing model of social life. (Idem)

The notion that the spectacle is not merely a 'product of the technology of the mass dissemination of images' but is an inherent part of who we are and how we conceive of and interact with the world is useful in the link between the physical and digital aspects of my research and reinforces the importance of both aspects being part of any discussion in this area (ibid.: 12–13). Since Debord wrote this work the mass dissemination of images has taken a quantum leap with the proliferation of image-based social media which can be accessed instantly by its many smartphone-based users; however, it is still important to situate the rest of society, beyond just the dissemination of images, within this model of the spectacle.

As such we must situate the fashion shows I describe within a world, both physically and digitally, of the spectacle: a world which has made the transition from 'having to appearing' (ibid.: 16). Essentially, as Debord tells us, the consumer becomes 'a consumer of illusion' as we subject 'all reality to an appearance which is in effect . . . labor's product' (ibid.: 32–33). This means that appearance itself has become a commodity, and performance more real than reality, while the commodity of appearance is increasingly fetishised (ibid.: 26). This idea works well with Baudrillard's notion of hyperreality, since the detachment from production, or the invisibility as Baudrillard would term it, leads to free-floating signs, which in this case are the attributes of appearance. However, as discussed, I suggest these signs are not as free-floating as Baudrillard describes them but rather are at the mercy of the *ocean currents* that surround them. Part of this is due to the existence of digital images of production being made available, which circumvent the obsoletion of production and instead grant it hyperreality. As such, this modified view of Baudrillard has been used in tandem with Debord to unpick the physical aspects of my research; their theoretical concepts will also be used below to assess the ever-changing modernity of digital interaction.

In terms of the two fashion shows I have described, they are both spectacles in their own right, within the vernacular, and a crucial part of the world of the spectacle. In a society where people's appearance is commodified, and that commodity is fetishised, fashion shows and the whole apparatus of the fashion industry act as a means for producing 'real images' which are 'transformed into real beings' (ibid.: 17). The images become beacons for aspiration and people purchase these images in order to modify their appearance. This can be as simple as viewing an image from the fashion show and deciding that it looks cool, leading you to purchase an item from that brand in order to alter your appearance and bring it closer to the ideas and identity of that brand, or it could be as involved as repeatedly consuming the images on social media and attending the shows.

Attending the shows themselves may appear to be more real than simply consuming the images through a brand's various media channels. One could argue that to attend the show you are seeing the real clothes and consuming a physical event which surely must be something more than merely an image. However, a fashion show is as much a performance as a piece of theatre, with the models carefully chosen, the clothes carefully adjusted and the mood, set, music and lights carefully choreographed. The designer is the artist who has painted a multi-dimensional performance for the crowd to consume, but this is not real, these are hyperreal images.

Debord's suggestion as to the nature of the spectacle is that we don't know that we are at the mercy of the spectacle and its machinations. It suggests that we are powerless to resist the images that are forced upon us, but I am not convinced. If this is true, then why do people buy certain brands and attend certain shows – to craft specific images from the plethora that form the spectacle. Whilst everything may well be pretence, we can at least be the masters of our own performance if we wish to mould ourselves into a specific image. Miller and Woodward (2012: 89) describe a group who choose to wear 'post-semiotic' blue jeans as an attempt to be invisible, but my research has focused on a group who want to stand out. Their subjects defy Sartre's notion of societal function; a garment has emerged which is ostensibly classless, equalising and invisible. In a world of blue jeans, one's apparel no longer 'proclaims the man', although of course in all things sartorial there will be those who prize certain denim over others. In contrast, my subjects are dreamers who defy societal norms and occupy a dandified category, again much like those wearing blue jeans undermining historical distinctions that once existed between professions, gender and class (Sartre 1993: 167). Therefore, I suggest that while the basic thesis of Debord stands, the advent of digital media, with its infinite content of freely available images, has accelerated the consumption of images to the extent that Debord's spectacle has fractured. Therefore, we must now consider not a single society of the spectacle but a society of spectacles.

While there will have always been those who did not fit, such as my network of dandies, it is now possible to restrict a vast quantity of the images that we consume to images that we want to see. As such we can tailor the images we consume to apparel ourselves. This leads to a monumental increase in the power of the individual but also of brands themselves who can create a spectacular relationship with a specific group of clients who are set on acquiring the image of that brand, albeit in a reflected and refracted sense. Whilst this is not individualism in the strictest sense, this does allow smaller networks of those striving to be individual to pay homage to a similar set of images.

The fashion shows do precisely this, playing to the gallery as it were, for the brand's set of acolytes. The power of the fashion show, in terms of its spectacular nature, is the sheer volume and quality of the images that are created, both at the very moment of its performance and in the aftermath. Joshua Kane is a digital master of this, teasing his online audience with images of small parts of the new designs before the show, and saturating his social media with images from the show in the immediate aftermath, allowing people to either relive it or feel like they were there if they were not. In addition, behind the scenes photos are often released later, and then, as specific parts of the collection come in to his shop, the images are posted again. Likewise, if he is wearing a new design, there is a sale, a new fashion show or almost any other excuse, then the images are again reposted. The repetition of the images doesn't confine the fashion show to a singular event but elevates it to a spectacular event which is reworked and relived in the images that are produced surrounding it, making it hyperreal and detached from a normal temporal reality. This is only considering the images produced by the brand itself, and many other images will be taken, posted and shared by attendees, acolytes and the fashion media. Yet for all this repetition, such brands have a particular image and need to appeal to a specific network of individuals.

Chapter 3

OTHER ELIZABETHANS
AND DIGITAL INDIVIDUALS

Alas! how most of the things in this world have nothing in their favour but appearances! The baldrick was glittering with gold in front, but was nothing but simple buff behind. Vainglorious as he was, Porthos could not afford to have an entirely gold-worked baldrick, but had, at least, half of one. His care for his cold and the necessity of the cloak became intelligible.
—Alexander Dumas, *The Three Musketeers*

If Porthos had been on Instagram, this unfortunate incident need not have occurred. Dumas' Musketeer could have displayed his partially embellished shoulder belt using artfully angled photographs which showed off the glittering gold front whilst keeping the buff behind invisible. As it was, his cloak attempted to craft his appearance through concealment but was undone by the unfortunate collision and subsequent entanglement with D'Artagnan. Whilst it is possible to affect such a manipulation of appearances, attempts to craft one's self misleadingly in the terrestrial world are easily exposed; in the digital world however, such exposure is much harder to engender. This, Sartre (1993) would tell us, is the essence of acting in 'bad faith', attempting to deceive others around you as to your station in life.

I encountered numerous individuals during my terrestrial fieldwork in London, however it was in the digital world that some of the most interesting individuals began to reveal themselves. Early in my fieldwork I began to use the image sharing social media platform Instagram, initially following tailors I had met but gradually adding my own content and building a rapport with other like-minded users. Following Holy (1988), I worked with Instagram as an observing participant methodologically echoing Wacquant's (2004) notion that one cannot understand boxing or what being a boxer is like without becoming a boxer. There are reflections of this modus operandi in Luvaas's (2016) work where he explores fashion blogging and street style photography by developing these practices as part of his research methodology. I was not content to merely observe other's interactions, or view the intersect of the terrestrial and digital world for my participants. Instead, I was determined to discover what it was like to be a committed user of this platform and as such I began to interact with it every day, posting images and spending hours every day online browsing and interacting, a methodological approach which I termed immersive cohabitation (Bluteau 2019). Such an approach built thematically on pioneering digital anthropology from authors such as Garsten and Wulff (2003), Miller (2011, 2012), Boellstorff (2012), Horst and Miller (2012) and Hine (2015), but my approach was subtly different. I slowly began to discover that there was a network of individuals, interested in sartorial matters, already established on Instagram that were producing images of themselves, their clothing and their outward appearance on a regular basis. It took me many months of daily interaction with Instagram to access this network, developing links with a sufficient number of its members to be accepted, and even longer to understand more thoroughly how the platform worked for the individuals involved. To begin with I was unsure whether the images produced by these individuals were mere vanity, a space to digitally peacock, or whether they were searching for affirmation, like-minded 'friends', inspiration, or the enjoyment of the creative process. It became apparent that the platform provided all of these benefits for any committed user, though the time drain and investment, not only of time and money (for the clothes which were desirable to view are not cheap) but also the psychological investment in constantly producing images of one's self to be judged by others, clearly took its toll on some users who intermittently took time away from the platform. I have painted it as a double-edged sword, which is certainly comparable to my experience of using the platform; however, this does not negate the joy it clearly gives many users. Yet despite this joy one cannot escape the fact that the digital landscape is one in which discourse is regulated and controlled – one where images are used to alter our perceptions of normality and reality.

Social Illegitimacy

Foucault's (1990: 4) 'other Victorians' is a concept used to understand the place within Victorian society for those people who do not fit into the idealised behaviours dealt with by Foucault's repressive hypothesis; those with 'illegitimate sexualities' (idem): 'The brothel and the mental hospital would be those places of tolerance: the prostitute, the client, and the pimp, together with the psychiatrist and his hysteric' (idem). This idea of social illegitimacy sat prominently in my thinking. If such a category existed, was it still relevant, and what did it look like? Throughout my fieldwork, ideas of the conservative in opposition to the flamboyant or those who dress to live, as opposed to those who live to dress, were crystallised as I explored both a terrestrial world and its corresponding digital landscape. Cole asserts that there is an assumption that 'an active interest in clothing' is 'feminine and frivolous' and that the study of twentieth-century men's clothing has reinforced this notion that men who 'dress up' are peculiar, and that 'implied in this peculiarity is homosexuality' (Cole 2000: 2).

Yet the participants I worked with do dress up, and it is a significant part of their lives and their day-to-day lived experience. These are men for whom the notion of the 'postsemiotic' garment is an abhorrence – clothing is important, with dress becoming an inseparable part of the body: a second skin. Despite becoming surrounded by a research world which took this to be the case, I am aware that this is not the generally held notion within the western world (or even the majority of London), at least not to the extent that I have observed. Indeed, the work of Miller and Woodward (2012) within the same city where I conducted my research shows us that a wish to blend in and dress invisibly is desirable to many. It is therefore my assertion that my participants are part of an 'other' – 'other Elizabethans' within the larger communities that they inhabit. For these other Elizabethans, in the spirit of Foucault, Instagram and the atelier would be those places of tolerance: the dandy, the gentleman, and the dreaming grocer, together with the tailor and his client.

The synonym implied here between Foucauldian sexuality and my study of dress is intentional. It seems to me that the account Foucault gives of his 'repressive hypothesis' must deal with dress (Foucault 1990: 15–49). Foucault does not mention it specifically, but discourse – taken in the context of a postdigital age (see Bluteau 2019: 2) – encompasses the (digital) image as well as a literal manifestation of an individual, including their dress. Therefore, if discourse evolves around sexuality to intellectually clothe the body, moving away from explicit confession to shrouded euphemism, then literal clothing must follow suit. A link, therefore, between physical appearance and notions of sexuality is inescapable.

Beyond reading the suit as an object of desire and repression, and dress a second skin, the notion of social illegitimacy percolated with my advancing engagement in the digital world. I began to wonder whether those who crafted themselves as individuals were, almost by definition, societal outcasts – with the digital realm supplanting Foucault's brothel and asylum. While it may seem tautological to suggest that there can be a collective of individuals, I use the concept of network based on the work of Kapferer (1969) and Boissevain (1978) which allows for the analysis of interaction between disparate individual actors. Their work shows how initially invisible links between individuals may be discovered and such connections may become more obvious over time when long periods of fieldwork are conducted. In the same way, my digital fieldwork enabled me to discover the links between the network of individuals that I came to work with. This allowed me to definitively connect a group of individuals into a tangible network which I came to be a part of, despite the fact that such a network was initially invisible.

A Network of Individuals

My digital journey, which would eventually lead to my discovery of the network of individuals in the digital world whom I would continue to conduct my research with, began with my interest in specific tailors whom I had encountered in the terrestrial world. I developed this concept of a network, building on the Actor-Network-Theory described by Latour, to understand a digital world where numerous actors, both human and non-human, interact in an amorphous network constructed of nodes of interest (Latour 2005). Law describes Actor-Network-Theory in the following manner:

> [we must] treat everything in the social and natural worlds as a continuously generated effect of the webs of relations within which they are located. It assumes that nothing has reality or form outside the enactment of those relations. Its studies explore and characterize the webs and the practices that carry them . . . the actor network approach thus describes the enactment of . . . relations that produce and reshuffle all kinds of actors including objects, subjects, human beings, machines, animals, 'nature', ideas, organizations, inequalities, scale and sizes, and geographical arrangements. (Law 2009: 141)

This theory does not perfectly fit the network which I encountered, however it is a useful place to start when considering a digital network made up of human users displaying their clothing, with both the human body and clothing functioning as equally potent actors in this digital space. At the start of my fieldwork I noticed how prominent a number of the tailors I had encountered in the terrestrial world were on social media, in particular the image sharing platform Instagram. I decided to investigate this phenomenon, one that I knew relatively little about, by joining the platform, making connections with these tailors (liking their posts and commenting upon them) and by taking and posting images of my own. Using Instagram is comparable to Slater's suggestion that men's leisure activities occupy a time and space disconnected with notions of home and work (Slater 1997, in Stevenson, Jackson and Brooks 2000: 206). This idea is used by Stevenson et al. to suggest the idea of 'ambivalent spaces' which they use to unpack the reading of 'men's "lifestyle" magazines' (Stevenson, Jackson and Brooks 2000: 206). Their example of lifestyle magazines packed with images of clothes and well-dressed men could be used as a comparison to suggest that Instagram is an ambivalent space; however, there is clearly a great sense of investment and passion felt by the users who produce high-quality, frequent content for their Instagram account. Through the process of becoming one of these users I gradually began to learn the language of hashtags and emojis that are employed by this specific network of Instagram users as well as the kind of images that would encourage more 'likes' and 'follows'. It was only after nearly twelve months of almost daily interaction that the existence of a network of individuals became apparent to me. Within the amorphous digital ether of millions of users and images interacting daily, networks of individual users interested in the same type of content gravitated towards each other. In the case of my digital fieldwork I became aware that there was a network of individuals interested in each other's content which was at least partly comprised of tailoring or high-end menswear. This interest extends to interaction with the network functioning as a digital quasi-societal mode for exchange, with 'likes', 'comments' and 'follows' being used as a currency of affirmation; a digital reciprocity – a contemporary form of Mauss's gift (1954). These social links are established and maintained with relatively simplistic and minimal modes of communication available for communicating this reciprocity. There is little space for the remedial use of 'overlays' as described by Goffman; 'judicious minor modifications in timing and tone, in stress and gesture . . . tacit meanings . . . contained in other meanings' are very difficult to communicate in only text-based comments, even with the like and follow function (Goffman 1971: 166–67). As such interaction needs to be taken at face value, or supplemented with the use of emojis to imply an emotion or inflection in tone. Evans' (2017: 132–34) work on emojis supports this view, and she uses the term 'metacomment' to argue that emojis function as a means of 'guiding the interpretation of the text', in text-based communication.

The network of individuals I established myself in is not linked in any tangible physical way, though some members may know each other in the terrestrial world; it is rather linked by the social connections made between individuals online, which over time form a complex digital network. Building on the work of Hine (2000), Burrell tells us that digital fieldsites require 'mental immersion and an engagement with the imagination' (Burrell 2009: 185). Burrell goes on to tell us that 'virtual worlds . . . may not be physically habitable' and that engagement with the virtual leads us to produce 'imagined spaces' (ibid.: 193). These are all valid points, but they do not effectively communicate the phenomenology of long-term interaction with a virtual world. One cannot, of course, expect one's terrestrial self to be fed and housed in such a digital space, but if we consider that we can have multiple selves, as Kondo does, then perhaps our digital self finds the virtual world perfectly habitable (Kondo 2009: 230–31). It seems to be the case that one's digital self continues to exist even when the connection to the terrestrial self has been severed. Furthermore, this notion of constructing an imaginary space to conduct fieldwork in is problematic to me. I suggest that instead of conceptualising the digital world as an imagined space, suggestive of the researcher projecting their notion of boundaries on an amorphous online network, that we conceptualise online spaces as a manifestation of a collective digital unconscious: that is, a space generated by the digital interactions that take place there, and which is maintained by the knowledge of such social connections (involving your digital self) even when one is not personally interacting in the digital space as a terrestrial being. In order to become a part of such a network you must make a sufficient number of these social connections, which require key users to be discovered first, and once accepted it is necessary to keep up with the daily interaction between members. It is these networks that police membership and pass judgment on the images that their members post. This is the pull for many Instagram users: the chance to belong to a digital network of like-minded individuals with whom you trust to interact and share your images. This is of course to some extent a fallacy to those users like myself who have Instagram accounts that anyone can view, but it feels like you are only sharing within your network, and it is certainly those other members who are being targeted.

The Image as Discourse

It became manifest, during my fieldwork, that within the world of Instagram the image itself constitutes a primary mode of discourse. There is of course text that can be associated with the posted images in terms of comments, both from the poster and others who view the image, but this is secondary to the primary mode of discourse – the image – which I wish to concentrate on here. Miller and Sinanan (2017) argue that images posted online must be analysed in terms of their local context. However, this is not so easy when the images are being posted to an international network. Perhaps then the network itself in this case, and the standards it upholds, constitute the local context.

Foucault's (1990) work on discourse does not directly deal with images but it is his theory that I will apply to my new definition of image-based digital discourse. Within my area of research concerning the digital world, one is at liberty to use discourse (in this case the image) in any manner which a specific user sees fit (any image may be posted by any user), although some images and comments deemed inappropriate may be removed by those who run Instagram itself. Indeed, Byström and Soda (2016) have compiled a book of images which have been removed from Instagram by the platform itself, deemed to be inappropriate content. Whilst only a relatively small number of images are included in this book, this curated collection is not used to argue against the fact that Instagram imposes censorship, but rather to explore the implications of such censorship on notions of power and the body.

> We quickly began to see patterns in the types of images that had been subjected to censorship. These included photographs of genitalia, bare butts, female nipples, period stains, liquids resembling semen or vaginal secretions, and pubic hair . . . The book evolved into a conversation about bodies – specifically, which bodies are seen as 'dangerous' and which ones are seen as 'safe'. Take, for example, two images of people wearing the same bathing suit; one has a shaved or waxed their bikini area while the other has not. The image of the hair-free body is less likely to be taken down. (Byström and Soda 2016: 16)

Foucault postulates that discourse is regulated as a means for control; in the case of Instagram this is achieved both by the censors of the platform itself and by the self-regulation of images which occurs within networks. Since there appeared to be a limited amount of Instagram censorship within my network, it was the regulation of discourse carried out by the network itself that I worked in which became the object of interest. A lengthy period of digital fieldwork was required for me to begin to unpack a link between these two ideas. It began to become clear that within the group of followers that I developed and the group whom I followed, the links between digital members became like a tangled mass of a many stranded kinship diagram. However, this may be better visualised along the lines of the network diagrams suggested by Kapferer (1969), but in this case linking individual accounts to form a network comprising numerous nodes of interest and loci. Now of course there are those outside this network who comment on and interact with the posts of this permeable yet disembodied collective of Instagram users. In the same way, those within the network may also be involved in other networks (they may have an interest in both tailoring and cycling for example). There will be users trying to break into a network, trying to reach Instagram 'fame' through amassing many thousands of followers, or simply, like me, attempting to be a somewhat recognisable 'face' within the network I had become a part of. Indeed, other users may just watch from the invisible shadows of the digital landscape, never posting content but allowing themselves to simply gaze at others' content. Furthermore, there will be those who may not be aware that networks even exist in the manner that I encountered them, but nevertheless becoming increasingly involved in the platform; this last category was certainly applicable to me at the start of my digital research. Now I understand that the concept of this ephemeral disembodied network that I have begun to talk about is a hard one to grasp, so I will try to articulate my understanding as clearly as I can.

The existence of networks within Instagram are not physicalised entities in the sense that they have been built into the platform by the designers. Instead, these are invisible social networks that have grown of their own volition and are bound by a collective interest, sitting in the vastness of the image-based ethnographic ether. These groups habitually 'like', 'follow' and 'comment' on each other's images, creating a relationship between users bound by digital reciprocity, although it must be understood that these are by no means solidly demarcated collectives. My digital research began with tailors and their clients and gradually grew to a slightly broader focus on tailors, tailoring and high-end men's dress, as I became part of a network that was interested in the same things: a diaspora of self-proclaimed dandies and sartorialists. There is a comparison to draw here with members of *la sape* reported by Gondola: 'Sapeurs find it necessary to speak, admire, and make others admire their clothing as if wearing it were not sufficient to communicate the desired message' (Gondola 1999: 37). There is a similarity here to the Instagram network I came to work with, where members are compelled to display their current outfit or collection of sartorial possessions to other members of their network. Individual users may well have had other interests, or a particular aspect or angle of men's dress that fascinated them, but nevertheless our interests were, at least in one key respect, coherent. Allow me to provide an example.

@westwoodcowboy

A prime example of a user who dwells in multiple networks is @westwood-cowboy who, as his handle may suggest, is a lover of the clothes of Vivienne Westwood and often posts images of himself (and his husband) in some of her most outlandish designs. However, he is also an aficionado of the hardcore cartoons featuring primarily leather-clad gay erotica from the artist Tom of Finland; images of this often feature on his feed. As well as this, a deceased pug named Mamma Biscuit whom the couple owned and dressed up in elaborate costumes is a common feature. This was clearly a much-loved animal and pictures of her appear frequently on the feed of @westwoodcowboy, especially referring to competitions that she was entered in. There are other images too but these are broadly three of the main categories. As such it is easy to see how a user such as this may belong to, or straddle, multiple networks. A sartorially inclined network, which is how I encountered him, one centred around Tom of Finland, and a further network that is interested in dog shows or more specifically pugs. The last two groups are digital communities which I know little about and can therefore only extrapolate approximately from my own research. There may be other networks to which this user also belongs that are invisible to the uninitiated, but I hope this illustrates the notion of differing semi-permeable networks with shared interests, all of which float in the digital ether bounded by their own interests but linked infinitely to every other group by the individual specific interests of the users.

Multi-sited Fieldwork?

I had imagined that the majority of followers that I would accumulate and interact with through Instagram would be UK-based. However, this belied the universality and cosmopolitanism of the network I eventually became a part of. I followed and was followed by users from the UK, Europe, the USA and, even further afield, South Korea. When the breadth of the network I became part of became apparent I initially wondered whether this constituted multi-sited fieldwork, but it quickly became clear that Instagram itself was the digital fieldsite for my research, and the geographical location of the users was not a crucial factor as they had all chosen to converge at a specific location within a digital landscape. Perhaps thinking about it as a 'flexible form' of fieldwork, following Wulff (2015b), would be more apt. For a long while I struggled to understand how people from all over the world managed to sift through the millions of potential images that one can view on Instagram to find those that interested them, or that were similar to the ones they were posting. However, through extensive interaction with this platform I began to slowly learn the manner in which it functions. I was intrigued that the search function, accessed through a magnifying glass symbol, showed me primarily fashion and clothing related images almost as soon as I began my research. It only later dawned on me that Instagram 'suggests' images based upon those you already follow, and the activity you conduct within their platform. This function is controlled by a sophisticated algorithm, updated to much furore early on in my research period with the platform no longer displaying posts chronologically but rather as a result of what they thought you wanted to see (Hunt 2016; Lua 2018). Even at the earliest stages of my digital research it appears, upon reflection, that Instagram itself helped me to find the network within which I began to operate, based presumably on the very first few accounts I followed, which belonged to tailors. On certain occasions the suggestions based upon some of those I followed with a broader range of interests led to some unusual items appearing within this 'suggested images' category.

@thebigsartorialist

This clearly happened when I followed @thebigsartorialist, an American medical doctor with a penchant for suiting; his Instagram bio states: 'Dan The Papa Bear of Men's Fashion Big Men! Big Suits! Big Ties!' I knew nothing about @thebigsartorialist when I first followed him apart from the fact that he seemed to post approximately three images of his outfit each day, almost always suits; he frequently sported bowler hats and, in a digital world of skinny male models he was, unusually, a much larger gentleman. An interesting side effect of my following @thebigsartorialist was that my suggestions feed (found through the magnifying glass icon) was suddenly filled, not with pictures of suits and suited men, but rather with a variety of larger men, typically partially clothed, from accounts that focused on (gay) bears. This change in content of my suggestions feed did not last long once I had followed a small number of more specifically sartorial accounts again, but it provides a glimpse into the other networks that @thebigsartorialist is involved with.

One of the interesting aspects of accounts such as @thebigsartorialist is that it is operated as a personal account by a real individual. Other accounts reuse the images of others as an extensive digital collage, or represent brands. This means that one can simply view the images in isolation or attempt to find out a little more about the person in question. For a long period of my digital fieldwork I approached the accounts of the users I followed in the isolated image-based world of Instagram only; however, towards the end of my research I felt the need to find out a little more about some of those users to whom I had developed more of an attachment. @thebigsartorialist is not famous, although having approximately 8,800 followers he is rather better known in the world of Instagram than me, yet I found with astonishing ease an interview he gave to an online blog called The Vestiary (Anu 2015):

> I'm a 43 yo 5'9" 280 lb virtually no-necked yet chronically over dressed, Irish Catholic gay powerlifting physician executive IT geek with a semi-Jewish sounding name. So essentially I don't tend to fit into anyone's pre conceived notions much. I enjoy powerlifting but people find it difficult to imagine a powerlifter in anything but a tank top and shorts. As a physician I am apparently expected to wear a white coat and look generally harried and dishevelled most of the time, or so my patients tell me. I work in Healthcare IT as well and there seems to be a general expectation we all dress like Wayne Knight in Jurassic Park. I'm a huge baseball fan but as a native New Yorker living in Boston, all those conversations get dicey quickly. (Idem)

It can feel at times as though one is a digital stalker, and to a certain extent I suppose this is true; indeed, one may hear the phrase 'to Facebook stalk' within the vernacular to describe the action of perusing another users' past posts and images, whether you know them in the real world or not (there are parallels to draw here to the phenomenon of online lurking: see Popovac and Fullwood 2018). However, it is an unusual sensation to make connections with other Instagram users within your network, some of whom you have almost daily interaction with (even if only a 'like') without knowing a great deal about them. It feels cathartic therefore to learn even the barest details about these users.

An intense curiosity can develop within these digital platforms between users, especially within Instagram where one might see the same users every day in the form of their shared images but have little traditional interaction with them. This curiosity is even more acute when trying to decipher information about them based on their digital activity beyond the sartorial as I have described with @thebigsartorialist. However, my typical activity dictated that the images presented to me were, for the most part, associated with suits, tailoring, high-end menswear or items associated closely to these categories.

One of the advantages of encountering users who don't sit neatly within the specific remit of the sartorial is that it is indicative of that Sartrean notion of being true to oneself (Sartre 1993). These are not constructed accounts looking to promote brands or manipulate the images of others but are individuals who attempt to construct their digital self as a representation of their terrestrial self. This is not to say that there is not a level of performance here – this is undeniable in a platform where one produces images of the self – yet some users display a consistent performance which makes it easier to connect with them.

In previous chapters I discussed how objects (including clothing) perform aspects of their production and how these objects can be thought of as more or less authentic in terms of a native category based on a variety of conditions such as cost, production, quality and provenance. This intertwined notion of performance and authenticity continues from the terrestrial world into the digital. Users of the social media platform Instagram with whom I interacted during the course of my fieldwork are interested in these same qualities and attempt to display them through the images that they produce. However, this is not as transparent an activity as it may initially appear. Objects can be photographed to highlight or conceal certain qualities or flaws. Clothing can be identified as a more desirable brand than it truly is or an outfit can be assembled and photographed to appear to be what the user is wearing that day, but in fact is only worn for the photograph or has been taken at a substantially different time. It is not always possible to ascertain the authenticity of the items in a post or how close the digital performance of a user is to their terrestrial self. However, over lengthy interaction it is possible to gain an understanding of which users give a consistent performance of their online self, and which appear to be analogous to their terrestrial performance; this seems to be considered as good practice. To give an inconsistent performance is, in Sartre's term, to play at the performance of the digital self and as such is to act in 'bad faith' (Sartre 1993: 185). In the digital world, such a display of bad faith is rewarded with less interaction and diminished reciprocity.

Sartre's Waiter

> Let us consider this waiter in the café. His movement is quick and forward, a little too precise, a little too rapid. He comes toward the patrons with a step a little too quick. He bends forward a little too eagerly; his voice, his eyes express an interest a little too solicitous for the order of the customer. Finally there he returns, trying to imitate in his walk the inflexible stiffness of some kind of automaton while carrying his tray with the recklessness of a tight-rope-walker by putting it in a perpetually unstable, perpetually broken equilibrium which he perpetually re-establishes by a light movement of the arm and hand. All his behaviour seems to us a game. He applies himself to changing his movements as if they were mechanisms, the one regulating the other; his gestures and even his voice seem to be mechanisms; he gives himself the quickness and pitiless rapidity of things. He is playing, he is amusing himself. But what is he playing? (Sartre 1993: 167)

'He is playing at being a waiter in a café', Sartre tells us and playing is to act in bad faith (idem). However, this is a complicated issue for 'the waiter in the café can not be immediately a café waiter in the sense that this inkwell is an inkwell' (ibid.: 168). Here Sartre is alluding to the necessity of transformation and the differentiation between 'I am' and 'I become'. To contend 'I am' is to act in bad faith since it denies the transformative nature of becoming. Sartre's waiter knows he is transforming but presents himself with this transformation disguised. Therefore, Sartre cryptically concludes, 'bad faith seeks by means of "not-being-what-one-is" to escape from the in-itself which I am not in the mode of being what one is not. It denies itself as bad faith and aims at the in-itself which I am not in the mode of "not-being-what-one-is-not"' (ibid.: 185–86).

This means that in the case of the aforementioned waiter, he acts in bad faith since one cannot be a waiter 'in the mode of being in-itself' because one is 'a waiter in the mode of being what I am not' (ibid.: 169). This means that the waiter is trying to fool his audience into believing that he, as a waiter, is a static being, a singular concept, rather than an individual who becomes a waiter every day. This cuts to the heart of Sartre's ideas regarding the individual and notions of being authentic to oneself, as well as speaking to forms of representation in the digital world. Essentially, it is a fine line of not playing at being something that one is not, but rather acknowledging the transformation into that role. This becomes especially important when we consider Goffman's idea that we perform every aspect of ourselves constantly in everyday life, a fact which means that these transformations are all performances, which is not problematic as long as they are acknowledged as performances (Goffman 1980: 28–82). This speaks to forms of representation in the digital world as it can be harder to discern the line between performance as a clearly transformative act and performance where the transformation made by the individual user is veiled. The nature of the connection between participants in a virtual world is such that digital users can act in bad faith with impunity. However, it may be the case that once one's digital self has existed for a long period of time, and there is a vast amount of content related to that self in the digital world, then notions of authenticity are not judged with regard to the transformation of terrestrial self into digital, but rather the consistency of the digital self's continued production of content.

This Sartrean notion of 'bad faith' is a crucial theoretical concept to apply to my fieldwork with digital media. Instagram, by its very nature, is a platform which encourages its users to act in bad faith, displaying themselves as the thing they want other people to see them as rather than a true record of their becoming the image they wish to present to the digital world. As such it is hard to ascertain which users within the Instagram network I conducted fieldwork with are being true to themselves and acting authentically and which are acting in 'bad faith' through playing (Sartre 1993: 180–86). However, through extensive interaction with the platform it is possible to gain a greater level of insight and understanding into the various members of a network and therefore gain a more solid comprehension of when a user is being consistent in their digital performance, and when this is a manifestation of the user being true to themselves.

However, this notion of being true to themselves needs to be appreciated in terms of being true to one's digital self, one of many potential selves. Kondo tells us how one can create selves through 'narrative', specifically in the case she describes through a 'selective life history' (Kondo 2009: 230). However, the images taken, edited and posted by members of the digital network I conducted research with are their own form of narrative:

> performances of selfhood allow us to continue the quest to further de-centre the self, not simply seeing a 'concept of self' related to other abstract domains of social life, but seeing how selves are constructed variously in specific situations, how these constructions can be fragmented by multiplicity and contradiction, and how constructions shape, and are shaped by, relations of power. (Ibid.: 230–31)

Essentially, Kondo is arguing for different selves being used in different situations, created from a specific narrative within the space that requires that specific self. Therefore, it is perhaps better to think of Sartre's notion of 'bad faith' as being untrue to the self that one is currently narrating. In terms of one's digital self, it can be considered specific and separate from one's terrestrial self. However, despite this possibility of multiple selves one still must acknowledge the 'I become' and not simply that 'I am' the particular self that one presents in any of these spaces.

These various notions of faith, play and the acknowledgement of transformation are crucial when considering the digital world of tailors and the network of individuals who surround them. Instagram is a space where a different self is easy to manufacture and maintain; however, while the images being viewed by one's followers may present this polished approach, you do not see through the screen to the production of that particular self beyond and all the difficulties that are associated with it. The inability to see through the screen also belies the ease and necessary time commitment for continual digital production of the self. This production of a digital self is an activity and, as Goffman tells us, 'When we examine the activity of a practiced pilot, sword swallower, skier, snake-handler or bomb defuser, it is perfectly plain that his capacity to be at ease with his activity now was preceded by a period, often quite long, when catastrophe seemed everywhere' (Goffman 1971: 248). This period of catastrophe, found in the terrestrial world where one prepares the self for publication in the digital, is easily disguised. These preparations are analogous to the 'obligation[s]' described by Sartre that the waiter must complete to aid his transformation in advance of becoming the waiter each day, such as 'sweeping' the shop floor and 'starting the coffee pot' (Sartre 1993: 168). One's online followers are only privy to the discourse which is published for them to see, and even though it is not uncommon to see two variants of an outfit posted, with a comment asking for advice, a preference, or simply 'what do you think?', the preceding period still exists. It is this period of transformation, from a terrestrial to digital self, which is crucial to how the larger digital network perceives the authenticity of a specific user. One must acknowledge the transformation to an extent or one is judged to be acting in bad faith, merely playing at being the sartorially inclined Instagrammer.

As Laing tells us, using Sartre's (1993: 167) example of the waiter, 'If or when "he" succeeds in pretending that he is "simply" himself, a mask will have become his face, and he himself will think that any time he acts . . . he is pretending not to be simply himself' (Laing 1971: 46). Essentially, Laing is reasserting Sartre's point, that everything is a form of performance, but if we fail to acknowledge this fact, then we begin to lose hold of our own notion of self; for Sartre this is 'bad faith' (Sartre 1993: 180–86). To connect with my network one needs to demonstrate that the user can produce a certain level of discourse, and that the user's digital self has a degree of authenticity, connected to their terrestrial self and demonstrated through an acknowledgment and display of the transformation between terrestrial and digital. Furthermore, one needs to convince other members of the network that they are, in fact, a real terrestrial user operating the account and not a business or a curated collection of borrowed images. This is similar to Slater's description of online users trading sexpics prizing pictures of 'real women' which typically meant images claiming to feature a 'wife/girlfriend' (Slater 2000: 137). Slater suggests the desire for this type of image stems from the erotic ideal 'that the woman is a truly desiring sexual subject rather than one paid to depict desire' (idem). This is the crux of the relationship between sartorialists on Instagram too, with greater kudos and respect paid to realistic depictions of one's life and current wardrobe than advertising products or presenting a faceless character.

During the research I conducted with Instagram, I observed almost entirely positive interactions. Users whose content was not to the taste of the network were simply ignored and not interacted with. This makes it difficult to use examples to unpack notions of play and bad faith. As such I am going to cast the digital net beyond Instagram to blogs and websites as well. These did not contribute to my primary digital study, but the intermeshed nature of the digital world means they are impossible to ignore entirely, and many prominent Instagram users in my network use Instagram as a tool partnered to a successful blog.

Articles of Style: A Blog

Allow me to present an example that may help to elucidate this Sartrean idea of 'play'. The world of digital menswear is rife with online blogs featuring everything from discussions surrounding which is the best Savile Row tailor to those espousing the superiority of the Milanese buttonhole. Frequently, a particular tailor or a set of images are discussed. One such blog appears on the website 'Articles of Style' which features a blog post about the tailor Joshua Kane (Trepanier 2015). The article itself merely serves as an introduction to Joshua Kane and the brand, accompanied by photographs of the tailor wearing his trademark look of intricately detailed three-piece suits, wide brimmed hat and personalised accessories. The fascinating aspect of this is the comment thread that follows the photographs and highlights the Sartrean concept of playing at being, in this case, a tailor. The photos can be viewed on Trepanier's (2015) blog or in Bluteau (2018: 119–29).

There is a raft of conflicting opinions expressed in the comment thread following this blog post. Some approve of Joshua Kane's style, others despise it, and then there are some who do not give a clear opinion of the style but seek to attack the construction of the garment or the aesthetics of the individual wearing them instead: a veiled form of personal critique. Some of the critique comes in the form of a technical discussion such as the following example:

Miguel:
I find it rather sad that most people here are hung up over the most asinine aspects of this man's look. Gender is a social construct people, just because he does not fit your neatly packaged preconceived notions doesn't mean he falters in the execution of his wardrobe … Is everyone going to seriously let some eyeliner and a curled mustache distract you from what is some really ballsy and extremely well executed pattern mixing. Yes maybe the exact aesthetic does not fit your fancy, however to let that inhibit your ability to appreciate the level of coordination in his outfit is just absurd. I mean just look at the post 2 … the large patchwork design of the pants, mixed with the thin stripes of the shirt, then the stripes in the tie, the flecking of the jacket, the width of the lapels, the form of the waist coat and how it frames the shirt/tie, just wow.

Bo (in response to Miguel):
Kudos to this guy for doing what he does, for sure (can't have everyone dress the same, I suppose). But when you really look at it (as others have said) the suits aren't technically correct, they don't look well-made at all, and if you really want to get into pattern mixing – well in look #3, this man is wearing about 3 or 4 different types of dots, two of which are essentially the same scale; isn't the first rule of pattern-mixing to vary the scale of your patterns? On top of that, in the checked suit look, there's almost no real variation between the thin stripes of the shirt and the tie pattern. And at the end of the day, I'm trying to keep this to simply patterns – don't get me started on the cut, supposed quality of the suits or the myriad number of accessories he's wearing (rings, scarves, pocket watch, tie tack, etc.). It would be one thing if this guy brought it with extreme quality with this rather outlandish look (as other guys profiled on the site have), but it just looks to me here like that quality and Proper attention to detail is missing.

Jim (in response to Miguel):
Respectfully, I disagree. Sure, we should ignore the fact that he's wearing eyeliner and has long hair, as that has nothing to do with his tailoring or his outfit. What we should not ignore, though, is the fact that his jacket is cut way too tight, so tight that I doubt that he would be able to button it up. The waistcoat is not well cut either, the patterns (such as stripes) are not matched well at seams and pockets (which they certainly should be with a bespoke garment), his shirt collars look too large for him and the whole outfit doesn't look as though it's well made or good quality at all.

Lucas:
Going from a previous post here, I've noticed none of the chalk stripes on the sleeves or pockets are aligned with the rest of the suit.

Papi Moscow:
Im no master tailor (yet) but there's some troubling points here. Im not even going to get into his grooming, etc, thats a personal choice. 1) The sleeve heads in look 3 seems terribly put together. i dont think its his posture, just not assembled correctly. 2) The whole point of BESPOKE is to have the wearer express their individuality while the tailor gives some balance and constructs a suit that is technically correct, regardless of color/fabric choice. This guys whole style screams Ready to Wear/Fashion which is fine if he has a ready to wear company, but it says in article several times he's running a bespoke shop. 3) The branding is just tacky. Im personally not spending upwards of 3k for a suit to be someone's billboard. The cut of suit, color & fabric choices should be enough advertising if the suit is well made. 4) Im all for originality & pushing boundaries but the suits aren't technically correct and some of the fabrics look downright cheap. Im not even sure if the lapels are handrolled. They seem to be fused. Again its only a problem because he has a 'BESPOKE' shop, not ready to wear or MTM.

There are some interesting points made here regarding how these comment posts intersect with a Sartrean notion of bad faith. There is clearly a set of unwritten rules which Papi Moscow believes need to be followed for the word 'bespoke' to be applied to your brand, such as hand-rolled lapels. Likewise, Jim and Bo have concerns over the cut and quality of the garments, something which they seem to have no concerns about judging through the photographs. In contrast, Miguel champions the alternative view of masculinity he sees Joshua Kane as embodying and compliments the pattern mixing and proportions of his tailoring. The main issues here, best described as challenging the faith in which Kane presents himself, centre around how these commentators think a bespoke tailor should look. To present too fitted an outfit, or too outlandish a set of pattern mixing, or too many accessories, defies a preconceived notion of the traditional bespoke tailor as one who understands cut, quality and aesthetics in a refined and reserved manner. It is interesting that the world of bespoke tailoring and fashion are seen as incompatible by these commentators, however this is precisely the niche which Joshua Kane has carved for himself. Perhaps because of this there is an insinuation that Kane is acting in bad faith by simultaneously presenting himself as a bespoke tailor, and a branded fashion icon of his own making.

Other commentators on these images are far more concerned with Kane's personal aesthetic look and seem uninterested in the clothes being displayed. In these comments it is clear that it is not his prowess as a tailor being questioned, but his masculinity, both in terms of gender normativity and sexuality.

zphyer6:
. . . I seriously thought he was a bearded lady when I clicked on the article.

Sam:
I love how clearly queer this guy is

Eric:
LOL this is just silly. Is attempting to look as feminine as possible whilst still sporting facial hair a new #menswear trend?

Evan:
Is he wearing eyeliner???

Eric (in response to Evan):
Yup. Noticed that too. It's hard to pay attention to anything else once you pick up on it.

Matchbook:
I seriously thought this was a girl with a fake mustache at first. Ugh.

Paoletti (2012, 2016) tells us how the strict binary colour differentiation of pink and blue for the vast majority of young boys' and girls' clothing and objects of desire, a process which has evolved over the past hundred and fifty years, helps to produce adults with a similarly binary constructed idea of gender. It is this which is being challenged here, with Kane being accused of acting in 'bad faith' by exploring perceived feminine aspects of appearance such as eyeliner – an aspect of personal presentation which is incompatible with these commentators' idea of masculinity, which should be reinforced and upheld by a bespoke tailor. However, not all the comments are in the same vein. Others are complimentary of the images, with comments such as those below offering support and appreciation of his individual style.

AK:
This is kind of amazing.

Dave Coakley:
I have the build of a rugby player so this 'Thin white duke' rakishly thin androgynous look just simply wouldn't suit me . . . but in an ever increasingly small world where everyone looks the same, isn't it great that such a guy exists. I think he's got tremendous unique personal style.

Solroc:
It's a bit disheartening to see such hate from people who are to be considered 'gentlemen' this guy is killing these looks because they are his own and, if I'm not mistaken, that is a large portion of this site. Wearing what you want, however you want. I say keep doing you Joshua, you've gained yourself a fan in me.

These posts reflect the full extent of the opinions expressed in the comments to the blog post on Joshua Kane. There is a preoccupation with historical style, and associated function or appropriateness as well as an obsession with production and associated notions of quality. However, what this comment thread highlights most acutely is this Sartrean notion of play. Some users here clearly think that Joshua Kane is playing at being a tailor or fashion designer (indeed, some seem to think one cannot be both). There are also numerous layers here, both explicit and alluded to, that highlight deeply held beliefs surrounding masculinity, identity and dress. This notion of play is linked to bad faith, for if they are playing at being the tailor, then they are acting in bad faith and trying to fool their audience. This is closely linked to the native concept of authenticity: those who believe Kane to be acting in bad faith and playing at being the tailor fundamentally conceptualise him as inauthentic. This native idea can involve many aspects of the person as we have seen above; Kane is outed not only as an inauthentic bespoke tailor but also as an inauthentic male.

Men Who Do Not Fit

It has long been the case that men who do not fit into traditionally conceived ideas of gender, whether through profession, dress or mannerism, are treated with confusion in a world of binary gender roles. The notion that exuberant or outlandish dress is somehow non-masculine and incompatible with traditional male gender roles is one that is relevant to my research. I suggest that this is the result of historical precedence where exaggerated dress and ostentatious menswear had been the preserve of, or at least associated with, modern 'queer subculture' employing dress as 'a vehicle for dissidence and disruption', as well as the more historical indulgent (Catholic) European metropolitan (Breward 2016: 116). This insinuation of effeminacy means that any overlap of traditional masculinity and one's enjoyment of clothing is still deeply entrenched in convention and sobriety championed by the most traditional of tailors on Savile Row (see Sherwood 2014).

In her work on gay identity and performance, Butler suggests that 'the parodic or imitative effect of gay identities works neither to copy nor to emulate heterosexuality, but rather to expose heterosexuality as an incessant and panicked imitation of its own naturalized idealization' (Butler 1991: 22–23). If this is the case, then perhaps it explains why the dress of western men has remained so static for the last century. Tailoring, drawn from military origins (Breward 2016: 39–76), has been the primary form of dress in this time, implying masculinity and uniformity, the antithesis of a world in which there are multiple notions of gender and sexuality. However, Cole points out that there have always been ways of using dress to subvert strict dress codes and signal one's sexual preference covertly, such as wearing a 'red necktie' in pre-Second World War New York (Cole 2000: 32).

However, these notions surrounding traditional masculinity in opposition to the effeminate are beginning to change. The suit as a work garment is less typical, and dress codes are becoming more fluid, despite their continued existence in many places. Furthermore, concepts of masculinity are shifting at an ever more rapid pace, perhaps influenced by the vast quantity of images that we now consume. Categories which are increasingly detached from gender and sexuality are now used, such as metrosexual and spornosexual:

> The typical metrosexual is a young man with money to spend, living in or within easy reach of a metropolis – because that's where all the best shops, clubs, gyms and hairdressers are. He might be officially gay, straight or bisexual, but this is utterly immaterial because he has clearly taken himself as his own love object and pleasure as his sexual preference. (Simpson 2002)

This description comes from the journalist who claims to have invented this portmanteau. Some years later he also coined the term spornosexual, a combination this time not of metropolitan and sexual, but sport, porn and sexual. He describes this new category of masculinity thus:

> With their painstakingly pumped and chiselled bodies, muscle-enhancing tattoos, piercings, adorable beards and plunging necklines it's eye-catchingly clear that second-generation metrosexuality is less about clothes than it was for the first. Eagerly self-objectifying, second-generation metrosexuality is totally tarty. Their own bodies (more than clobber and product) have become the ultimate accessories, fashioning them at the gym into a hot commodity – one that they share and compare in an online marketplace. (Simpson 2014)

However, my fieldwork suggests that current metropolitan masculinities in London cannot be confined to bounded groups such as these; although I submit that Simpson makes a good observation of shifting trends, this is too concrete. I therefore suggest that we have gone beyond any specific or particular form of masculinity and must therefore predict the advent of a post-particular man.

An earlier work by Simpson (1994), subtitled 'Men Performing Masculinity', raises some interesting points in a similar vein, regarding the shifting and dissolving notions of traditional western masculinity in modernity: 'I am keen to suggest that male narcissism, once explicit and separated from the imperative to disavow homoeroticism, might be a model for a "new type" of masculinity' (Simpson 1994: 15). He suggests that 'the increasing use of naked men to sell products . . . [is] evidence of the discovery of the male body's desirability' (ibid.: 13). This is comparable to Foucault's (1980: 57) description of the 'exploitation of eroticism' found in the advertising of products such as sun-tan lotion, but Simpson (1994) is highlighting the fact that men's bodies specifically are becoming increasingly naked and eroticised. However, this is problematic for Simpson since 'traditional male heterosexuality, which insists that it is always active, sadistic and desiring, is now inundated with images of men's bodies as passive, masochistic and desired'. This, for Simpson, conflicts with the traditional view of the homosexual as an 'inauthentic' man (ibid.: 5) – similar to the third category of gender explored by Kulick in his work with Travesti (1998: 124–25): 'Homosexuality, if it is to exist at all, must be segregated: it must be the Other which male heterosexuality defines itself in opposition to' (Simpson 1994: 4).

This lack of clear demarcation between male sexual preference in attributed characteristics of maleness led Simpson to his assertion that new types of masculinity have come into being, the metrosexual and the spornosexual. However, I am not convinced by his justification for replacing a set of out-dated categories with a set of new ones. There are now infinite masculinities to perform, regulated and fuelled by the rabid consumerist society which is at the mercy of an immeasurable tsunami of images. In the words of Debord, 'the real consumer becomes a consumer of illusion' (Debord 2012: 32). This illusion which we consume and clothe ourselves with offers no one particular form of masculinity, and even the notion that there are rigidly bounded categories has begun to dissolve. Masculinity has lost specificity, and in an increasingly digital world has become post-particular.

This lack of a specific single type or notion of masculinity, and the subsequent advent of the post-particular man, leads me to approach the performance of masculine identity, specifically through dress, in a manner which focuses not on overarching tropes of masculine dress but more specifically on notions of individualism in male dress.

Looking Forward

This chapter marks the point in this book where a transition occurs between research that began in a terrestrially bounded fieldsite, and the realisation that the field did not exist in terrestrial isolation but instead projected beyond these confines, and could therefore be viewed in four-dimensional postdigital space. This journey that began offline and led to an incorporation of the digital world will continue in successive chapters, mirroring the continued development of my 'self', both digital and terrestrial, as my time in the field elapsed. This is not to say that this book can be neatly divided into two halves, the first offline and the second online: it is more nuanced than this. However, from this chapter onwards there is a focus on the enmeshed nature of the digital in the blended fieldsite which I have worked in.

It became apparent that a particular type of image was the most desirable to my semi-insular network. These particular images would gain more approval, 'likes', 'comments' and 'follows', effectively reinforcing (in a Pavlovian sense) their status as a more desirable form of image. If in a Foucauldian sense we consider these posted images as discourse, then, in the manner of his discussion of sexuality (Foucault 1990: 36–49), the nature of what is considered to be beautiful, desirable or correct in this semi-insular world of tailoring and menswear aficionados is dictated and ratified by the collective control of this image-based discourse. In essence, if nobody 'likes' your image (or it receives far fewer 'likes' than you are expecting), then you are unlikely to post a similar image again. This makes the assumption that everyone's goal is to achieve validation for their posts. This is probably not a universal but is difficult to overlook or escape for the frequent user. This ideal form, like the discourse surrounding sexuality that Foucault describes (idem), not only controls the discourse, but through this control alters how this community conceives of a fundamental set of beliefs, from the nature of aesthetics, to political leanings and notions of the body.

Instagram, unlike the blog post explored earlier in this chapter, was a friendly place to work – at least that was my experience. In the aftermath of my fieldwork there was a much publicised case of a teenage suicide linked to images of self-harm consumed through Instagram. This did not surprise me – the closed nature and self-fulfilling discourse produced by certain networks is clearly comparable to my research even if the timbre of content is not. The sartorialists I worked with were positive, and supportive of one another. Indeed, any critique of an individual was dealt with in a passive manner: by not engaging with this specific individual, or unfollowing them entirely (there are parallels here to Rocamora 2015: 416–17). Such an attitude permeates the network and therefore regulates who is allowed to make sufficient links to join. Such insights were not immediately clear and only after eighteen months or so was I able to gain an understanding of how human individuals and non-human objects interacted in this amorphous digital space, one where individual actors who have no physical link can exist in a network of interconnecting loci.

Chapter 4

GAZING ON (IN)VISIBILITY

... the papers want to know whose shirts you wear ...
—David Bowie, 'Space Oddity'

Lacan's Gaze (2018) is a pervasive concept within the social sciences, but when we frame this with an ethnographic field concerned with fashion, tailoring and Instagram, the desire to see and be seen becomes all encompassing. The multiplicitous loci of human views, reciprocal glances and unseen stares, whether terrestrially or digitally bounded (or both), are intrinsic to this field and some of the relationships which such gazes engender have been discussed in the previous chapter. Here, instead of conceiving a mesh of interwoven views, sightlines and gazes, this chapter will conceptualise my fieldsite in terms of visibility and invisibility. This decision allows for the field to be viewed more holistically than in the previous chapter where individual operators were discussed.

The Repressive Digital Discourse Hypothesis

Foucault's (1990: 15–49) 'repressive hypothesis' details how discourse has been used as a tool that allows sexuality to be repressed, liberated and controlled. He gives an example of the evolving notion of appropriate detail within Catholic confession to illustrate how the prohibition of language, implicit or explicit, works to alter a society's cognition of a specific event or act: in Foucault's example sex, and in my work the correct form of the digital image. This prohibition can be limited to a certain place or time, controlled by location or those present in it, but nevertheless permeates deeply into the cognition of those whom it effects.

> Consider the evolution of the Catholic pastoral and the sacrament of penance after the Council of Trent. Little by little, the nakedness of the questions for-mulated by the confession manuals of the Middle Ages . . . was veiled. One avoided entering into that degree of detail which some authors . . . had for a long time believed indispensable for the confession to be complete: description of the respective positions of the partners, the postures assumed, gestures, places touched, caresses, the precise moment of pleasure – an entire painstak-ing review of the sexual act in its very unfolding. Discretion was advised, with increasing emphasis. The greatest reserve was counselled when dealing with sins against purity. (ibid.: 18–19)

Whilst Foucault's example of the confessional is specific here, the digital discourse present in Instagram can equally be controlled and manipulated through a similar repressive hypothesis. Furthermore, Foucault's depiction of the body as a sexual entity and eroticised canvas is one that is particularly pertinent in a digital world where the body is on show within image-based digital media: 'An imperative was established: Not only will you confess to acts contravening the law, but you will seek to transform your desire, your every desire, into discourse' (ibid.: 21).

Within the digital world of Instagram, discourse is not merely the text-based comments and interactions that one can observe and actively engage with, as I have, but the primary form of discourse are images that are pro-duced, manipulated, shared, reposted and commented on. Essentially, by controlling discourse, in this case a prohibition against the production of certain images, the network (steered by powerful members of the network) dictates what kind of image is deemed correct, appropriate or beautiful. For networks that concentrate on menswear and the masculine clothed body, this has an enormous impact on a wide range of issues, including sexuality, gender, construction of the clothed body and authenticity of the individual.

The Body: The Erotic Canvas

Foucault (1980: 56) discusses the body as an eroticised canvas, firstly present-ing the example of 'auto-eroticism' with 'restrictions on masturbation' which begin 'in Europe . . . [from] the eighteenth century'. He uses this example to demonstrate how the body is both a site of personal physical control and external social control, in this case most likely from watchful parents, and how this objectifies (through 'surveillance and control') both the body and its inherent and associated sexuality (idem). Foucault (ibid.: 57) elaborates on this example and suggests that such scrutiny inevitably intensifies 'each individual's desire, for, in and over' their own body. A conflict therefore develops, with control of the body being fought over both between 'parents and children' as well as the child and these various 'instances of control' (idem). This leads to the 'revolt of the sexual body', as Foucault (idem) calls it, and rebellion again such 'encroachment' of personal control.

This process does not happen overnight, indeed Foucault's example of this rebellion – the 'exploitation of eroticism', both 'economic (and perhaps ideological)', found in pornography and 'sun-tan products' – is unlikely to be found to any extent in the eighteenth century where his example began (idem). Yet despite the slow speed of this change, the point remains that the 'form of control by repression' has been replaced with 'control by stimulation' (idem). This notion of stimulation and repression, in opposition, as potentialities for imposing power on the body (and for one to imbue one's own body with power) that can be projected outward, fascinated me. I began to approach my own notion of clothing as a second skin through a Foucauldian lens and to ask questions as to the nature of the clothed body (and the digital self) as an equally eroticised canvas.

One key idea that seemed to be missing from Foucault's (1980: 55–62) analysis of the body here was an omission of any mention of the clothed body. Foucault's body, it seemed, was in a permanent state of undress. This troubled me, and I began to consider how his ideas might be relevant to an analysis of a clothed body. My initial thoughts were of the Punk movement in Britain around a similar period to this publication by Foucault (idem), where clothes were used to define an alternative identity very clearly through a dramatic modification of the wearer's body through dress, not only altering the physical body of these Punks but also the perception of these new bodies from those who looked upon them (see Bruna 2015 and Lamotte 2015 for a historical comparison). In terms of a Foucauldian notion of power this is a very clear display of 'control by stimulation' which I suspect felt particularly stark to a post-war generation of parents for whom dress was primarily a means for modesty and practicality where control came from 'repression' and to some degree conformity (Foucault 1980: 57).

The heavily safety-pinned garments that so shocked 1970's Britain (see Smith and Sullivan 2011: 28–29) are, by means of their ability to modify one's perception of the wearer, an elegant segue into applying Foucault's ideas to my own research. Clothing is not merely a surface to the body which had little impact on the true nature of the person wearing it, but rather a deep and important indication of the nature of the person, perhaps better thought of as shallow or surface ontology. This was a topic that I discussed with the tailor Mark Powell at the very start of my fieldwork. I asked why he had become interested in suits, to which he replied immediately that when he was growing up: 'The girls like a man that looks good'. Before going on to espouse the merits of a sharp suit, I pressed him on how he dresses now and whether he always wears suits or is ever more casual, which he didn't give a definitive answer to, but shrugged his shoulders and leaned back in his chair before proclaiming: 'You don't feel right if you leave the house looking like shit'. The precise nature of what this meant was unclear, but it was clearly a personal judgment as to whether he felt suitably attired for the given day. However, it struck me that this statement not only reflected a personal belief about looking one's best, but also the power of clothing and appearance to alter one's state of mind. However, this thinking, further to enriching the complex ongoing depth-ontological analysis that I was conducting, led me to a discussion as to the nature of the individual and the importance of thinking about the individual in the context of my research. This led me back to Foucault.

The King's Body: An Intersubjective Approach

When Foucault (1980: 55) describes the concept of the 'king's body' in the seventeenth century, this king's body is not simply a 'metaphor, but a political reality' which was physically required for the functioning of the state (idem). Foucault goes on to describe how in the nineteenth century it is the 'body of society' that takes metaphorical and literal control of states and that as such this new body has to be protected by a raft of new 'remedies and therapeutic devices' (idem). These include: 'the segregation of the sick, the monitoring of contagions, the exclusion of delinquents. The elimination of hostile elements by the supplice (public torture and execution) is thus replaced by the method of asepsis – criminology, eugenics and the quarantining of "degenerates". . .' (idem).

This idea of a single social body that metaphorically and literally held and represented the power of the state intrigued me, especially in terms of the notion that I have been previously discussing: the individual. Since this single public body is policed in its behaviour and actions by the collective set of diktats laid down by the body of society, it appears to be, in effect, self-policing. Yet this cannot be so, for even in Foucault's example of society post regicide, the doctors and lawyers and other powerful figures take over this control. This, it struck me, is the perfect climate to breed uniformity, since if it appears as if the body of society is collectively making judgements and rulings as to what is and is not permissible, it gives a much greater power to those authorities really making the decisions. In this case it is my digital fieldwork with Instagram which I am specifically referring to; however, these

ideas could also be used to discuss the nature of the terrestrial fashion industry and notions of cool.

All discussions of this type must inevitably include the nature of the body
both in private and in public performance. If, as I have already postulated,
clothing must be taken as an important and inherent part of the body, a second skin, then a public body governed by the power of society must have an
impact on the very nature of clothing, in terms of use, appropriateness and
intellectual engagement within the society in question. This stance must be
held if we are to take Foucault's theory on the change from the 'king's body'
to the 'social body' (idem). However, I think that this is an outdated model as
it omits any thorough analytical appraisal of the role of the authentic individual, and specifically the other Elizabethans I have encountered. Individuality
cannot be synonymous with uniformity, and while in the past there were
certain written and unwritten dress codes which espoused a certain type of
conformity for certain occasions, rules that were very difficult to break, the
world in which I conducted fieldwork was concerned with subverting these
rules in search of individual identity: a goal made possible through clothing.
Within Instagram and the world of high-end sartorial menswear one does
not necessarily need to be socially important to be an 'influencer'. Indeed,
there are echoes here of Durkheim's 'cult of the individual' (see Marske 1987:
10–11). However, despite this and despite a greater freedom there is still a
web of control lurking in less plain sight than the king's body yet still visible
if one looks hard enough.

The Clothed Body

I began to wonder whether Foucault's omission of clothing in terms of his
analysis was an unintentional product of his extensive studies within institu-
tions. The naked body, it appears to me, is at least partly a medicalised entity
and I suggest that Foucault (1980: 55–62) may himself be guilty of using
the medicalised gaze that he claims as an agent controlling a vast sway of the
population on behalf of the political body: 'Naturally it's medicine which has
played the basic role as the common denominator. Its discourse circulated
from one instance to the next. It was in the name of medicine both that
people came to inspect the layout of houses and equally, that they classified
individuals as insane, criminal, or sick' (Foucault 1980: 62).

This medical gaze, then, has the power to identify and dictate the reality
of an individual. However, this gaze is presumably associated with the ana-
tomical, and does not take into account the reality of clothing and dress as
hugely important aspects of the body and associated identity. Indeed, for me,
the clothed body is an equally erotic canvas as Foucault's naked body (see

Entwistle 2000; see also Steele 1997). Within my research it became apparent that clothing was not merely a means of keeping the body warm, dry and decent, but functions as an invested skin, a carapace if you will. This second skin has the ability to mould the individual, broadcast information about them, hold memory and function as an unescapably important aspect of the body, one that both complements and functions in opposition to the hidden naked body.

Furthermore, throughout my research I began to notice the prevalence of the sexualised clothed body in the society I was investigating. I came across a dating website called Uniform Dating with the tag line 'do you wear a uniform in your job or just love people in uniform?', aiming to partner people according to their desire to be in a relationship with someone who wears a specific garment to work. In addition, one of the highest grossing books and films in recent years has been the *Fifty Shades of Grey* series which focus on a young woman entering a sadomasochistic relationship with a suited businessman, and was being heavily advertised in London as I was conducting my fieldwork. The author has endorsed a range of sex toys and perhaps most interestingly of all one of these includes a necktie so that one can re-enact scenes from the book:

> Transform your fantasy into a reality with Christian Grey's Tie. Made from luxurious silver and grey quilting, this versatile accessory is perfect for wearing in public to display your kinky intentions, and whipping off in a hurry for impromptu bondage. A fully functioning and stylish tie that won't stand out to those not 'in the know', wear it in public to let your partner know what's on your mind, and when you're alone, slip it off to experience tie-and-tease. ('Fifty Shades of Grey Christian Grey's Tie' 2017)

This example is a serious acknowledgment of how the clothed body has entered our consciousness as an erotic canvas – although I suspect for many of my informants the fact that Christian Grey's tie is made of polyester would be somewhat off-putting. Clothing displays wealth, power, taste and a whole raft of other characteristics. These, I would argue are not a smokescreen hiding the true body but are, in fact, a clear display and therefore essential part of the complete body. As such we must consider the body, not naked but as a clothed entity. This naturally falls within a discussion of depth ontology, and while Miller and Woodward argue that clothing is chosen for its ordinariness and ability to act as a post-semiotic cover-up, many of the participants I worked with do not want to be invisible (Miller and Woodward 2012: 89). This then brings us to a crucial question as to whether there can be vastly differing notions of depth ontology across a city. It seems that this is indeed so, and perhaps this leads us elegantly back to the digital aspect of my research. If communities with a coherent notion of things such as depth ontology are becoming more disparate in tangible terrestrial communities, perhaps they increasingly seek networks of validation in the digital world.

Throughout this research I began to wonder why depth ontology within the western world generally places the true reality of the person below the surface. I questioned whether in the history of western intellectual thought, particularly that of the social sciences, past practices such as physiognomy, anthropometry and even phrenology have made any notion that truth can be obtained from the surface appearance of a person an uncomfortable concept for modern scholarship to swallow.

Foucault tells us that the body as a sexual entity has become increasingly covered, both linguistically (through discussing the unclothed nature of the body in increasingly less detail) and intellectually over time, leading us to a historical state where clothing was designed solely to cover the body, not express the nature of the wearer (something still found in totalitarian regimes). Exceptions to this, where clothing has always been used to express identity and sexual availability in certain circumstances, such as prostitution (see Cole 2000: 20), are contained within the category of Foucault's 'other Victorians'. The hypothesis that language used regarding the sexual act relayed in confession (and subsequently in a wider dialogue too) became increasingly cloaked in metaphor and suggestion led me to a parallel, Foucauldian influenced reading of men's fashion history (Foucault 1990: 18–19). I began to question the notion best summarised in the colloquial phrase 'buttoned up', implying a conservative, or overly formal character, a phrase which can also sometimes be used in the vernacular to imply a slightly repressed character. This notion of the conservative seemed to my mind appropriate as a basis for an analytical approach to tailored menswear in England.

The two-piece, two-button, dark blue or dark grey suit with notched lapels is certainly the archetypal modern suit (see Breward 2016; see also Hollander 1994). Practically any tailor or menswear shop selling suits will be able to sell you one of these off the peg. They appear in shop windows as advertisements and in magazines on the backs of models typically advertising something other than the suit. They are the formal wear equivalent of the post-semiotic garment of Miller and Woodward's (2012: 89) blue jeans: unremarkable and invisible. The reason why I have linked this notion of invisibility to Foucault's (1990) work on sexuality is multifaceted. There are questions regarding power and the body linked to desirability and dress that I will unpack later, but in this instance, I want to explore the symbolic association between the conservative nature of men's formal dress and a repressive hypothesis. The suit, as an item of men's formal dress, has remained fundamentally unchanged since Victorian times, and while the vast majority of men now own and wear casual clothing on a regular basis, the suit is still an important garment either for work or at least for various formal occasions. Wulff (2008) uses Fabian's

(2002: 23) concept of 'typological time' to eloquently answer the question of why 'Romantic ballets, having been around for almost two centuries, are still performed' (Wulff 2008: 523). The constant reproduction of these ballets is a representation of the 'quality of states . . . unequally distributed throughout the world'; the same could be said for the continued wearing of tailored suits (Fabian 2002: 23, in Wulff 2008: 522).

It seems strange that the formal standard for men's dress has remained so comparatively unchanged, at least in terms of structure and perceived formality, for so long. This is in comparison to female dress, which has changed far more drastically since the Victorian period, not only in terms of style but also the nature of construction. It may seem odd at this point to deal with dress in such obliquely dichotomised manner. There are of course numerous items of unisex clothing available for consumption – indeed, some designers increasingly will sell little else – however, in the world of tailoring and formal wear these gendered boundaries to dress are still obvious and profound.

In Mark Powell's Shop

On another occasion, early in my fieldwork, while visiting the tailor Mark Powell in his Soho shop, I asked him about digital platforms and specifically his own (at that point minimal) presence on Instagram. He has since made a very profound digital transformation including a new website with an online shop and far more frequent posts on his social media platforms. Such a line of questioning, as ever with Mark, didn't elucidate the particular issue in question but rather gave him license to talk about something he was more interested in. In this case, a question regarding his own brand's digital position provided me with an illuminating answer as to his notions regarding authenticity and the individual.

> JB: So I was wondering how much you use social media, do you think it's important in this industry?

> MP: Yeah, we had a mate of mine building us a new website for us as a favour, but then they got another job and we were left with it half done so we're trying to find someone to finish it.

> JB: Ah cool, and are you going to be able to shop on your new website?

> MP: Yeah maybe, don't know yet, but that's what we were thinking, we get lots of enquiries from abroad so it might be good.

> JB: And what about social media, Instagram, Facebook, stuff like that, how do you find using stuff like that?

At this point I was expecting Mark to tell me about how he used social media to publicise his brand; however, instead he gave a much more personal insight into his use.

> MP: Well I follow lots of accounts that are all guys in suits, ya know, there are so many of them now and if I can't sleep or before I go to bed I'll scroll through.

At this point his phone is out and he's leaning over the table to show me his feed:

> MP: The thing is that they just all look the same, they think that just by giving them a hat and a sharp haircut that it's individual but everyone looks the same. It just all looks the same. There's that new tailor in over in Shoreditch James or something, who uses scissors as his logo, bit like the ones on your hat (gestured to my hat), Jonny something.

> JB: Joshua Kane?

> MP: Yeah that's him, with the hat, everything overtailored, too fitted. We were doing that years ago, but not any more.

I didn't think this a good time to tell him that my hat was indeed from Joshua Kane.

> JB: And what you do is different?

> MP: Exactly, yeah, it's about having style.

A key tension is exposed here about the construction of the individual, with Mark stating that the construction from outward influences devalues the individuality of the act. However, it seems that this is a layer of hypocrisy here, not least since Mark Powell subsequently produced his own range of hats. However, this circumvents the point, which is that for Mark it is the choice of an individual to come to him to be dressed. Indeed, he spoke of dealings with clients where he gave them the illusion of making their own choices about their bespoke designs whilst actually guiding them to a style that looked good.

This conversation continued with Mark and his assistant Shivaun telling me about some of their clients. This whole discussion made me question Mark's notion of authenticity. He clearly believed that his own designs and personal sense of style were somehow better or more authentic than the vast majority of images that he saw on social media. However, whether this was because he had earned this mantle from long years of experimentation in the industry, or because he had a unique look, was difficult to say. It is perhaps understandable that a designer or tailor would believe their designs are superior to the competition; they are after all a salesman for their designs. However, it felt more than this, as though he was trying to prove that his clothes were more individual than the competition and to some extent more authentic in the sense of being chosen by connoisseurs; although no particular justification was given, it was as though it was simply a given. Mark's designs are certainly beautiful; however, to my eye he has his own derivative look, borrowing style cues from Edwardian cuts, Mod culture and 1940's gangster chic. There are stock details and style elements that appear repeatedly too and a knowing use of exaggerated style and proportion to his cuts; to those in the know a Mark Powell suit is easy to spot. However, I struggled to ratify in my own mind how this made it any more or less individual or authentic. Despite this Mark clearly had a different idea, and whether this was merely a confidence in his own look or something more complex, it had taken me aback and sharpened my engagement with the increasingly important notion of authenticity. Fundamentally, there appears to be a perception among certain tailors and designers that one's own clients are expressing individuality whist anybody else is simply following norms and as such are inauthentic individuals.

The Authentic, the Individual and the Hyperreal

Authenticity is a multi-stranded behemoth of complexity both within the corpus of anthropology but also within my own research. There has been work conducted on the phenomenon of fake clothing (Crăciun 2009, 2012; Pipyrou 2014), but this is not an issue when dealing with tailors directly. It is important to note that this concept of authentic in opposition to inauthentic or fake is relevant to the idea of connoisseurship presented by Fillitz and Saris (2013: 1). It also seems that even within the hallowed rooms of London tailors, where the quality of the bespoke garments is roughly equivalent, there is a level of snobbery where each tailor is depicted as the best by themselves and their team. However, the digital world that many of these tailor's clothes come to inhabit is rife with the continual question of authenticity. Digital image manipulation, and a carefully taken photograph, can transform the look of a garment, hide defects, or even provide viewers of your online profile with a fictional account of the outfit you were wearing on a particular day. I myself regularly post images to my social media ostensibly as a record of what I am doing at that very moment when in fact it could have been taken weeks in advance, or even with no intention of actually going out in the particular garment. There is the commonly used hashtag #latergram which indicates to the observer that an image has not been taken close to the time of posting, and others such as Joshua Kane repeatedly reuse images particularly of his fashion shows to keep the images 'alive' across his platforms. This naturally calls into play the Sartrean notion of 'bad faith' and raises questions as to the authenticity of the digital individual in their presentation of themselves online (Sartre 1993: 180–86). However, this is not a simple question since before we question the faith and authenticity of the individual that presents themselves to us via the digital world, we must first question the reality of this digital space. In his work on the virtual, Baudrillard questions whether hyper-reality is a better way of thinking about the digital world (2003: 41–45). The question is whether the postulated critique of being inauthentic to one's digital self (in a Sartrean way) can be levelled at a virtual world that is hyperreal. If we take Baudrillard's assertion that 'the virtual now is what takes the place of the real', then perhaps within the digital world of free-floating signs and signifiers, being authentic to oneself has little to do with reality (Baudrillard 2003: 42). In this case it could be that Sartre's bad faith needs to be re-evaluated; perhaps the man who is playing at being a waiter is, if he plays this role in the digital world, more authentic to his identity as a waiter than he could ever hope for in the terrestrial world where he would be acting in bad faith.

> . . .is the virtual that which puts an end, once and for all, to a world of the real and of play, or is it part of an experimentation with which we are playing? Are we not playing out the comedy of the virtual to ourselves, with a hint of irony, as in the comedy of power? In the end, isn't this immense installation of virtuality, this performance in the artistic sense, a new stage on which operators have replaced actors? (Baudrillard 2003: 42)

Here we are told that play, far from being an action of the actor that has tried too hard to inhabit their idea of individuality, is actually the action of an operator. This operator is removed from reality by the hyperreal, but this gives them the opportunity to create a new kind of truth, one where play is the mechanism of being authentic to one's constructed self. Perhaps it is the case, if you will forgive the bastardisation of Oscar Wilde's wit, that if you give me a mask I will tell you the truth.

#joshuakanejourney

Approximately a year after the Joshua Kane AW16 Houndsditch fashion show I attended another of his shows, this time at a much larger venue: the London Palladium. Attending this show allowed me an alternative view, not only of the brand's growth a year on, but it also allowed me to approach the show as an established member of the Instagram network, and afforded me the opportunity to dress to fit in, as I had a better idea of what to wear to such an event. Crucially, my established online presence allowed me to analyse the build-up to such a show through an additional optic.

The show itself was even more spectacular than the previous year, the venue was larger and set in a stylised 1910 railway station, with a string quartet on stage, and the collection of forty-six looks was a mix of men's and women's styles. The show ended with a short piece of ballet under a gentle fall of snow, to the highly evocative strains of Barber's adagio for strings.

In light of Baudrillard's above assertion that 'operators have replaced actors' in the virtual world I want to use my observations from the digital world surrounding this Joshua Kane's AW17 show to analyse this idea (idem). Both in advance and in the aftermath of the Journey fashion show there was immense digital activity from Joshua Kane's social media. This activity ranged from the first indications that a new show was on the horizon, a casual selfie with the caption 'working on something big' superimposed on it, as well as short video clips of him sketching designs, never giving away much detail. Images and videos from previous shows were re-shared too, highlighting the link between previous shows and the impending one.

As it got closer to the beginning of the year it was announced that Joshua Kane would not be showing his collection in the January London Collection Men's fashion week as he had done in the past but rather later in the year. The date for the show was subsequently announced and it became apparent that the new date positioned his show in the more prestigious London Fashion Week. Once it was barely a month till the show was to be held, teasers became an almost daily occurrence, growing in specificity and the associated level of excitement with every passing week. Images of the set being built were shared, as well as discreet images showing portions of one of the outfits that would appear on the runway: the same image that was later displayed on enormous posters outside the London Palladium as part of the advertising for the show.

The show itself was spectacular, both in the Debordian sense and the vernacular. However, as with everything Joshua Kane, the conversation did not end just because the show was over. The hashtag #joshuakanejourney allowed one to search through images that had been taken at, or were somehow related to the show from other Instagram users and Joshua Kane himself posted numerous times over the days following the show, ranging from short posts giving close-up details of looks from the show to longer, more emotive pieces like this from the day following the show:

> The #joshuakanejourney . . . last night I wanted to do something different, I wanted to break the mould of how fashion should be presented and how people are able to access it, how exclusivity can be removed and create something much more exciting and emotive. I want to create an experience that stands

Illustration 4.1. An image taken during Joshua Kane's Journey catwalk show at the London Palladium, showing models in suits and the flat caps that featured heavily in this collection. The image was posted to Instagram on 17 February 2017 by the author. © Joshua M. Bluteau.

alone, in every aspect as beautiful as another. Although fashion and tailoring is my back ground I want my performance to be so much more, designed for the amazing characters that come to visit me everyday. Design an experience that captures their imagination and that they never forget.

Last night we filled the London Palladiums 2270 seats to present my 'Joshua Kane Journey' presenting a mix of acting, live music, fashion, art, dance and more. This project took me six months of blood sweat and shears to design and i (sic) am privileged to say the creatives who have been by my side are second to none!

There are far far to (sic) many to mention, but from my staff in 68GPS doing the longest hours ever, to all the amazing teams and individuals by my side

I am truly honoured to share this experience with you and thank you from the bottom of my heart for making this all possible. Without my family and girlfriend none of this would have ever happened, I can't put into words how much it means to me. (Shared on Instagram from the @joshuakanebespoke account on 18 February 2017 as the caption to a picture of the ballet dancers' final lift)

As well as this, new pictures were posted as the items from the show became available in his shop and in the online store, which did not occur in a single move but rather as a drip feed of a few items at a time. Such a masterful use of the virtual world, across numerous social media platforms, and additional websites, to keep an audience engaged, shows precisely the distinction Baudrillard is highlighting between 'actors' and 'operators' (Baudrillard 2003: 42). Kane is an individual actor in a personal sense, but his interaction with the virtual world as a brand moves him into the realm of operator, one who is able to manipulate an audience, both evocatively and temporally, to keep them continually engaged with his product and the constant possibility of new information or details being released at any moment which his clients may be able to use to craft themselves: information which is used to craft both terrestrial and digital selves.

#jkcruise – Invisible Shadows

Following the Joshua Kane Journey fashion show at the London Palladium, the showing of his next collection was very demure, though the same could not be said for some of his designs which included a hot pink leather biker jacket, ruffled shirts and a collection of skateboards. This show, entitled Cruise, made me consider how the terrestrial and digital world intersect, and where my place is, as a participant and researcher in both worlds exploring notions of visibility and invisibility in images which are posted to social media.

Dilley has explored 'aspects of invisibility and the unseen' in the photographs taken by Henri Gaden, a French colonial officer (Dilley 2019). He gives the example of 'shadows on the wall' providing a glimpse of the 'unseen presence of the photographer', where there is no more tangible optical record of this presence in the photograph (ibid.: 11). Instagram images are naturally far more numerous than these French colonial photographs. However, whilst many more images will be taken per published image, Instagrammed images (much like the curated images discussed in Dilley's article) that make it to publication are carefully chosen to perform a specific narrative for the one publishing the image (ibid.). This is not only due to the image itself being carefully chosen, edited and published at a specific time to weave a narrative around the digital self of the user, but it also supplies us with a far more 'real', in a terrestrial sense, view into their supposed current surroundings. This fosters a sense of terrestrial and temporal connection even if the taker is invisible.

Cruise was held at Joshua Kane's newest store; a small capsule collection was displayed on mannequins around the shop floor and there was a DJ and small free bar. When I arrived for the event, accompanied by my partner, the shop was shrouded in pink drapes but the door was open and the thump of electronic music drifted out into the quiet evening street. At the door, manning the roped off entrance, was Fran, a model and close friend of the brand (who had been photographed in early Joshua Kane's campaigns), wearing a Joshua Kane suit in dusky pink and stilettoes. She smiled as we approached and greeted me by my first name, which was surprising as we had never met, or at least we had never met physically, but had corresponded over email and had clearly seen each other's digital online presence before as we both recognised each other: 'Joshua' – 'Fran, it's so good to finally meet'.

We chatted briefly and she let us in. Once inside the light levels were low, but this darkness had a pinkish hue from the drapes, like walking through Turkish delight. The fact that neither myself nor Fran had ever met in the terrestrial world before but greeted each other with familiarity demonstrates our visibility in the images present in each other's overlapping digital networks. Within this gloom between thirty and forty people milled around, many clad in the wild fabrics of Joshua Kane's designs, chatting, drinking and looking at the clothes. Through this melee of bodies photographers manoeuvred themselves, hugging those they were searching for like long-lost friends, rearranging groups and taking photos before sliding off to look for their next victim. At one point one of the roving photographers approached us and asked for a photo and my Instagram name: a prime example of the terrestrial world meeting the digital.

The images that were later posted to the social media accounts of Joshua Kane were carefully curated, with images chosen to display the high-profile attendees. As such I, and other people I met at this event whom I know were photographed, did not appear. This is an example comparable to the 'strategic invisibility' described by Dilley (2019: 6). With such a 'strategic invisibility' there also comes a strategic visibility, with the content of selected images being carefully chosen, and if necessary cropped or edited to produce a desired image for publication (idem).

I would like to draw parallels from this example with the shadow of the photographer captured on Gaden's film as described by Dilley (ibid.: 11). I suggest that in the case of Instagram there are the digital shadows of individuals present at the event of the image being taken, but invisible in the image posted. However, such individuals may be visible on different Instagram feeds at the same event. For example, while I and other attendees were invisible from Cruise on Joshua Kane's social media accounts, we did appear on our own Instagram accounts. So, while we would be invisible to the casual browser, one who looked a little deeper and perhaps searched for the show's hashtag, #jkcruise, might begin to see these additional individuals becoming visible. The digital world has grown to the extent where events, such as the one I describe above, are accessible to those who are not terrestrially present: no longer through a single digital image, or even multiple digital images from a single Instagram account, but rather through multiple searchable images from numerous users' accounts. This gives a multi-dimensional view into a terrestrial event from a digital platform and provides the potential for a dilution of strategies of visibility and invisibility through a number of users all using different parameters for what features in their images.

The plot thickens too. As we made our way home from Joshua Kane's Cruise show, I was stood on a London tube train, wearing my outfit from the show – a short Joshua Kane black and white houndstooth shawl collared jacket, a blue wide-brimmed hat and a short vintage necktie with a tiny spotted pattern that I had tucked into the placket of my white shirt. As I stood there, swaying gently as the train hurtled through the underground tunnels and juddered violently every time the wheels passed over a set of points, I asked my partner to take some photographs of me that I could later post to Instagram. A man approached, jovial, if perhaps a little over-refreshed, and asked to be photographed with me. We obliged, and this seemed to satisfy him, as he then proceeded to make his way down the train to find a seat. What you cannot see in the image I chose to post is my partner taking the photograph, or the gentleman who wished to have his photograph taken with me, both of which are visible (albeit one in a reflection) in the alternative version to the photograph that I posted. This, to borrow from Edwards, demonstrates that even in the digital world, 'photographs can spring leaks' (Edwards 2001, in Dilley 2019: 3).

Chapter 5

@ANTHRODANDY

. . . a man's life is laid out and preserved most clearly in a drawer of silk stripes. The rest is ephemeral. One of my earliest sartorial memories is of my father teaching me to tie my shoelaces and tie on the evening before my first day at school . . . I imagine that the final act before the lowering of a coffin-lid is the straightening of the tie on the body and the gentle brushing aside of hair.

—Christopher Breward, *The Suit*

Two weeks into my fieldwork we buried my Gran, my father's mother. I bought a new jacket for the occasion, a Vivienne Westwood black suit jacket, with an asymmetrical front and three amber buttons. It was a little too big for me, in a comfortable way, though long in the sleeves as though the jacket itself expected a rakish occupant would roll them back, but not that morning. That morning I woke from an uneasy sleep and when I reached for my spectacles I saw the garments I had laid out the previous evening silently waiting for me.

It was the first funeral of a family member that I had attended as an adult and I was a little unsure what to expect. In my mind, I had imagined a filmic scene where a sea of black umbrellas shielded the overcoats and the mourning weeds of those gathered from the worst of the weather, where all colour had been banished: a world of gothic architecture and black plumed horses. This, however, was not what I experienced. All the men of the immediate family were sombrely suited, though not everyone was wearing black and few wore black ties, though nobody was without one. The non-family were mostly elderly and attired in a wide range of colours and garments, and though typically more smart than casual they did not project the sobriety of the relatives. One particular aged gentleman caught my eye when he stood for communion dressed in a wild mix of pink chinos and purple jumper. My mind initially drew comparison to a Liquorice Allsort, but then, I reflected, perhaps this was an apt choice of colour, especially for a lady whose wreath, sat atop her coffin, was comprised of vegetables.

The cortege moved off from the Catholic church, with no horses in sight, and the priest followed on in his bright red two-seater sports car. It had been a strange day, a sad day too, but it made me reflect nonetheless about men's dress and why this was a topic that so fascinated me. At the time I took field notes of this event as a matter of course and as a purely personal document. However, it is an event that I have repeatedly returned to in my thinking. I questioned the place of the black suit as a transitional garment of funeral wear: is it a protection against the sombre day or a means of encouraging a collective sense of loss? Furthermore, I reflected more personally on the precise garments that I wore. Will that new jacket always carry the memory of that day within the folds of its fabric? Will the tears that fell on the sleeve be worn like campaign medals by an item of clothing that can remember its own history? Indeed, Svašek (2007: 243) claims that:

> matter has emotional efficacy, and that material objects distribute the primary agency of their producers and users who experience and construct them as mediators of their own desires, fears and convictions. Objects are thus often perceived as subject-like forces, which – like human subjects – exist in time and space. Experienced through the senses, they express and evoke emotions and make themselves 'known' as bodily felt and imaged internalized presences.

Svašek (ibid.: 229) is here talking about 'material objects that consist of human remains, or that are casts of human body parts' such as death masks and the ever-popular anthropological artefact – shrunken heads. However, this explanation of objects being empowered with emotional efficacy is precisely how I conceptualise the aforementioned funeral jacket damp with tears, a palpable, and very human remain. Yet even without this physical bodily remnant to imbue the jacket's fabric, clothing can still be conceived in this way: objects which can not only 'express and evoke emotion' as Svašek (ibid.: 243) tells us, but also objects which can take in and hold emotions in their own right. It is worth noting that while I took photos of my outfit both for this funeral and the funeral of my second grandmother further on in my research period, it seemed too personal to post these images to Instagram, though I have seen such posts from others.

Certain items of clothing, I contend, can carry emotions with them and exude them whether worn or hanging in the wardrobe. These items sit in a complex loci of human object interaction, where we imbue the object with emotion, and experience it in return. There is both an intangible psychological aspect to this and an acutely physical one too; the colour, cut, weight and fit of a garment, along with what one finds left in its pockets, all form part of this complex notion of shared emotional bond between wearer and wearee.

The Ties That Bind

This sense of garments and objects becoming imbued with emotion and laden with a shared history was something that continued to fascinate me throughout the entirety of my fieldwork. This is a concept which Breward (2016) unpacks with wonderful eloquence in terms of his tie drawer:

> There are thirty-six ties in my tie drawer. Four bow-ties and a cravat hang in the wardrobe. Most of them were acquired between 1990 and the present. The majority are silk-jacquard woven. Three are wool and four polyester. Five are knitted (one by an Italian monk), and three are embroidered. Two are cotton. They range through blacks, blues, greens, browns, silver, yellows and pinks. Rolled like paper scrolls or canapés in their square wooden box they present a pleasing regularity: scientific specimens in a sartorial museum . . . Some ties have strong associations of time and place, or represent lost ensembles suits and shirts long ago handed to the charity shop): the remaining accent of a half-forgotten sentence. And whilst many of them resist 'fashion,' they are also located firmly in a trajectory of style: like architectural remnants or ghostly revenants of bygone taste . . . there are of course ties that mark the more serious moments of life, the job interviews, the crucial work presentations, the weddings, civil partnerships, christenings, significant birthdays, funerals and memorials.

> These memento-mori sit further back in the drawer, marking passage, absence and loss. Superstition suggests I shouldn't dwell on them. The act of tieing them brings a heaviness and solemnity, a sense of apprehension. They are rolled more tightly than the other ties in the drawer. (Breward 2016: 133–34)

Introduction to the Reflexive Individual

I don't have a tie drawer. I have a shoe box, a far cry from the immaculate rolled sartorial sushi that Breward (idem) describes above. My tie box squirms like a nest of silken serpents, constantly threatening to overflow and spill their jacquard tails across my floor. This is not to say that my collection is any less capacious than Breward's though it is certainly less well ordered. There are nineteen ties in my shoebox, thirteen bow ties and a single cravat, not to mention a cornucopia of pocket handkerchiefs. My ties, though less well ordered and lacking numerical superiority, are perhaps as varied as Breward's: everything from an emaciated Alexander McQueen ribbon of midnight blue silk with flared ends festooned with a print of tiny light blue skulls and smears of paint, all the way through to a pair of vintage Turnbull and Asser kipper ties whose width is so vast as to prohibit their use unless one wishes to look like a clown, or they are worn beneath a waistcoat. In between these two extremes is a selection of more typical styles, each with its own individual story, reason for being there and associated historical baggage. Interestingly, and mostly devoid from Breward's account of his tie drawer, many of my ties have had a former owner. Whilst some of my ties have been bought new, many are second hand and a few inherited. The same goes for the majority of the tailoring in my wardrobe. This adds a new layer to the discussion regarding an item of men's clothing having shared history and carrying an acquired emotional weight. Wulff (2002: 77) notes how ballet costumes that are reused in numerous productions bear the former inhabitants names on the label and demonstrate a history, 'symbolic capital and patina that is quite different to the social meaning of most other used and tattered clothes and shoes'. I suggest that there are similarities here with second hand bespoke tailoring which bears the name of the original owner on the label, or inherited items from family members.

The focus of this chapter will therefore be a reflexive look at the researcher as an individual; this is very firmly a reflexive approach but incorporates certain aspects of autobiographical and autoethnographic theory (see Coffey 1999; Chang 2008; 2013; Holman Jones, Adams and Ellis 2013; and Adams, Holman Jones and Ellis 2015). This methodology is crucial in situating my work as anthropology at home as well as acknowledging the personal aspect necessary in crafting a digital self as a methodological tool. However, this digital aspect of my research moved me away from anthropology at home, and prompted a synthesis of autoethnographic and reflexive methodologies. I could frame this as a form of autobiographical anthropology, conceptualised by Okely in the following manner:

> Reflexivity may seem comfortably neutral for some. That depends how it is interpreted. In its fullest sense, reflexivity forces us to think through the consequences of our relations with others, whether it be conditions of reciprocity, asymmetry or potential exploitation. There are choices to be made in the field, within relationships and in the final text. If we insert the ethnographer's self as positioned subject into the text, we are obliged to confront the moral and political responsibility of our actions. (Okely 1992: 24)

Essentially, Okely (idem) is promoting the notion of the researcher as not removed from the research but embedded in it. She tells us that 'the reflexive I of the ethnographer subverts the idea of the observer as an impersonal machine' and goes on to postulate that 'autobiographical accounts of field-work are not confined to self-understanding in a cultural vacuum. They show how others related to the anthropologist and convey the ethnographic context' (Okely idem). In addition to Okely's (1992) work on reflexivity, I will also draw from a wider corpus of anthropological literature concerning reflexivity to inform my methodology, including the work of Turner (1979, 1980), Clifford and Marcus (1986), Bourdieu and Wacquant (1992) and Zenker and Kumoll (2010). In contrast to the previous comments concerning autoethnography, my use of a reflexive methodology is more specific, focusing on how I conducted crucial aspects of my research. This included crafting a digital self and conducting digital fieldwork as an observing participant, using this digital self as a methodological tool which could be employed experimentally in the digital landscape, providing the potential to elicit responses from informants, as well as providing a phenomenological account of digital self-making both in the digital and terrestrial worlds. This includes an acknowledgment of the performance, creativity and awareness of self required for research in the digital landscape. This is a very important idea for my work since in both the digital branch of my research, and that concerned with material culture in terms of clothing, the relationship between myself and the object of study is a very personal and enmeshed one. In the digital world, I create and display images of myself as a means of gaining access to the network I wish to research. In terms of material culture both the digital and terrestrial aspects of my research involve me interacting with clothing as well as purchasing items and clothing my own body with these garments. As such it is impossible not to discuss these aspects of my research without approaching them in a reflexive autobiographical manner.

This chapter will begin with a reflexive look at how I established my digital presence as a researcher with the platform Instagram. This will include the character 'anthrodandy', whom I created as my digital persona, the manner in which I produced content to post on my feed and an exploration of the language used in this digital world including emoji use. I will look at the experiences of myself as a researcher to gain a deeper understanding of the physical processes and associated digital world of an individual interacting on a daily basis with Instagram. This chapter will end with a broader reflexive analysis encompassing both digital and physical aspects of my research, exploring how one begins to build a rapport with research subjects.

anthrodandy: The Beginning

At the start of my fieldwork I created the Instagram account and associated character of anthrodandy. This event at the time was merely an experiment, a foray into the anthropology of the digital and an attempt to understand the processes of interaction within this digital space in which the tailors I had begun to work with were operating. This low-key inception belied the totality with which an engagement with digital research would come to permeate the ultimate methods and product of my research. During the period of my field-work there was a tangible change in the way digital media were used by the tailors I worked with physically (and some whom I only interacted with digi-tally). Even those who had been initially prolific became more so, employing additional features as soon as they were available while others who, at the beginning of my research, appeared less technically aware, became increas-ingly confident and present within the digital world. These changes were not only fascinating, serving to hold my anthropological interest within the digital world, but also unintentionally mirrored my own digital development.

You may wonder why I chose the epithet anthrodandy for this account, and not my real name. This choice stemmed from two things; firstly, the pre-liminary digital research I had conducted suggested that the only Instagram accounts which typically use the offline name of the owners were related to brand names or shops that were being represented digitally. Secondly, almost all the other accounts, run by individuals as personal accounts, had portman-teau-esque names typically consisting of two (or more) words run together which somehow described the user or the aspiration of their digital persona. Those that I have encountered through my digital research include: dapper-trendie, the.style.professor, welldresseddad, thebigsartorialist, westwoodcow-boy, pearlsandpoisonlondon and stylescoundrel. In contrast to Burrell's work, almost all of my digital 'friends' were older than me (Burrell 2009: 193). My chosen nom de plume was partly influenced by a desire to fit in with this network of users who had assumed chosen names, and partly as a means to identify myself as both a researcher and an interested sartorialist. As such I went with the combination of the words anthropologist and dandy to create anthrodandy. While this was a hastily chosen name, it has seemed to take on a life of its own in the two years since it was spawned, not only taking on a digital life with a presence and character, but also becoming a new word in the vernacular of my physical friends, and perhaps beyond too. Despite its tentative conception, anthrodandy is now alive in both the physical and dig-ital world and seems to have become accepted.

The first post I made as anthrodandy was a daunting experience. A few years previously I had a personal Instagram account which was hidden to all but a few friends, but it was seldom used and I quickly tired of it. In contrast, anthrodandy had a concept, one that morphed throughout my fieldwork certainly but nonetheless there was a purpose to the images that I created and published. This account was open for anyone to view and concerned itself with menswear and specifically, in line with the manner in which tailors and their clients seemed to use the platform, the account holder wearing items from their wardrobe.

As I stated above my first post was a daunting experience, not only due to the knowledge that anyone could see it, but also perhaps more crucially because my participants could see it too. Despite this it rather felt like no one was watching to begin with, and my posts felt like screaming into the wind at the top of a dark mountain: an isolated, lonely and ultimately pointless endeavour. Indeed, in my first few posts the only people to like my images were my mother and my partner; perhaps I need not have been so worried after all. Interestingly, the first glimmer of interest and the encounter which persuaded me to continue a digital arm to my research came not from Instagram, but Twitter. At the inception of my project I had created a Twitter account as well as an Instagram account where all my Instagram posts would be automatically duplicated, but I was also using it experimentally to comment on and interact digitally on a second platform, a method which I refined to being purely Instagram-based as my research progressed. During the early period of my digital research I wrestled with what to post, how to phrase tweets or compose images. The whole landscape of digital linguistics, etiquette and time was foreign to me and I struggled to think of what I could post about my life and wardrobe which would be of the least interest to others in the digital ether. As such on the afternoon of 4 October 2015 I tweeted:

> Just ordered #THEGOSTICK hat from @joshuakanebespk online shop. Very excited for it to arrive.

This was not strictly true, I had ordered a hat but it had been a couple of weeks previously when they had been put on sale in celebration of London Fashion Week, and I had already received it. This would not have been an issue had the following reply not been posted within fifteen minutes from Joshua Kane himself, but only after he had already liked and retweeted it:

> @Anthrodandy you did? Did you receive confirmation ??

This was both amazing and terrifying in equal measure. The very fact that I had been contacted by the tailor himself, who at this point I had not met in person, in such a short period of time and with a seemingly encyclopaedic memory of his outgoing orders, was astonishing to me. I tweeted a hasty reply:

> @joshuakanebespk Whoops, old tweet that didn't send. Got confirmation a few weeks ago but been away. It should be waiting for me at home :)

This was a slight fabrication, but highlighted to me the importance of time within a digital world and the importance of the learned language of temporal markers such as the hashtags #latergram and #ootd. #latergram implies the image was taken some time ago and is only just being posted now, whereas #ootd is an abbreviation for 'outfit of the day' and implies that the image shows what the poster is wearing on that actual day. The notion of time being distorted through the use of digital social media has been discussed by Miller (2011: 78) in his description of the sensation of time disappearing when one gets engrossed with one's social media. Miller calls this phenomenon 'time suck' (idem). Joshua Kane responded to my tweet by liking it, and a few days later I posted my sixth picture on Instagram, which was the hat, and it too was liked by Joshua Kane: our first digital interaction. This may seem like a series of detached occurrences, but this highlights the nature of digital communication across a social media platform and indeed across various platforms, termed 'polymedia' by Madianou and Miller (2012a, 2012b). A disparate selection of posts, likes, replies, public comments and private messages all intersect in the digital spaces shared by the two in conversation. As such another online user may be able to glean some or all of the conversation, but aspects of it may be hidden or more difficult to access. In contrast, for the two in conversation, they do not need to join the 'digital dots' because despite the ostensibly disparate messages and nodes of conversation the devices used to access these spaces (typically smartphones) notify the owner when they have been contacted (in any manner and on any platform) by the other user they are conversing with. This creates a greater fluidity to such communication than it is possible to describe here in prose. It is most closely comparable to receiving a question via a text message on one's mobile phone and then waiting to see the sender in person before replying; there is a fluidity to the conversation belied by its use of more than one mode of communication.

In addition, it creates a complex system of layers of intimacy. The ability for digital communication to construct and maintain notions of intimacy ranging from maintaining family or work connections through to sexual relationships has been noted by Miller and Sinanan (2014: 48–81) in their work on webcams, and there are comparisons here with how my informants use digital technology. Seeing people in different digital places and having them converse with you through a variety of media and in a variety of styles fosters a sense of almost familial confidence. They are always carried with you on your pocket-sized device and are easily accessible. It is possible within a few seconds to discover their latest post and as such the feeling that you know what they are doing at that very moment, though of course there is no guarantee that this in fact represents their reality, only the reality of their digital character.

One of the potential problems with such diverse communication methods is the assumption that you have read all the messages and symbolic acts of reciprocity and are fully abreast of the latest developments in your digital social world. This may not always be practically possible, and as such you may be unaware that certain conversations are occurring if you have not been keeping up with the continual flow of correspondence. The closest comparison I can think of to this is being telephoned to discuss the contents of a letter which you have not opened yet. This takes an astonishing amount of engagement and a full-time commitment to your digital world. Indeed, by the time I was fully engaged with my digital fieldwork I was spending multiple hours a day browsing and interacting online.

The immersive nature of the research endeavour I was about to embark upon was unknown to me at the beginning of my digital fieldwork. I had begun with the idea of working across the platforms of Instagram and Twitter but it soon became apparent that this was an unfeasibly vast endeavour to undertake so I confined myself to Instagram, the platform used most by tailors. Whilst based in Instagram I did link my account to Twitter so that everything posted by me on Instagram would also be duplicated with a post to my Twitter. My journey with Instagram and my creation of anthrodandy began slowly. My first post was of a deconstructed Dolce and Gabanna suit I saw in a TK Maxx, reduced, but still rather beyond my price range. This was followed by four rather grainy and badly edited pictures of myself including one sat on my balcony in a vintage Tootal dressing gown. Perhaps unsurprisingly I wasn't deluged with a tsunami of likes or comments. Then I posted a picture of my new Joshua Kane hat, and received a like from Joshua Kane himself. This was the first part of my digital education and made me think more closely about the digital language that is on offer to those who know how to use it. Through images, and the text you associate with those images, you can draw greater interest from those with similar interests; you simply need to highlight these links.

Learning the Language

Over time, my confidence and digital fluency improved and I moved from a very stilted and unsure digital representation of myself to one with a greater sense of continuity, presence and self. As mentioned above, I now concentrated on Instagram and as such I was able to learn the intricacies of the platform and the networks I came to inhabit intimately.

A great deal of this change came through my development as a researcher and through the consistent process of creation (creating new posts), response (to feedback on the posts), and browsing (other user's posts). This led to an evolving methodological approach building on the work of Hine (2000,

2015), Miller (2003a, 2011, 2012), Miller and Slater (2000) and Horst and Miller (2012), as well as drawing on Holy's (1988) notion of the observing participant. Using an amalgam of these ideas I developed a methodology that I have termed immersive cohabitation (Bluteau 2019), where the participation of the researcher in the same digital tasks as one's participants forms the core research method around which all other strands of research are to be formed. These additional strands included the reflexivity of the researcher with regard to these tasks, and a more traditional observation of the participants through the available digital data. Oddly, it seems that such a methodology is rare within the wider corpus of digital anthropology, with most concentrating on an analysis of digital technology and its users rather than an analysis of the researcher using it. Often researchers who do engage with social media as a research methodology, such as Haynes (2016) and Costa (2016), still use it as means to access more typically ethnographic data on how their informants use social media. However, Luvaas' (2016) work on street-style photography and blogging serves as my primary methodological inspiration as he employs an autoethnographic approach to his fieldsite, becoming a street-style photographer and fashion blogger. This methodological process has allowed me to refine my ideas with regard to the nature of the image as a form of discourse, building on Foucault's (1990) notion of discourse and its regulation as a means for control. The use of the digital image as primary discourse as well as the associated comments and responses as a secondary form of discourse allow the network to regulate the content it views due to a collective expression of approval or a lack of interaction. Further to this development of an understanding of digital discourse as a method for control I gained an understanding of how these images are physically captured, crafted and broadcast.

The full 850 images which I produced across this period of digital fieldwork can be viewed digitally on Instagram by searching for @anthrodandy. Initially, I presented poorly edited images with minimal hashtags in a naïve style that bore little resemblance to later posts. Over time I learned what type of image, both in terms of editing style and content, was favoured by those in the network that I worked with (see illustration 5.1). This is not to say that the vast majority of images shared by those in this network are identical; this favoured form of visual discourse is not prescriptive, but requires style, individualism and detailing with an individual flair to be deemed of good quality. Users tend, therefore, to develop their own style which adheres to the unwritten rules of the network. These rules seem to include minimal editing, and if the images are edited it is in a naturalistic style as one might find in a high-end men's fashion magazine. The images primarily appear in colour, although occasional black and white images are well received. Tailoring is the

Illustration 5.1. An image of the author wearing a Mark Powell gingham waistcoat and Alexander McQueen bow tie. This image of a torso, dressed in tailoring with a neck tie, typifies one form of highly desirable image in the Instagram network where fieldwork was conducted. This image was posted to Instagram on 23 September 2016. © Joshua M. Bluteau.

preferred content, ideally with someone wearing it, though close-up images of unworn tailoring and accessories showing particular details are also happily accepted (see, for example, illustration 5.2).

Images used to feature the outfit one is wearing, or a portion of it, are favoured, and these are often in the style of a body shot (taken by the poser or by another person) with the head out of shot (see illustration 5.3). Such photographs highlight that the purpose of the account is to emphasise the importance of the clothing in the images rather than the wearer. However, it is also important to at least occasionally include images with the face of the account holder shown to add an authenticity to personal accounts, and give a face to connect with other users (see illustration 5.4).

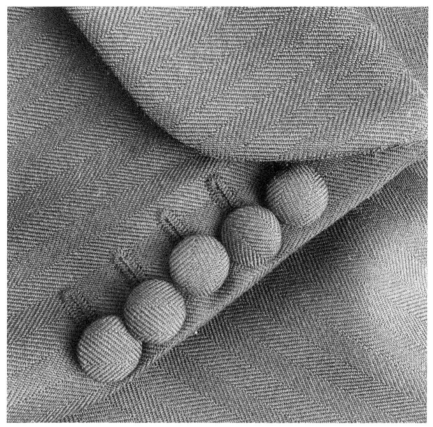

Illustration 5.2. Close-up of a cuff from a bespoke suit made for the author by the offshore tailors A Suit That Fits. Cuff features five covered buttons and a turnback – sometimes referred to as a gauntlet cuff. This image was posted to Instagram on 16 February 2016. © Joshua M. Bluteau

This may seem contradictory since I have stated that the most desirable images are those without a head. This remains true; however, the occasional appearance of the user's face suggests that the account is being operated by a specific individual, and that it is not simply an account of curated images. This idea is comparable to Haynes' (2016: 88–114) description of how one can create authenticity online in order to foster visibility, assuage suspicion and build trust. Questions can be posed in the comment below the image which can elicit a favourable response, and sometimes an image which is more personal but has little to do with the general scope of the account is posted which allows for a more intimate connection with those who follow you. One of the ways I did this was by posting occasional images of myself riding my mountain bike.

Illustration 5.3. Close-up torso shot of author. This headless style of image was popular in the digital field. This image features a Joshua Kane shawl collar houndstooth jacket and vintage paisley pattern tie. It was posted to Instagram on 8 March 2017. © Joshua M. Bluteau.

Through my extensive digital research, images such as illustrations 5.1, 5.3 and 5.5 seem to get the highest number of likes – although it is still important to show your face from time to time. Each individual element is important but it is the overall effect of all these items working in harmony that is the crucial element here; the overall image must feel well balanced and the individual colours or patterns of various elements must work well together. That is not to say that it needs to be boring – indeed, I have observed some outlandish ensembles with very positive feedback – but it needs to fulfil these criteria. In addition, higher quality images tend to garner greater positive feedback too; you can see that in my image the detail around the white stitched buttonhole on the lapel is a little grainy, which is not ideal. However, it is difficult to gain

Illustration 5.4. Image of author, this time including the face. Note, the jacket worn here is the same as in illustration 5.3. Demonstrating how specific items can be worn in different contexts and dressed up or down is part of displaying one's knowledge and sartorial skills to other online users. This image was posted to Instagram on 3 June 2017. © Joshua M. Bluteau.

this level of detail without a digital SLR camera set up and good lighting. In order to embrace the ethos of the platform almost all of my images posted to my Instagram are taken with my iPhone camera, a good tool but certainly not the tool used by many accounts which are producing magazine quality high-definition images. There is a fine balance between accounts which have the look and feel of being a personal project of the account holder, and those which have a professional feel with images being taken not by the user themselves but by an exterior photographer. This can give the feeling that the account is concerned with the persona of the user rather than their clothing or combination of the two, though like everything in this digital world there is overlap of all categories.

Illustration 5.5. Close-up torso shot of author wearing a three-piece Tommy Nutter glen check suit, vintage pocket watch chain, William Hunt spotted tie and bespoke tab collar shirt. This image was posted to Instagram on 30 August 2017. © Joshua M. Bluteau.

Of course, there are exceptions to the rule of the perfect image, as a mode of discourse, which I have discussed here, and which I unpacked theoretically in the previous chapter through a Foucualdian optic. An 'ideal' image which I have alluded to here does not really exist, however there is a type of image which seems to be replicated, posted and liked with a greater frequency than others by members of my network – for an example of my interpretation of this form of image see illustration 5.5. In addition to this form of image there are individual users who post images in a certain idiosyncratic style unique to them, which may garner a lot of attention and approval, but only if, as before, the network approves of the form of the image.

One of the interesting aspects of the platform is that once you have built relationships with other users, they will begin to like your images almost irrespective of their quality or content. This is because they know you and have embraced you as part of their network, though you are unlikely to garner new attention from users who do not currently follow you. How long these relationships last without the production of certain types of content I do not know.

The physical process of preparing an image for posting on Instagram can be brief or laborious. It may be a selfie or a photograph taken by another person which you post with minimal editing on a whim, showing your followers what you are doing at that time. This is perhaps the simplest post and one which I do not complete often. The majority of my posts are premeditated, where I decide that I want to post a particular outfit, or showcase a specific accessory. This can often be because it is a new acquisition, or there is an element which hasn't featured in a while, or there is some kind of topical link. I begin by choosing the outfit, accessory or combination of items and getting dressed. This is where the fiction begins, for it may be that if I want to take a picture of a suit such as illustration 5.7, I don't need to put the trousers on. So, once I am dressed, or partially dressed as it may be, it is time to start taking photographs. The majority of my posts are taken by myself which, depending on the image, may entail a degree of contortion which is not always easy in a tightly tailored jacket. A lot of the images which I take showcasing specific items, as opposed to the more impulsive photographs taken while I'm out, are taken at home in whichever flat I'm currently living in. Sometimes I take these outside too, but this is less common, and in such cases I am more careful to wear trousers!

Allow me to set the scene, I have dressed as shown in illustration 5.7, in a grey chalk-striped suit jacket with a grey velvet collar from Oxford-based tailor Clements and Church, though second hand to me, with a red patterned pocket handkerchief from American brand Jos A Banks, a birthday present from my partner's grandparents, a white shirt with a tab collar which I had made for me by a company called A Suit That Fits, and a green-based abstract floral tie from Christian Lacroix, which I picked up second hand from eBay; as to the existence of trousers, I will leave that to your imagination. Once I am dressed I need to find a location in my flat which has ideally nothing in the background and is in good natural light. I avoid using a flash as it tends to overexpose the image which is not a look my network enjoys. In this case, after several minutes striding from room to room taking in the myriad of possibilities I chose the bathroom. At this point the composition of the image itself can start to take place and it is also the point where I run into a difficulty with my iPhone. My iPhone has both a forward- and rear-facing camera, which is helpful since the forward-facing camera displays its image on the screen allowing the framing of a selfie to be accomplished with ease. However, I have learned that the rear-facing camera is of significantly higher quality than the forward-facing one and as such this is the one I use. This does mean that I need to use a mirror, or guesswork, to frame the images

I am taking. Once I have found a mirror, framed the image and contorted myself to get the phone far enough away from myself to get everything in the frame, and then managed to get my finger onto the shutter button I can start taking photographs. Illustration 5.7 demonstrates a reasonably easy image type in this regard; I am blessed with arms long enough to accomplish such images without too much issue. However, in other situations where I want a full body shot or a more specific shot of an aspect of a garment, and there is no one else around to assist me, you will find me balancing my phone in mugs or pressed against window sills with Blu Tack and employing a timer to capture the image that I am looking for. If this isn't practical I have become adept at increasingly elaborate contortions to try and frame items of my dress just so. Once I have taken a few images I will typically review them in full size on my phone, and at this point I may adjust the ensemble I am wearing.

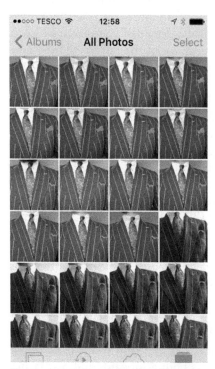

Illustration 5.6. A screenshot from the author's smartphone showing a series of photographs that have been taken of an outfit prior to the selection of a specific image for publication. © Joshua M. Bluteau.

As you can see in illustration 5.6 the first eight images feature a pure red Crombie pocket handkerchief, which I then swopped for the patterned Jos A Banks one which featured in the final post. What you cannot see in that screenshot is that before the red Crombie one I had also taken photos with a green spotted Paul Smith handkerchief which, on reflection, I did not think worked. After these amendments to my outfit, additional photos will be taken, I will review these and either make amendments to the outfit again and take more images or keep the ensemble and try images from a different angle. Eventually, once I am satisfied with one or more of the images I have taken I will finish, change out of the outfit and either change into an outfit for the day or into another outfit I want to photograph and the whole process begins again.

I have now acquired the image I wish to post, or a selection which might be suitable for posting. At this point I may decide to post an image immediately, but it is much more

Illustration 5.7. Close-up torso shot of author wearing the same outfit featured in illustration 5.6. A Clements and Church striped suit with Christian Lacroix tie and a bespoke tab collar shirt. This image was posted to Instagram on 1 April 2017. © Joshua M. Bluteau.

common for me to take these images in advance and to keep them stored on my phone for posting at a later date, though typically I post an image within a week of taking it. At a time when I think I will get a good response to my post I scroll through my stored photos; illustration 5.6 shows what this looks like, though I took at least three times the number of photos shown here to get the one I eventually chose. I select one and open it in Instagram; at this point there is a whole host of possible ways to edit the photograph, one of twenty-three filters can be added over the image or it can be manipulated in terms of its brightness, contrast, saturation and numerous other ways. Happy with my chosen editing I add a comment and finally press the button to post. Illustration 5.7 is the result of that particular effort, and it is an effort.

The process of preparing these images can be extremely laborious, and while I learned to speed up the process I also spent more time thinking about my next post so that by the end of the second year of digital research I was almost continually considering what outfit combination or image location would be good for my next post. It had become all-encompassing, almost as if the persona of anthrodandy had begun to leave its digital home and bleed into my terrestrial life. As such you will frequently find me attired in a manner which is atypical for a researcher at home writing up, partially suited or half clothed in an outfit, stood on chairs or in the bath, pressed against the window in a large hat or contorted on the shared stairs to my flat trying to catch an image of a pair of shoes. The windows in my flat are very large; I do wonder what the neighbours think.

> Pattern mixing in this #latergram #suit with #velvetcollar from @clementsandchurch #bespokeshirt with #tabcollar from @asuitthatfits #pocketsquare #pockethandkerchief from @josabank and #tie from @lacroixofficiel #mensstyle #mensfashion #menswear #dapper #dandy #bohochic #sharp #suave #tailor #tailored #tailoring #chalkstripe #suited #suiting #tabcollarshrt #devilsinthedetails
>
> the.style.professor So many distinctive details here including the lapel and the shirt collar. . . 👌
> neillkatter Aww cool
> joaquinfernandezprats Dope!
> monsieur_bespoke Awesome :)
> anthrodandy @the.style.professor I do love details
> haberdashers_ Me gusta. 👍
> steve_highbarger Terrific large tab collar and tie!
> anthrodandy @steve_highbarger thanks v much

The text below illustration 5.7, that I posted on my Instagram, is the comment I included with it, an optional addition to any Instagram post, but one which most users use to at least say something about the image. I always include some text and particularly in my more recent posts it tends to be in this form. A short comment on the image followed by listing the Instagram accounts of the brands of the items that I am modelling, identified by the @ symbol. Any statements beginning with the # symbol identify these words or phrases as hashtags which means that they can be searched for within the platform of Instagram. This means that if I wished to search for images related to men's wear I could search under #menswear and I would find any images (including mine) which include this hashtag. Utilising this form of signposting allows a much greater audience of users who may be potentially interested in your image to gain access to it. At the beginning of my digital fieldwork

I was confused by the notion of the hashtag and which ones I should use to classify my posts; however, over time I learned through perusing and engaging with posts of others in my network.

The style in which I composed my comments evolved over time, from a very basic to the more complex form that you see above. Typically, by the latter end of my digital research every comment contained a basic set of hashtags with a preceding comment and additions or subtractions depending on the specific image. This standard set included:

#mensstyle #mensfashion #menswear #dapper #dandy #bohochic #sharp #suave

In addition, the following hashtags were often included:

#tailor #tailored #tailoring #suit #suited #suiting

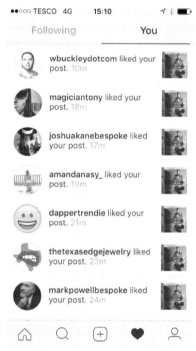

Additional hashtags were included depending on the context, which in the above image included mentioning some of the specific items in the photograph such as the pocket handkerchief or the fact that the shirt had a tab collar. The beauty of using hashtags on a platform such as Instagram is that they act as a search tool for grouping similar images. As such one can click on any hashtag and be taken to a list of every other image which has used that hashtag in its description. This allows users to find other users sharing related content. Naturally, there are a variety of interpretations of how to use these hashtags, and as such there will be a mix of images in any one of these lists. Below my comment I have included the comments that I received from other users on this post and my replies. As soon as the post is live on your Instagram you begin to get feedback either as likes, comments or follows. Illustration 5.8 shows what this page looks like on the iPhone screen for a post from July 2017.

Illustration 5.8. A screenshot from the author's smartphone showing a series of notifications on his Instagram app following an Instagram post on 25 July 2017. The post featured a Boomerang image of a look book he received at the Joshua Kane Cruise show. Note both Joshua Kane's and Mark Powell's accounts have liked the post. © Joshua M. Bluteau.

The Emoji

Emojis are an enormously important part of communication across social media but they are used particularly frequently on Instagram. It may be the case that emojis are used in lieu of, or in complement to, text-based comments in Instagram because the platform treats images as the primary form of discourse. These emojis act as a pseudo-symbolic language which seem to have learned meaning(s) for the initiated of the network that uses them. Despite the existence of this language being chronologically post-Foucauldian I still consider it as a significant part of the digital discourse which takes place within Instagram and which I unpacked in the previous chapter. Evans suggests that emojis have evolved to replace pre-existing internet slang; however, it does not appear to me that emojis are used in this way by my network (Evans 2017: 25). Rather, they are used to facilitate what Goffman would describe as 'overlays' (Goffman 1971: 166–67). In lieu of being able to modulate tone and inflection, as one would in spoken communication to imply emotion and nuance, digital text-based communication has evolved to use emojis: 'Emoji users are more effective communicators. . . Their messages have more personality, and better convey the emotional intent of the text message. In turn, this leads to greater emotional resonance in the recipient' (Evans 2017: 35). These emojis can function as descriptors, literal translations of the image being represented, euphemistic images with a codified implicit meaning, or as symbolic representations of emotion: an ideogram. These emojis 'can help make online communication "thicker", by way of offering a stylized way of "translating" accents found in facial expressions or gestures in an interpersonal meeting' (Garsten and Lerdell 2003: 177).

The beauty of many of these emojis is that, at least on a simplistic level, they transcend traditional linguistic boundaries – a useful feature when image-based digital media are not confined within geographic boundaries. However, while they may function in essence as a hieroglyphic international digital language, their meanings may be much more specific within digitally closed groups where these meanings must be learned.

There are hundreds of potential emojis to choose from when deciding on the contents of a post or comment, with new ones being added frequently, including ones to encompass different skin tones and gender orientations. However, there is a small set of this vast alphabet which is used frequently by the members of my network and as such I will provide a brief description of the meanings of sixteen of the most commonly used ones below.

– Smiley face: indicating agreement or approval or the fact that it makes you happy.

– Thumbs up: indicating agreement or the fact you like the post.

 – Ok hand signal: indicating that you like the post (more enthusiastic than thumbs up).

 – Hands clapping: again, an indication of approval (more enthusiastic than Ok sign).

 – Hands together: sometimes referred to a prayer or high five, symbolic of a thank you.

 – Sunglasses wearing emoji: means 'cool'.

 – Heart: indicates love, or that you love the image.

 – Smiley face with heart-shaped eyes: again, a symbol of love, but with a more personal connotation.

 – Scissors: tends to be used by tailors as a representation of their tailoring shears to indicate a good cut or their creative prowess.

 – Top hat: can be used to literally represent a hat, if one is in the picture and you like it, for example, or as an allusion to the notion of the dandy and an appreciation of the image's style.

 – Rocket ship: something is happening fast, going places or is futuristic and forward-looking.

 – Fire: this is amazing, as in 'smoking hot'; can also be used to identify the person in the image as attractive.

 – Explosion: similar to fire, this is fantastic.

 – Crying with laughter: something is funny or a joke has been told; typically holds an ironic or tongue in cheek double meaning.

 – Kiss: indicates affection or love; typically used when the digital presence is known in real life.

 – Target: used to identify a post which the commenter thinks is just about right, the phrases 'spot on' or 'bullseye' would be comparable; usually employed when the proportions or components of an outfit choice are deemed to be close to perfect.

The use of emojis is a hugely useful tool of communication across an international platform, but they are also potent symbols of intimacy when used in specific ways. The first five emojis I list are the most typical and tend to be rather generic in use; one could comment on any user's post with them happily. However, the other more obscure emojis I have listed are more typically markers of a deeper connection with a user. These are used to demonstrate a greater level of connection than you would with a user you didn't know either personally in the terrestrial world or with whom you didn't have a significant digital connection. This is all part of a complex system of levels of intimacy and associated etiquette found within digital communication, which Garsten and Lerdell would term 'netiquette' (2003: 174).

Style Scoundrel

Throughout the whole process of interacting with the digital world, it began to dawn on me that far from being purely a self-indulgent exercise of navel gazing, it was rather the pursuit of building relationships that began to dominate and shape my time and my manner of interaction. While there are numerous people who clearly view and interact with my Instagram feed, some do so on a much more familiar basis. It is these building relationships that I wish to explore here to ascertain the ways in which digital relationship building differs from relationship building in the physical world.

I discovered and followed stylescoundrel early on in my research, though it was not until some weeks later that I received a follow back. Fundamentally, I know very little about him, as his biography on Instagram only tells us that he lives in Las Vegas, Nevada and that his Zodiac sign is Libra. The only other information I know about him is told through his image posts, and there are more than 1200 of them. From these I have learned that he is obsessed with the designer Vivienne Westwood; almost all of his posts concern her clothes and which particular ones in his expansive collection he is wearing today. Some posts concern new purchases and feature him in different locations but the vast majority are taken from the same perspective as a reflection in a huge mirror in a green room that I assume to be his home, but may not be. The only other individual to crop up with any regularity is his cat, called London Calling, London for short.

It quickly became clear that we shared a love of the designer Vivienne Westwood, and some of her clothes that I own appeared in my posts, though I have neither the extensive collection nor the financial resources to come even remotely close to the level of collector that stylescoundrel clearly is. To begin with our level of interaction was limited; I followed him, and liked some of his posts, slowly learning a little more about his style. Then on 14 April 2016 he liked one of my posts and followed me back. I responded to this by 'liking' a number of his posts and in return he liked twenty-six of my previous posts and left two comments. This was an enormously interesting segue in the development of our digital relationship. It also taught me that the use of the 'like' button was not merely a tool for displaying approval or pleasure over another user's posts but could also be used in a more subtle and complicated way to forge stronger ties. Whilst I conceptualised the digital 'like' as a simplistic form of an 'overlay', following Goffman (1971: 166–67), there is no exact terrestrial equivalent. The closest terrestrial comparison to the digital 'like' would be seen in non-verbal cues, perhaps the tiniest inclining of the head in recognition of someone's shoes, or a gentle smile in response to a beautifully knotted tie.

My relationship with stylescoundrel continued in much the same vein for some time, both of us periodically liking the other's new posts until 1 August. Then he sent me a comment on one of my early posts showing a picture of vintage Penguin books I had seen at a market on the Southbank in London. He simply said 'Vintage Penguins are the best!', and I responded with '@stylescoundrel I agree, such gorgeous colours and typeface'. This seemingly acted as a social marker (much like a conversation about the weather) that implied an acceptance to correspond as in the following minutes he left comments on three other old posts of mine. These ran as follows:

IMAGE 1
stylescoundrel: 🖤🖤🖤🖤🖤
anthrodandy: @stylescoundrel 😃

IMAGE 2
stylescondral: 🖤👍
anthrodandy: @stylescoundrel 👏

IMAGE 3
stylescondral: Beautiful Vivienne Westwood Krall shirt
anthrodandy: @stylescoundrel thank you, I do love it 👍

As you can see from these exchanges, they were very short, and in only one case referred directly to the image, when talking about the Krall shirt: a high-necked shirt with a three-button collar from Vivienne Westwood. The other two comments were purely made up of emojis. I include this example here as it is from one of my earliest digital friends with whom I developed a digital relationship over time. At the time of these comments I was still unsure how emojis were used or what they meant, so to receive so many in comments in such quick succession was intriguing, but it was only later in my fieldwork that I began to realise the significance of exchanges such as this. After the three comments and my replies (each reply prompting a new comment), stylescoundrel proceeded to like almost every one of my previous posts that he had up to that point not liked, a significant number. Whilst I have compared the use of the digital 'like' to terrestrial non-verbal cues earlier in this section, this is slightly different when a very large number of one's posts are liked by another user in quick succession. In this case it is a much more active display of approval and typically indicates a desire to develop a digital connection.

Comments such as those above made up of emojis may seem ephemeral or even standoffish for those used to terrestrial forms of social interaction, but in a digital world which is mainly driven by simply 'liking' other's photographs, 'following' and leaving comments becomes much more significant. It is perhaps also important at this point (and before moving onto the more semantically complex discussion concerning emojis) to analytically appraise 'like', 'follow' and 'comment' as three notions together.

These are three actions which occur through all major social media platforms, and have come to be established to such a degree within the vernacular of not only digital but also terrestrial language as to have numerous acquired and implied meanings beyond the bare unencumbered command of pressing a button online. Naturally, on a purely base level of intellectual interaction, 'like', 'follow', and 'comment' are simple things to understand. Presumably, this is why they have been chosen by the designers of digital platforms to fulfil the needs of many across a whole variety of languages and cultures who share access to the internet. 'Like' (as applied to a post) signals a generic approval, sympathy with, acknowledgment of or a slightly more detached notion of support. For example, if a tailor posted a picture of a suit that I liked, or even coveted, I might 'like' it. In contrast, if the same tailor posted a picture of themselves with a caption saying that they were having a bad day, I might also 'like' this. However, I began to unpick through this research that this action is not approving of, or taking a schadenfreudeian joy in their unhappiness, but rather it is a sympathetic action, despite the action in question being termed a 'like'. It very quickly became clear to me that the levels of meaning in online digital interaction are as subtle as they are convoluted and as complicated as they are instinctive. It is for these reasons, at least to some degree, that the emoji has come to the fore to such a degree for the Instagram platform. In addition to a 'like', the nuanced use of comments and follows allows for relationships to be built through signalling connection and a desire to remain connected. This is crucial for building rapport.

Building a Rapport – Layers of Intimacy

The nature of my research, being a blend of digital and terrestrial, means that there is no one model for the building of a rapport with individuals; however, methods I would like to explore in this section include the manner in which I have communicated with Joshua Kane over the period of my research, especially highlighting the use of multiple platforms for communication.

This began with a visit to his shop where I introduced myself and chatted to Joshua Kane himself, about his brand and my research. I had quickly learned in the course of my research leading up to this point that a researcher can gain much better access to tailors if they become a customer too. Wulff (2012: 164–66) notes the importance of rapport in establishing and maintaining relationships with informants, particularly in terms of revealing something about oneself to the informant in order to establish rapport. In the case of the tailors I worked with it seemed that making a purchase opened a similar door to greater rapport. This purchase demonstrates a personal (as well as) financial investment in the brand which in my experience elicits a far better response from the tailor in question. Naturally, my funds were not bottomless and I was extremely limited with what I could buy at full price from any of the tailors that I visited. However, I was fortunate enough to be awarded a modest grant to support my studies and I used this fund to make a small number of purchases from Joshua Kane over the year of my fieldwork. On this first visit, I purchased an enormously long black and white knitted scarf which was at a sale price and a white bow tie, he had even let me try on one of his wonderful coats which I had lusted after. A couple of days after that visit an email appeared in my inbox.

'Good morning fellow Joshua', it began, and proceeded to enquire after my health and remark how pleasant it had been for someone with both an aesthetic and research interest to visit the shop. It was, of course, from Joshua Kane himself. This genuine tone turned playful and then teasing, barely disguised with an earnest manner. I could almost see Kane's eyes twinkling beyond his emailed words as he told me that they had a busy week of fittings ahead and that the coat I had tried on in his shop – the last of that size – would almost certainly be sold. He did, however, confide that he would much rather it found a home with me alongside the accessories I had already collected, and as I had already visited the shop that week he would be prepared to offer me a special discount. He reasserted that this wasn't usual practice, but he could see it was a piece of tailoring I loved and did not want to see it go to an unloved home. Rarely have I felt more beguiled; then my eyes found the numbers. The typical retail price for the coat at that time was £1650 (although it has since been reissued and the price increased accordingly to £2000), but for me it was offered at £1200, the same as an opening price point suit.

This made me feel physically sick. I could not comprehend spending that much money on an item of clothing no matter how beautiful. However, as the nausea began to subside somewhat, I reflected that this would be an excellent way of cementing my relationship with Joshua Kane as client and researcher and that it might be the best way to spend the majority of my research funds to begin a working relationship with such an interesting tailor. Even more importantly, it was a truly beautiful coat. About a week later I went back to collect my coat which I had already paid for over the phone. Joshua Kane himself wasn't in the shop but an assistant with an identically waxed moustache disappeared downstairs to get the coat for me which was placed with much ceremony in an enormous coat bag. It felt surreal to finally own a garment I had coveted for a long time but never imagined owning. I held very tightly onto the garment bag all the way home (see illustration 5.9, for an image of the coat).

The day after I had collected the coat another email arrived. Once again it was Joshua Kane, this time apologising that he had not been there in person when I had visited this shop to pick up the coat, but he was excited to see a photo – an allusion to our shared Instagram use. A few weeks later, another

Illustration 5.9. Image of author en route to Joshua Kane's AW17 show at the London Palladium, wearing a Joshua Kane houndstooth Fawcett coat, oversized black and white striped Shaw scarf and navy blue Gostick hat. This image was posted to Instagram on 17 Febraury 2017. © Joshua M. Bluteau.

email arrived, this time from the shop manager informing me that their current collection was coming to an end and that they were offering special discounts to select clientele. This time a three-piece houndstooth suit was offered at 50 per cent discount and various other suit styles and fabrics were mentioned. A long email exchange followed and whilst research funds were running low, I eventually settled on a houndstooth jacket to match my coat.

I once again made my way to Shoreditch and #bloodsweatandshears. By this point I had attempted to establish myself as both a familiar face and a customer, a combination which seemed to facilitate the greatest access to this particular tailor – an approach that needed to be carefully crafted and evolved individually for each contact I made.

I arrived at the small shop in the pouring rain, so entered through the back door which opens into the Spitalfields market itself, allowing the last few minutes of my journey to be shielded from the weather. As I entered I could see Joshua Kane, talking to another customer. Joshua was dressed in a customary skinny fitted suit, this one was rather demure for him, blue with occasional pin head sized white dots woven through the fabric, single-breasted two-button, with a slim notched lapel. Unusually for Joshua Kane, this was teemed not with the usual shirt and tie, but rather an aqua coloured t-shirt ('dress down Friday', he later quipped) and a slim scarf tied around his neck. Spotty socks, visible beneath intentionally cropped suit trousers, ran in to round-toed burnished Oxfords with just a hint of brogueing on the toes.

The other customer in the shop seemed to have just dropped in for a chat on his lunch break, and to check whether an order of his was ready for collection, although it later transpired that he didn't really want to have to carry it around all day and wanted it delivered instead. Whether this was a real request or just playful teasing, I wasn't able to fully establish.

Joshua Kane greeted me and introduced JB (or 'yet another Joshua' as Joshua Kane referred to him), whom I had corresponded with over email and who I knew, from his Twitter feed, was the shop manager. Under his guidance I perused the items on display and he explained that a number of items were in the sale, pulling out a number of waistcoats and a suit for me to try on. A particular waistcoat in red imperial wool with black lapels caught my eye and was such a good price, as I was told, that I purchased it then and there, but left it at the shop to collect with my houndstooth jacket which I had been told would probably need alterations. Eventually, Joshua Kane finished with the other client and jauntily strode down the stairs into the basement to retrieve my jacket, as the client left he passed me: 'Great coat, I've got one in camel'.

I was, naturally, wearing my new houndstooth coat. Joshua Kane reappeared and once again the suit bag was opened with much reverence; I slipped my arms into the heavy fabric in front of a full-length mirror so I could view my new acquisition. The fit was poor, it fitted my shoulders well and the sleeve length was good but other than that it was like wearing a houndstooth sack, boxy and unflattering. Joshua Kane appeared behind me and began to pin the back seam drawing the fabric together and tapering the jacket. Joshua Kane asked: 'Do we want to see a gap between the arms and the jacket?' It was a rhetorical question, but the impetus was on me to make the choice. 'The good thing is that you've got a waist so we can give it some shape, not like me, I'm just a beanpole, straight up, straight down'.

I looked back at myself in the mirror and he had indeed highlighted my waist and shaped the jacket to me. It looked good, and with a nod of approval I slipped it off very carefully to avoid disturbing any of the pins. The jacket was placed back in its bag and hung temporarily on one of the rails in the shop as we continued to chat. At this point I was about to leave when another person burst into the shop through the back door. At first I thought it was a customer but it soon transpired that it was one of Joshua Kane's good friends from school; they greeted each other and I was introduced. Joshua Kane picked up my jacket and pottered downstairs at this point while his friend and I browsed some of the items on display. 'I don't know about you', he said turning to me, 'but I don't know where I would ever wear that'. He pulled out a red velvet dinner jacket with a gold dragon patterned shawl lapel. 'No', I said, 'I'm not sure either'. This was not, however a malicious slight, but a playful ribbing which continued when Joshua Kane had bounded back up the stairs. 'We could make you look great in that', Joshua Kane retorted mischievously.

Once again at this point I was about to leave the shop but the friend produced, rather incongruously, from his bag a miniature set of table tennis, complete with bats, net and ball and insisted we all play. This seemed to capture the imagination of Joshua Kane, and while JB the manager looked on with a slightly pained expression, Joshua cleared the counter where the till was situated, erected the net and pulled out his phone to change the shop's music from gentle background music to James Brown. Over the next ten minutes we all took turns playing with the ball invariably bouncing off one of the walls and rolling down the stairs on more than one occasion. 'Clean up in aisle three', shouted Joshua Kane with a laugh on one occasion.

Eventually the game came to an end and I left the shop; it had been an unusual visit but an interesting one. It definitely felt like I had entered a new stage of relationship with this tailor. As I departed Joshua Kane said: 'So now you've got three pieces from us in two fabrics'. It felt like I was becoming a collector, a feeling which was certainly being fostered by Joshua Kane himself; I was becoming part of the club.

This section demonstrates very clearly the development of intimacy with Joshua Kane both physically and in his use of multiple platforms of communication. Here emails and Twitter have been used to send messages as well as the more typical interaction he gives my Instagram posts which feature his clothes. This multiplatform communication heightens a sense of intimacy (despite the nature of digital communication being terrestrially disconnected) and is used to give a sense to those you are communicating with that they are part of multiple aspects of your life. This increase in intimacy was later manifested when Joshua Kane would occasionally send me messages which were not related to any specific purchase. For example:

17/09/16 – Twitter message from @joshuakanebespoke

How's it going chap! Love the content in the red imperial

04/11/16 – Twitter message from @joshuakanebespoke

How's it going sir!! Been ages since you visited!

23/12/16 – Twitter message from @joshuakanebespoke

Looking forward to your visit!
Went on sale at Brushfield street for the last week there today. . . 50% on lots of beauties! Let me know if you like a deal 🖤

These unprompted messages could cynically be read as a clever marketing strategy and good business sense, which I am sure it is, but this sense of connection makes it feel more personal than this, especially when Joshua Kane's attempts to make me buy new items from him seem to be more overt in private Instagram messages I have received from him. On one notable occasion this involved a red velvet jacket with lapels faced in a gold jacquard dragon print – this seemed a little ostentatious for even my taste. There are elements in this exchange reminiscent of Rapport's (1998) chapter concerning the 'Hard Sell' he experienced following winning a scratch-card competition. However, with Joshua Kane there is a playfulness to the selling, and a well-judged sense of rapport between himself and clients, a tactic which engenders a familial sense of connection, and one which would certainly have been effective in persuading me to add more pieces to my collection had I been able to afford them.

All these methods of communication, alongside the times I met Joshua Kane physically, assisted with the building of a rapport, one that is present in physical life and in our digital communication, including the simplest of emoji-based Instagram exchanges. This ever-increasing demonstration of intimacy was further highlighted the next time I visited Joshua Kane's shop and was shown downstairs for the first time into an area that was typically off limits to customers to view the designs from the Langtry runway show that had happened a few weeks earlier and were not on the shop floor yet but available to order. Rails of blue crushed velvet jackets, quilted lapels, studded leather and items that had not even appeared in the final runway were at my fingertips; I had both physically and socially been accepted into a inner level of intimacy.

In other cases, a digital rapport can be built without ever physically meeting, for example I earlier describe an exchange of comments and emojis with stylescoundrel, demonstrating the digital reciprocity which began our Instagram relationship. Since this exchange of emojis we like practically every one of each other's Instagram posts. It is these moments of digital interaction which are equivalent to the rapport building found in the terrestrial world. This may seem far simpler than the development of my relationship with Joshua Kane but this is an entirely digital relationship, examples of which form a large portion of my Instagram friends and research participants, and while this may appear to be a simpler form of rapport building, it is important to bear in mind the heavy time investment required to build such digital relationships.

Chapter 6

TIME TO LEAVE THE FIELD

I spend my cash on looking flash
And grabbing your attention
　　　　　　　　—Adam & The Ants, 'Stand And Deliver'

There is a kaleidoscopic nature to the digital world. With every twist of the lens or flick of the finger, the image we are presented with reloads and a different permutation of the present is presented to us, the user. This distortion is a phenomenon which platforms such as Instagram actively promote, as the notion that we are looking into the 'presents' of other users every time we take a look at our feed is intoxicating, and we are beguiled.

This phenomenon highlights the disjuncture between temporal and digital realities of the present. The manner in which digital media alters and augments notions of time is a significant finding from my research and adds to the pre-existing anthropological understanding of time. Time is manipulated by digital platforms and over long periods of interaction this bleeds into one's terrestrial understanding of time. If I post in the middle of the day I get a very lacklustre response, but early morning (8 am) or after work (6 pm) posts provide good feedback, presumably because they catch people commuting with nothing else to do but browse social media. However, the best feedback I find is from posts at 2 am, whether this is because I am picking up international users or because there are fewer posts at this time of night meaning mine receive greater visibility the following morning I don't know, but this discovery fascinated me. I subsequently altered my own sleep patterns. Editing and posting an image to my Instagram is almost always the last thing I do before going to bed. This naturally has altered my own sense of time, and my place within it, but it is a more nuanced interpretation of time which I wish to explore next with regard to social media.

Instagram acts as a tool which manipulates a multiplicity of temporal realities. It manifests as a modern digital form of a Polaroid instant camera, indeed its logo, though frequently updated, still takes styling cues from Polaroid and similar cues are found in the square shape of the posted Instagram images and the style of image offered by some of the available filters. Additionally, there is an assumption written into much of the text accompanying the posts of many users which project the notion that these images represent what they are doing at precisely the moment that they are posted. This assumption can be actively cultivated through the accompanying text or assumed through the omission of a comment saying that it is an old photo. Within the language of Instagram there are certain temporal markers which identify whether an image is indeed a realistic representation of the current temporality of the poster or whether it is an older image. These include #ootd indicating that the image is one's 'outfit of the day', #latergram indicating that this image is not a current one but has been taken some time ago and is only being posted now, and #tbt meaning 'throwback to' or sometimes more specifically 'throwback Thursday', again indicating that this image is an old one, typically taken from further back in time than the latergram. If temporal markers such as these are omitted then it can be hard to judge when an image was taken and given the ostensibly instant nature of the platform it is easy to assume that an image is from that day if not that actual moment, not from days or even weeks earlier. This is an occurrence which I myself fell afoul of in the earlier stages of my digital research, when I would meet people who followed me on Instagram and I was not wearing the outfit I had posted a matter of hours earlier (often because it had been an image I had taken days before); they would express an interesting mix of emotions, a combination of disappointment and a sense that they had been cheated: 'you weren't wearing that earlier'. It was as though the illusion that Instagram was indeed instant needed to be maintained, whether contrived or not, and definitive temporal markers used when an image was older to preserve the precarious equilibrium. It is very easy to make the assumption that the vast majority of images posted on Instagram are not instant, but are carefully crafted images taken in advance with large amounts of time spent on them, both in the conceptualising, taking and editing of said images, rendering the narrative crafted by the progression of images to be entirely fictitious. However, this assumption (whilst perhaps true in some cases) ruins the fundamental joy of the digital platform. There is a surface pleasure to simply viewing the images that are posted and interacting with them to show one's approval or not.

In contrast, I contend that there is a deeper pleasure to the voyeuristic gaze which not only looks at the images in a detached manner but rather looks through the images to the user at the other end of the digital lens. There is a comfort to being confronted by the images of familiar faces on a daily basis, and there can be a sensation of abandonment if they do not appear for a length of time. Indeed, an apology often occurs from users who have taken some time away from Instagram upon their return. Furthermore, the consumer of these images learns over time the style, nuances and digital personality of a particular user. In addition, while some users are quite protective regarding their non-digital private life, others are much more open and one can glean aspects of their terrestrial life too. Work, partners, family, holidays and vacation time can all feature on Instagram accounts primarily focused on the intricacies of an individual's dress and their love more generally of menswear. These diversions create a sense of the ontological depth of an authentic individual as well as building the bond between image producer and the gazer which exceeds the bond one would expect for such minimal active interaction. These loci of connection are bound together with the assumed truthfulness of the temporal projection made by such users. The gazer buys in to the narrative being produced by the user and follows it like an abstract story, a series of vignettes into their digital friend's life. One could feel hoodwinked and cheated if these posts turned out not to be genuine in the sense of their temporal position. This creates an important bond of reciprocity between sharer and gazer in the network within Instagram, where it is important to highlight the 'truth' and position of an image which is being posted.

There are alternatives to this, such as the case of curated collections: accounts which consist of images which the user has not necessarily taken but they like or approve of and are reposting for the interest of their followers. However, these accounts lack a sense of the account holder which means that there is no physicalisation of a user at the other end of the lens to connect to. As such, there is not such a palpable connection and it feels as if the account could be using images chosen by an algorithm. In this case the notions of authenticity, temporality and interpersonal connection are almost non-existent. It is important to note that accounts such as this exist, but I have for the majority of my digital research concentrated on accounts with visible operators, which I would term personal accounts.

Finally, let us return to the physical reality of the process of posting on digital media. Even if a post is as instant as it can be, which in this case indicates it has been taken, edited and posted in as short a time frame as possible, and it is truly documenting the present of the user, we do not see the reality of the taking of the picture or the editing: we simply see the finished posted result. Therefore, in the most temporally accurate digital reality we are, at best, living a few minutes behind the subject. This makes more complex a simplistic reading of Fabian who asserts that 'the temporal conditions experienced in fieldwork and those expressed in writing . . . usually contradict each other. Productive empirical research . . . is only possible when researcher and researched share time' (Fabian 2002: 71). He goes on to say that 'only as communicative praxis does ethnography carry the promise of yielding new knowledge about another culture. Yet the discourse that pretends to interpret, analyse, and communicate ethnographic knowledge to the researcher's society is pronounced from a "distance," that is, from a position which denies coevalness to the object of inquiry' (idem). Fabian (idem) is saying that the 'other' which the anthropologist studies is typically located in a non-contemporary time to their own. He suggests that those we study and write about are located in a constructed past that is not contemporary with the present the ethnographer lives and writes in. This, he suggests, is not a valid way of gaining productive data. However, this does not take into account the notion of multiple presents. My understanding of digital time will build on Dilley's (2014) work on chronologies when considering the letters of Henri Gaden, letters which would have taken weeks if not longer to reach their recipient. In this case there is both the present where Gaden writes the letter, the present he is writing about (which could be either the same present as he is writing or a past event at which he was present), and the present where the letter is received and finally read. As Dilley puts it:

> Three types of chronology, which run simultaneously through this book, should be borne in mind by the reader. The first is the chronology of events as they occurred in historic time; the second is the chronological sequence in which these events were written up in letters to family and friends; the third encompasses the time delay between the writing of the letter, the period taken to deliver the letter to the recipient and the subsequent responses to the correspondence. (Dilley 2014: 2–3)

This is profoundly similar to my understanding of how Instagram creates different chronologies or alternative temporal realities. These chronologies are necessitated by the function of the platform. There is the present in which the image is crafted, taken and edited, though this could be divided even further if an image is taken far in advance of the editing process. There is the present where the image is posted, and finally the present when another user views your posted image. These alternative chronologies allow users to manipulate where they are, geographically, emotionally and aesthetically, to create their own digital narrative. Now of course I am not suggesting that all users manipulate their chronologies in a malicious way to adulterate the experience of those who gaze upon them, though I am sure some do. What I am acknowledging is the disjuncture between temporal and digital realities of the present. This is crucial to how we must understand the intersection between digital and temporal fieldsites. Even if it is not an intentional mask, those viewing your posts at a different time will experience your 'present' as the posted image in their 'present' as gazer. It is however important to note that in a recent change to Instagram, posts are no longer shown chronologically on the feed of other users' posts that one browses, but rather in an order selected by an algorithm placing those with the highest level of activity at the top. This may in due course alter even further the way in which concepts of time and the present are viewed by users of this platform. It is now the case that Instagram itself is constructing the digital reality of what you get to see based on what it believes you want to see, or possibly by what it wants you to see. This naturally adds further dimensions of complexity to an already difficult construct of digital reality.

These different chronologies can, however, be a very useful business tool for those who are able to effectively utilise them. Tailors such as Joshua Kane are masters at this, constantly showing images of past campaigns to keep the garments on sale fresh, allowing images to be taken of their work in progress and behind the scenes designs, hinting at new projects, or just letting their followers know that they will be on the shop floor in person all day that day. Despite these different chronologies the notion of 'present' is still a problematic one to engage with in an ever increasingly digital world. Those producing the image may do so in one present, and those who view it may do so in another, but where does this leave the image itself? Baudrillard (2003: 42) conceptualises the virtual world as belonging to the realm of hyperreality, and perhaps this is a prudent way to think about where these digital images sit in time when they are not being gazed upon. If this virtual digital world 'takes the place of the real', then time for these images is not real but rather they sit in a hyperreality of infinite possibilities of present (idem).

Additional features became available through Instagram during the period of my fieldwork, including a feature known as Instagram live. This allows a user to broadcast video and sound live to any of their followers who are online about what they are doing at that very moment. This is to me the most voyeuristic aspect of the Instagram platform and the most intimate. While it is of course controlled by the user who is filming and broadcasting, they are making a very real emotional and temporal connection with their followers – literally letting them in to their life. This adds to the discussion on chronologies, reinvigorating the instant nature of Instagram, a feature which was becoming more distant as images were chosen more carefully to be posted.

Taking the Field Home

There are significant challenges to digital working with regard to knowing when to leave the field as well as issues surrounding the addictive quality of social media. Coffey (1999: 101) describes fieldwork as a form of 'courtship' which inevitably comes to an end when one leaves the field. Coffey and Atkinson (1996) note the sense of loss that one can feel at leaving the field, and Coffey (1999: 106) notes that the guidelines suggested by Lofland and Lofland (1995: 63) are not always straightforward to execute, and that the emotional strain felt by the researcher can be difficult. Burrell tells us that when fieldwork is located in 'cyberspace' then 'entering the fieldsite is no longer a process of crossing the boundary from outside to inside' (Burrell 2009: 193–94). This highlights the permeability I discussed above and exemplifies why leaving such a space, which Hine would conceptualise as a product of imagination, is more difficult than a terrestrially bounded fieldsite (Hine 2000). Wood recalls feelings of betrayal upon leaving the field, and wrestles with how to write about his experiences without adding to this already existing feeling of betrayal (Wood 2011). Haynes (2016: 106) explores the notion of social media as a tool for 'performing relationships in absence', something which would enable one to physically leave the field whilst mitigating some of the betrayal described by Wood (2011). However, this assumes that one is simply using social media as a tool for communicating between terrestrial selves. In my research, the fieldsite was digital, and occupied by digital selves, which means that the relationships existed within the digital space; it was not merely used as a communication tool. In a similar way to Wood (idem), Cohen suggests that 'the "intrusion" of extraneous personal experience makes spatially and temporally bounded "fieldwork" a chimera', essentially arguing that such an ideal is impossible (Cohen 1992: 339). Consequently, when one considers fieldwork in a digital space, an amorphous imagined space, arriving and leaving are both physical acts made astonishingly easy by modern handheld technology, and yet are incredibly emotionally, intellectually and psychologically challenging. One does not simply arrive and leave on a boat or an airplane, but one must actively make the journey in and out of cyberspace leaving a digital self behind in the ether. However, this is the crux, for after long periods of digital fieldwork this digital self is not content to remain behind in the digital world, but instead begins to bleed into the temporal world, altering the way the temporal self acts, thinks and appears.

I was discussing the digital aspect of my work with a number of colleagues a few months after I had left my physical fieldsite. I was asked: 'but how do you leave it, isn't it always there when you wake up?' This was a good question, and one which prompted a deeper analytical reflection on the nature of the digital fieldsite and the impact of its study on the researcher. Coffey (1999: 97–113) notes the difficulty and emotional strain of leaving any fieldsite after a protracted period of research. However, the specific issues of leaving a digital fieldsite have received minimal attention or anthropological discussion. The precise issue which my colleague was alluding to in this question was one which appears to be increasingly common amongst ethnographic researchers: the connection with physical participants through digital social media, whether this be Facebook, Twitter and Instagram or specific messaging platforms such as WhatsApp. This connection ensures that an avenue of communication can be maintained or reopened with relative ease once the researcher has left the physical field. However, for my work which is so deeply entrenched within the day-to-day workings of a digital world, Instagram was not merely a means for communication but a fieldsite in its own right, and the residence for the digital identity which I had created. This problematised stepping away from the field, since my digital field is not a geographically bounded physical entity but rather a portable reality which I carry everywhere in my pocket. This ease of access and the habitual nature of my research meant I found it very difficult to leave my digital fieldsite once I began to write up my research and I therefore developed a number of strategies to deal with the complexities of the digital field.

Firstly, I developed the principle of permeable fieldsite boundaries for analytically distinguishing between digital and physical fieldsites. The traditional ethnographic fieldsite which is geographically remote and physically bounded is by my definition impermeable. Traditionally, once the anthropologist has left the field they are no longer able to interact with their subjects in any temporally equivalent manner. They can visit again, write letters or interact with artefacts they have taken home with them but they cannot communicate with their fieldsite and those living there in real time. Communication, where possible, takes a considerable time to travel and there is therefore a disjunction between researcher and subject; this allows for easy separation once the field has been left. With the advent of modern technologies, communication (including email, video calling, text messaging and the sending of images and video) is instantaneous, allowing researchers to keep in a much more temporally relative contact with their fieldsite, and much has been written on the phone and mobile phone as either a phenomenon or an ethnographic tool, to be used both during and after the period of fieldwork (Sunderland 1999; Horst and Miller 2006; Hahn and Kibora 2008; Mcintosh 2010; Archambault 2012; Jeffrey and Doron 2012; Kenaw 2012; Johnson 2013; Schiffauer 2013).

In such a case where the field can still be accessed through mobile communication even after a researcher has physically left, I would define the fieldsite boundary as semi-permeable, with the barriers between researcher and subject beginning to dissolve once the researcher has left the field. In the case of a digital space itself being one's fieldsite, the boundaries become fully permeable, with the researcher's geographical location having no bearing on their ability to interact fully with their fieldsite. This meant that in my case, once I had left the terrestrial arm of my research and returned to my university to begin writing up I was still fully immersed in my digital fieldsite. This was not initially problematic; however, as I became fully immersed in the process of writing up a number of issues began to become manifest. This led me to develop the aforementioned set of strategies. It is also important at this point to highlight the difference between mobile phones which enable phone-to-phone text-based and audio communication and smartphones which allow instant access to the internet with a plethora of available applications to access far more complex forms of communication; my research dealt with the latter.

Secondly, once I had securely established my own understanding of how my digital fieldsite was different to traditional physical fieldsites I realised that I would have to carefully plan and execute my eventual detachment from the digital field. I was conscious that in a world of continual instant communication to suddenly disappear, or 'ghost' as it is known, would not only be personally challenging but may indeed damage any future research possibilities I wished to complete in this digital field. As such, I decided that the best way to achieve the distance required for a successful analysis of the data whilst not ghosting my digital friends was to select an arbitrary digital data set, essentially only analysing my digital content before a certain date. I initially thought the rather pleasing mix of my 800th post, accompanied by me garnering my 500th follower, which I achieved on 25 August 2017, would be a cathartic response to the intellectual conflict surrounding this issue (see illustration 6.1).

However, I decided that it would be more empirically sound to conduct two years of digital research and as such I would finish on 3 October 2017. This is not to say that I would become a 'ghost' after this point; I had decided that I would continue to interact with my digital participants and post new content, but this would be in a less intensive manner than during my period of research, where I had endeavoured to post every day. It

Illustration 6.1. A screenshot from the author's smartphone showing his Instagram page after his 800th post on 25 August 2017. © Joshua M. Bluteau.

also felt appropriate at this point to acknowledge the passage of the previous two years and as such I posted illustration 6.2 and the following text.

> It's been two years since I joined Instagram. Thanks everyone for all the support. Here's to the top half of my outfit from the previous post. #latergram featuring this #tommynutter #threepiecesuit #glencheck #powcheck with #vintage @turnbull_asser #kippertie @charlestyrwhitt shirt and @crombie1805 pocket square #mensstyle #mensfashion #menswear #dapper #dandy #bohochic #sharp #suave #tailor #tailored #tailoring #suit #suiting #suited #savilerow #savilerowstyle #savilerowfashion #doublebreastedsuit #sprezzatura

It was odd to step away from this digital world which had formed such an enormous part of my everyday life both for the year when I was conducting physical research alongside it and in the year when I had returned to my university to begin writing up. However, I did not step away completely and my

Illustration 6.2. An image posted to the Instagram account @anthrodandy by the author on 3 October 2017, featuring a Tommy Nutter glen check double-breasted suit and Turnbull and Asser kipper tie. © Joshua M. Bluteau.

interaction became more limited, with posts and interaction only occurring when a garment or outfit particularly appealed to me for posting or when taking a break from writing. I had considered closing my Instagram account or at least archiving all the images to make them invisible from other users at the termination of my digital fieldwork. However, Uimonen highlights the precedents and benefits of maintaining a digital platform and presence which can be viewed in conjunction with a final published hard copy detailing one's digital anthropological research (Uimonen 2016: 246–47). As such, I maintained my Instagram account with the same level of access available as I had during my fieldwork. The interaction I had with Instagram post-fieldwork was certainly not as rigorous or compulsive as it had been on a daily basis for the majority of the previous two years. In this time the longest period of absence that I had was in May 2017, where for four weeks I was without my iPhone as it had developed a fault and was sent away for repair. In this time I made a conscious decision to not interact with Instagram at all, a period of time which is best described as a digital detox, and felt a strange sense of relief at not being beholden to my handheld device, not only in terms of the relentless feeling of needing to produce image-based content for Instagram but also a more general feeling of connection with a slower temporal world where information and communication was less instant. The result of this for my digital following on Instagram is that I lost approximately ten followers per week across those four weeks, and gained few new ones in that time. However, I reflected that this was no different than leaving a terrestrial fieldsite for a period of time and losing contacts through loss of interaction of other means over the absence. This did not particularly bother me as the goal of my digital research was never specifically to amass followers, but I thought this was an interesting aspect to the digital network that I was working with. This negative overall response to taking time away from one's digital persona acts as an incentivising tool, encouraging users to develop regular patterns and consistent production levels of the image-based discourse around which the platform is based. As such, it is good etiquette within the network that I studied to apologise for a period of absence. For example on 9 August 2017 @aloisio.ricky, who at that time was the *New York Times* art director, posted a picture of himself in a blue suit in one of his trademark poses after an absence from Instagram and wrote:

MEA CULPA. . .

My sincere apologies for having been away so long. . .

And me utmost gratitude to all those who inquired both publically and privately about my whereabouts (and encouraged me to return)!

As John Lennon once said: 'Life is what happens to you while you're busy making other plans.'

Thus, I gingerly dip my toes back in these briny IG waters!

The following day he posted another image of himself in the same outfit but a different pose:

MAY WE PROCEED?
Two posts in two days. . .
It's a start!
Your comments and heartfelt
encouragement are sincerely
appreciated . . . what amazing individuals you
truly are!

he first comment garnered 615 likes and 242 comments, many enquiring as to the health and wellbeing of @aloisio.ricky, and even more expressing joy at his return. Comments like this were typical:

ellalondon Yayayayay!!! Just
opened up Instagram and this
pic was first in my feed . . .
made me soooo happy

After my four-week period of absence I also felt the need to offer an apology to the network, so I posted illustration 6.3 with the following comment.

Apologies to everyone for my absence on here, dead phone to blame, but I'm back now! #ootd @turnbull_asser #doublebreasted #jacket #blazer in this stunning fabric with #vintage #knittedtie and @edeandravenscroft #shirt #mensstyle #mensfashion #menswear #dapper #dandy #bohochic #sharp #suave #suit #suited #suiting #tailor #tailored #tailoring #madeinengland

There is a pleasing circularity to this section on apologising that after my (above) apology @aloisio.ricky commented:

You are DEFINITELY back!

Illustration 6.3. A screenshot from the author's smartphone showing an Instagram post by the author on 22 May 2017. The image features a Turnbull and Asser double-breasted horizontal stripe blazer and vintage knitted tie. © Joshua M. Bluteau.

It is clear that there is a powerful social and emotional link between digital users, with expressions of concern for other users' wellbeing, and the necessary apology to other members of one's network after an absence, being widespread practices. It is with this in mind that I discuss the nature of these digital links between users in the next section, where I question how best to describe the users one is linked with online. Are they friends, 'friends', digital friends, or perhaps not friends at all?

Meta Friends

How one describes the members of the network whom I interacted with on a daily basis is an interesting linguistic choice. Miller describes the online platform itself as a 'meta friend', choosing to emphasise the interaction between user and platform over user to user interaction (2011: 170–72). This does not convince me as a sufficient manner to deal with the individual users whom I interacted with through my digital research. There is something friend-like about social media platforms, always willing to interact with you, but if such a platform is a meta-friend then the other members of my Instagram network must also be termed meta-friends. However, the invocation of the prefix 'meta' implies that these online acquaintances are an abstract form of friend, somehow less tangibly real than those one has made through terrestrial physical interaction. I prefer to refer to those whom I have formed online relationships with as digital 'friends' and in doing so actively engage with Baudrillard's notion of hyperreality (2003: 42). In this way, I am not suggesting that online acquaintances are an abstract form of friend, since there is a 'real' physical person at the other end of the digitally linked relationship. I am instead suggesting that the method of communication between these two physical entities alters the terrestrially bounded notions of time, privacy and social interaction, augmenting traditional notions of relationship building and reciprocity. The consequence of this is the typical digital methods of building relationships which I have detailed above, interactions which occur at a hyperreal level where speed of communication, temporal coevalness and personal privacy all occur in a more liberal and rapidly shifting manner within the boundary of the network you are a part of.

It is worth acknowledging that after a long period of interaction with Instagram and the other users in my network a small group developed, within the larger network, who would 'like' practically every post which I made, regardless of content. These posts often concerned a more personal aspect of my life than a simple headless shot of my current outfit would convey. It might be a picture of me with my partner, or a picture showing something I was interested in, or even myself dressed more casually. Such images would not garner many likes compared to the standard type of image which I would post, however certain 'friends' would always like them. This indicates to me a deeper sense of friendship and connection, which extends beyond the Foucauldian repressive discourse, where only images fitting in with the networks shared aesthetic are 'liked'. Whilst I have not met any of these individuals with whom I feel this connection in person, I feel as though the digital relationship we have is closer than the digital relationship I have with some of my terrestrial friends.

An Addictive Medium

Digital social media is by its very nature an addictive medium, though the precise nature of digital addiction is debated (Griffiths 2012). The nature of a platform where any one of the millions of users from all over the world could be uploading content at any second of the day means that it does not matter when you last checked your smartphone for an update, there will almost certainly be something new to look at, even if you last looked barely a minute ago. This fact, coupled with the ease of use and portability of handheld electronic devices, means that it is easy to get drawn into an addictive, quasi-ritualistic cycle of checking for updates. This is certainly the experience that I had from my research and it compares well to the notion of 'time suck' as described by Miller (2011: 78): 'Friends in England often refer to Facebook as a 'time suck' – which is a pretty neat way of describing one of its most considerable powers'.

In addition, the requirement to be continually presenting images of oneself in new outfits means that there is a great impetus to continually purchase new items to showcase to your network. There are elements here of both a voyeuristic commodity fetishism and a personal connection to this desire to keep acquiring new looks for your network to pass judgement on. Throughout my period of digital fieldwork I certainly felt this pressure to present new purchases or unseen parts of my wardrobe to the network, an action which over time necessitated a continual stream of purchases. Fittingly, Miller tells us that there is pressure 'to live up to a fetishized ideal that now regulates off-line as well as on-line practices' (2003a: 16). This is certainly comparable to the way in which I experienced my relationship with both digital and terrestrial worlds, with my buying habits, sleep pattern and appearance changing in response to my digital networking. The vast majority of my purchases throughout this period of fieldwork were second-hand, though carefully chosen, often bought for minimal amounts from the online auction website eBay. However, the 'time suck' described by Miller (2011: 78) which had, for me, begun solely in Instagram now began to bleed more widely into associated digital spaces, as I found myself surfing other websites to acquire knowledge, garments and accessories to be shared with my Instagram network. This naturally placed a self-inflicted financial burden on me as a researcher, but it left me with a collection of artefacts which I can interact with (and wear) terrestrially, but which I have also displayed in the digital world, a process which has enhanced my understanding of the phenomenology of wearing and owning high-end tailored clothing and accessories. This became a crucial part of my methodology, without which I would not have been able to understand the way in which members of my digital network understood the items which they were publishing images about.

> Most of the more substantive recent studies of new technologies are actually used (e.g. Miller and Slater 2000; Woolgar 2002) to emphasize the degree to which on-line activity and off-line activity have major, often unexpected, effects upon each other . . . however . . . new technology practitioners are extremely concerned that there SHOULD be consequences for off-line life . . . the key testimony to the importance of what they claim to have achieved in on-line practice. (Miller 2003a: 16)

This need to continually display new items (or at least to have a large enough wardrobe to allow for a circulation of looks) is not only an exercise in vanity but the network itself reinforces the sense of a shared standard or quality of image which needs to be upheld. In addition, certain images can elicit hugely powerful responses from others in the network, who make it feel as though the act of publicising what you are wearing is not purely a selfish one, whereby one fishes for approval, but one which actively helps other users too. This notion of inspiration is important for understanding the nuanced difference between simple creation of the image, and the digital connection with others. For example, after I posted the images shown in illustration 6.4, the flared sleeve cuff of a Mark Powell ready-to-wear jacket, I received the following private message from @the.style.professor:

> You just inspired me to have my tailor add flared cuffs to a mod-looking jacket I had ordered – thanks!

Comments like this demonstrate how a network of individuals support the production of images in an active manner, more akin to the terrestrial sharing of ideas than meaningless digital peacocking. I had in this case become, as my network would term it, an influencer. Equally, I have had users commenting on posts I have made to tell me that they have the same item and how much they love it. This experience of shared fabric, both owning something literally cut from the same cloth, and being able to discuss and acknowledge such a

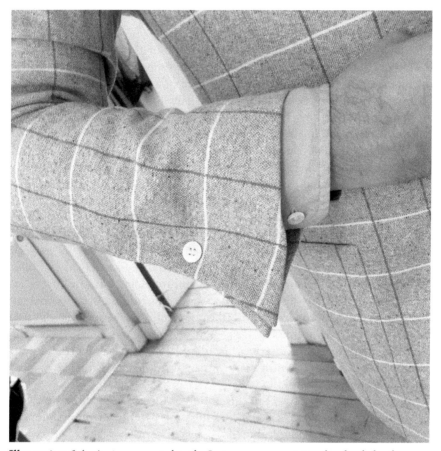

Illustration 6.4. An image posted to the Instagram account @anthrodandy by the author on 25 August 2017, featuring the flared cuff of a ready-to-wear Mark Powell checked suit jacket. © Joshua M. Bluteau.

connection in a shared digital space, is very powerful. Bourdieu would tell us that 'taste classifies, and it classifies the classifier' (Bourdieu 1996: 6). This is an idea used by Slater in his work on the sharing of sexually explicit images online: he suggests that 'displaying knowledge of the other's taste' constitutes an 'intimate rather than competitive' relationship (Slater 2000: 136). This supports the findings of my research, where a network of individuals with similar interests develops, and fosters relationships by sharing images that appeal to the shared tastes of the network. It is through processes such as these that Miller suggests that far from being a socially isolating phenomenon, digital social media actually allows us to make more friends (Miller 2011: 198).

The Voyeur

I have already alluded to the voyeuristic nature of the social media I conducted my digital fieldwork with. I have written about the experience of feeling like a voyeur by gazing through the screen of a smartphone into the lives of those that I follow, being able to glimpse the unintentional details which are included in carefully crafted photographs through which an observer can tell a little more about these individuals' lives. There is a comfort in this type of familiarity which develops over time, the daily cycle of seeing the faces and outfits of a small number of individuals who have never met terrestrially, but who form a substantial part of one's day-to-day life. Naturally, any anthropologist interested in the body as an object of study is engaged in a quasi-voyeuristic study, one which considers the body as an object of intellectual desire. Kulick comments on what he describes as the 'masochist anthropologist' who is concerned with studying the 'powerless', a fact he analyses through a Foucauldian lens of 'fantasy, desire and pleasure' (Kulick 2006: 933–34). This is a voyeuristic reading of anthropology, but one that is an important critique. My fieldwork differs from this reading of anthropology in that I was directly concerned with the powerful, affluent and well-dressed. In this case there is a different form of voyeurism at work, one where the researcher studies up, but this does not negate the existence of a relationship between researcher and subject that is situated within a landscape of 'fantasy, desire and pleasure' (idem).

There is a secondary aspect to this notion of the voyeur – those who gaze upon the individual taking a selfie. Whilst the practice of photographing oneself is ubiquitous amongst those I conducted research on, and fairly widespread more generally in urban western settings, catching sight of someone contorting themselves into the desired posture for a selfie, arm outstretched, face posed and body just so, can feel like an incongruous view to an onlooker. This is not the view the selfie taker wants the world to see, despite the fact that they exhibit such behaviour in the terrestrial world; rather, it is the carefully crafted image which appears later on social media which is the image the selfie taker wants people to see. As such, taking selfies has always been something of a conflicted endeavour for me, one necessary for my research, yet inherently embarrassing; very few people are able to look as cool as they do in the finished picture while actually taking the selfie.

There are numerous layers to the nature of voyeurism that occur through interaction with the digital field, from the two previous examples I have discussed to the live video broadcast of Instagram live where you can see through the 'eyes' (or at least the camera phone lens) of the individual you are following at that very moment. The existence of such voyeuristic gazes, with users of such digital platforms potentially being gazed upon at any moment, help to continually reassert the importance of performance and the native notion of authenticity discussed in greater depth in previous chapters. One is never immune from the gaze of those following you, and as you do not know when anyone is looking at your images, or not looking at them, one's online 'self' is held in a digital panoptism: a digital prison (see also Foucault 1995: 195–228 and Rabinow 1991: 206–13). This knowledge alters the way in which one's selves interact in the digital and terrestrial world, in an endless stream of creating content in the terrestrial world to craft a digital self who needs to constantly perform.

In the early stages of my fieldwork I had considered using an Instagram account with no personal content to simply observe the posts of the tailors I wanted to work with terrestrially. While this was not the methodological route I chose to take, I reflected that there are other users who do just this. Such a reflection, along with my own evolving methodology with regard to my digital presence, led me to formulate the concept of active and passive digital engagement. The active engager posts images on their account and interacts with other users through likes and comments; this is how I behaved during my digital fieldwork. The passive engager posts images in the same way as the active, but engages no further with the discourse of the platform. They will never (or scarcely) comment on others' posts or reply to comments. They may still like others' posts, but this is done as a form of passive reciprocity and does not truly identify images which they approve of. These categories are not definitive, but sit on a sliding scale of digital engagement from the very active to the very passive.

Throughout my digital fieldwork I found myself moving from a position of passive engagement to one which was increasingly more active. This had a great deal to do with my own confidence in my place and identity within the digital platform, but it was facilitated by the contacts and relationships which I formed through my long engagement with Instagram and the fellow users in my network as well. However, as I mentioned above there is a third category, those who simply view others' posts without creating any content of their own or interacting further.

This third category which I will term the passive invisible user is the ultimate example of the voyeur which one never encounters, for one cannot interact with them, yet sat under the surface of the digital landscape they are there, watching. In terms of the digital networks I have described, and specifically the one I conducted research with, I gained access to that space through a history of interaction and reciprocity, teamed with the demonstration of a cultivated shared taste. It is hard to know without doing comparative research, but I hypothesise that it would be possible to conduct similar research, discovering the network as I did, and gaining anthropological insight as a passive invisible user. However, this methodology would provide the researcher with a far less balanced understanding of the digital fieldsite. Without the experience of creating and producing content I am adamant that one cannot gain a fully complex and nuanced understanding of Instagram in terms of its function as a social space and the utilised processes of knowledge and discourse creation.

The existence of this narrative of the voyeur, present in the digital landscape, became highlighted throughout my digital research on a few occasions when images of mine were reposted. This is a process where an image that one user has posted is copied and posted by another user, typically with an acknowledgment to the original poster. When this happens, the user wishing to repost usually asks permission; however, on one occasion Mark Powell's Instagram account shared the following image (illustration 6.5) of me in one of his suits, without asking. However, as it attracted 541 likes, far more than I have ever achieved on one of my posts, I have no reason to complain. This occurrence, and a few others like it, made me question who really has control of the self as portrayed in the images one posts online. In this case is Mark Powell asserting ownership over the image and the identity of the self, contained within, as he designed the clothes being pictured? Is the image of @anthrodandy wearing a Mark Powell suit or a Mark Powell suit being worn by @anthrodandy? The subtle differentiation casts doubt over notions of the constructed self as well as narratives of individualism, performance and the native notion of authenticity. We can, therefore, study the constructed selves of individuals on Instagram and examine how a researcher can create a self to exist in an online network, but once others start to use these images, questions must be asked as to who really controls these digital selves.

Illustration 6.5. A screenshot from the author's smartphone showing an Instagram post by the account @markpowellbespoke on 19 October 2016. This image was originally posted by the author to his personal account on 26 September 2016 and features a Mark Powell three-piece ready-to-wear gingham suit and Joshua Kane hat. © Joshua M. Bluteau.

Conclusion

Unpacking My Bags

Real buttonholes. That's it! A man can take his thumb and forefinger and unbutton his sleeve at the wrist because this kind of suit has real buttonholes there ... Once you know about it, you start seeing it. All the time! There are just two classes of men in the world, men with suits whose buttons are just sewn onto the sleeve ... or – yes! – men who can unbutton the sleeve at the wrist because they have real buttonholes and the sleeve really buttons up. Fascinating!
>—Tom Wolfe, *The Kandy-Kolored Tangerine-Flake Streamline Baby*

This epiphany from journalist Tom Wolfe is one that I too experienced during my time in the field. Working buttonholes, although mostly confined to bespoke in Wolfe's day, are still a luxury touch, found mostly on high-end ready-to-wear, made-to-measure and bespoke tailoring. However, with changes in manufacturing techniques a working buttonhole can now be machined at a much lower cost, with the result that working cuff buttons are now found on a wider range of tailoring. For true aficionados, there are now three classes of men, to mirror Wolfe: those whose buttons do not undo, those whose buttons do undo, and those whose buttons undo and have hand-stitched buttonholes.

These nuances are easy to spot once you know how to look, and Instagram makes such looking far easier. Instead of catching the briefest of glimpses of a burnished horn button and handstitched silk threads as a bespoke suit brushes past you in the street, these details can now be seen in high definition, artfully posed and entombed in digital aspic for posterity.

Beyond buttonholes the buttons are important too with both the material and number of holes in the button causing flurries of interest from cognoscentes' watchful eyes. Horn, mother of pearl, and corozo are the most common on bespoke tailoring, although precious metals (sometimes stamped with a symbol or crest) and fabric-covered buttons are also worthy of interest. Four holes in the button is typical but many Savile Row houses prefer two-hole buttons, another way of spotting a rare item. There are other details too; from pad stitched lapels and gauntlet cuffs, to lapped side seams and frog mouth pockets, almost every aspect of a tailored garment has the potential for a subtle design detail that will mark out the maker and wearer to others in the know, but only if such options are selected. Many of these details sit within an historic narrative borne out of practical purpose or are remembered and reworked in homage to an earlier iconic wearer. Certain houses have their own fabrics and cuts, while others have small idiosyncratic details that mark them out – but such options are not compulsory and beyond the fit, quality of cloth and construction the precise maker can be hard to read. As O'Connor tells us, 'cloth and clothing are culturally constructed commodities with complex symbolic properties . . . linking past and present . . . carrying fundamental values' and crucially having the ability to 'consolidate identity' and 'mediate social relations' (O'Connor 2005: 41). In the world of tailoring the power of the suit means different things to different people. It can be as simple as a uniform, used to dress appropriately for a job interview, or can be employed to display one's sense of self, sartorial knowledge or wealth to those who know what details to look for. London gave me access to a wealth of tailors, suits and suit wearers, while Instagram allowed me to widen this gaze and see beyond the terrestrial into a network of sartorialists and artisans. I have immersed myself in the aesthetics of tailoring and emerged, much like Wolfe, with the ability to see in a different way.

So now, as this book moves to its twilight chapter, it is time to unpack my bags, both theoretically and literally. In earlier chapters you came with me as we visited shops, met tailors and purchased wares. The most significant of these, both financially and emotionally, was the houndstooth double-breasted coat from Joshua Kane. As I travelled home on the train with the coat nestled in a large black garment bag, tightly held in my gently trembling hands, I occasionally inched the zip open so I could peer inside the dark bag to catch a glimpse of the fabric inside. It was not until I was home at last, and alone, that I hung the garment up and gently slid the zip the full way down. A moment followed where I forgot to breathe and then reaching into the bag my hands found the shoulders of the coat and my thumbs slipped into the folds of cloth, unhooking the coat from its hanger and, in one swift motion, pulled it into the light.

Up close, my face mere centimetres from the cloth, I could see the large houndstooth pattern, of black and white interlocking shapes. A centimetre closer and the fabric was made up of individual woven threads that gave the garment a weight, texture and depth that I had not been expecting. I inhaled and the soft scent of clean wool flooded my nostrils – ancient and ecological – transporting me out of time for just a moment with a strangely comforting tang akin to, yet abstracted from, a walk through crisp seaweed on a cold beach. I laid the garment on my bed, and looked at it as it looked at me. We were strangers, but I knew from that moment that this would always be my coat. My hands passed over the cloth, feeling the texture under my fingertips. Next I made my way to the cuffs; five horn buttons engraved with the Joshua Kane crest were there, each one working and I unbuttoned them in turn. The cuff gaped and I returned the buttons to their holes, restoring the neatness I had undone. Under the lapel there was a flower loop and, turning the coat over, I found that the belted back and vent both had buttons and working buttonholes. My joy blossomed with each discovery. Finally, with reverence, I stood and for the first time owning such a garment I deliberately slid my arms into the sleeves, and let the cloth engulf me. The lining was cool against my skin, the wool at the collar a little scratchy and the weight pressing down on my shoulders comforting. The coat fell to just below my knee and as I looked up into the full-length mirror in front of me the hem danced with my move-ment as the garment showed me its personality. I was in awe. I stood there looking at myself while the minutes passed. Then quite automatically I began to take photographs of myself perhaps as a way of capturing the moment or perhaps to simply make sure it was real. As I slipped the coat off a little later and hung it on its hanger, within the protective confines of its bag, it felt like putting an old friend to bed.

People look at me differently when I wear that coat; perhaps it has a trans-formational effect on me, perhaps it is simply loud and ostentatious, or per-haps it may just be a good coat. In any case, unpacking it for the first time was the first step in a relationship that is ongoing, that involves @anthrodandy (for of course it is his coat too), that collectively holds shared memory, and, phenomenologically, results in a coat that fits a little better with each wearing.

Such experiences have formed a key tenet to my methodological approach and wearing as ethnography cannot be understated. Yet this book has pro-voked in me a number of broader reflexive thoughts that must be discussed before our journey together ends. So, to unpack the theoretical bags that have been carried through this book, five questions will be asked.

Is an Anthropology of Dress Important?

While there are accounts of dress in the wider anthropological corpus, it is a topic often overlooked or lacking thorough analysis (with the exception of Luvaas and Eicher 2019). The manner in which we dress every day, whether on our own at home, going out, or attending special occasions, is a central tenet of how people conceive who they are. This could be, as Miller and Woodward (2007: 341) tell us, that people prize comfort and the post-semiotic invisibility that blue jeans offer, or it could be, as Newell (2016) suggests, that the wildly coloured suits of members of *la sape* help to establish prestige for the wearer, and allow entry to a family-like support network of other *sapeurs*. Equally, for my informants, as a network of individuals who define themselves by how they dress, clothing is used to craft a sense of self, and this chimera of cloth and man can communicate with others who share such a form of self-representation. Dress, then, is a tool for self-expression, to craft identity and afford access and belonging in a shared network.

This is hugely important, not only to the individuals that I conducted research with, but to a wider western society. In a digitally saturated modernity, the continual bombardment of images, particularly from the fashion industry, alters and manipulates notions of desire, gender and appropriateness, ultimately changing how we think about ourselves, how we dress, and what this means. Even those who rely on their post-semiotic denim and are not conforming to notions of cool are, perhaps unintentionally, perpetuating and reinforcing the image that the fashion industry adopts as a warning to make sure its acolytes continue to buy. Miller (2003b) suggests the possibility that the internet could 'defetishise the commodity', through a suggestion that many items we once paid for (specifically music, pornography and games) are now becoming open-access and free. However, in the case of clothing I suggest that the precise opposite is taking place. As more and more retail is conducted online, we are buying beautifully photographed images of garments rather than the tactile (and textile) original. This leads to a hyperreal exchange, for a hyperreal object, whose details you may appreciate more due to the way the images of the object appeared online. Far from de-fetishising, such a process fetishises the garments for sale, elevating them to hyperreality and exponentially heightening their desirability. Whether this is problematic or not remains to be seen. For the houndstooth coat unpacked above the experience of finally acquiring it was certainly heightened by the obsessive hyperreal engagement that I had engrossed myself in for a number of months before the opportunity to purchase. This garment matched the hype, but undoubtedly alongside the functional garment of cloth and thread I had also purchased something larger – a performance made up of viewing the garment on a mannequin in Joshua Kane's window, of seeing it walk at a fashion show and, of course, seeing it in high-definition images repeatedly restyled and reposted on Kane's social media channels.

This process of purchasing performance set within a hyperreal landscape is crucial to rationalising the pursuit of an anthropological investigation into dress and adornment in a western-centric digitally saturated world. However, there are other elements too, which make such a study vital to our understanding of visual anthropology, urban anthropology and the individual. Clothing does not act as merely functional objects, but can become invested with emotion and memory by the wearer, ultimately forming a symbiotic relationship. This is also related to its sign-value, and the various details of said garment which, far from being post-semiotic, can be semiotically loud, to those who can read these semiotic signs. My fieldwork has led me to observe the importance of dress and adornment, in how people think of themselves, and in how others think of that person. This is in sharp contrast to the concept of depth ontology which I have referred to throughout this book – shallow ontology is at work here, with judgements being made regarding the nature of a person through the way in which they present the outer layer of themselves: their clothing. As such, dress and adornment form a fundamental facet of how every interaction occurs, through the crafting of identity, the making of social relationships, and narratives of power which exist throughout both terrestrial and digital worlds.

What Does It Mean to Be an Individual?

Everyone I worked with during the course of my fieldwork, both digitally and terrestrially, made claims regarding their own individuality. However, despite this regular access to a network of self-proclaimed individuals the true nature of what it means to be an individual remained murky. Throughout this book I have examined notions of authenticity through an analysis of Sartre's (1993: 167–86) concepts of 'play' and 'bad faith', with the suggestion that if one is deceiving others as to one's station in life (an inauthentic act), then that person is an inauthentic individual. However, my use of Sartre is reliant on his concept of 'function' (Sartre 1993: 167), one which no longer reflects the metropolis in which I conducted my fieldwork. Despite this I have continued with these concepts as a means for understanding the way in which my informants think, rather than the way in which the rest of society thinks about them. The idea that everyone has a function which one must dress for, or that one can be subversive by dressing differently from one's prescribed function, is at the centre of how many of the individuals I worked with conceive their dress as a means of self-expression, even if those around them do not view their conformity or rebellion in the same manner.

These suggestions are only valid when one considers the terrestrial branch of my research; when we journey into the digital landscape there are additional layers of complexity with regard to the notion of the individual which must be unpacked. My digital informants interact as part of a network, which is made up of those with a shared interest in sartorial matters, with the members typically identifying as some form of other. I have termed this 'other' as 'other Elizabethans' but my informants may identify themselves as dandies or gentlemen. In any case they are bound together by their collective desire to share their individual identities with others who are similarly individual. The irony here, especially in terms of Instagram and its controlled discourse, is that these self-proclaimed individuals end up producing content which is very similar to each other's, valuing the same types of image and imbuing objects with a hierarchical sign-value.

There are a number of elements here which require detailed analysis: firstly, how we decide whether one's digital self is authentically individual; secondly, if there is any such thing as an individual; and thirdly, what this tells us about masculine identity.

The nature of a digital self, as an authentic individual, changes as the digital self matures. To begin with, the authenticity of the individual is dependent on the terrestrial self creating a digital representation of themselves. At this point Sartre's notion of 'play' and 'bad faith' hold. However, as the digital self matures and acquires its own agency, notions of bad faith become blurred. As such, we must look for other means to identify these digital selves as authentic individuals.

Kondo (2009: 230) suggests that selves are created through narrative, and this is the best way of thinking about the crafting of digital selves on Instagram. Consequently, a discussion regarding the authenticity of these digital selves becomes reduced to a discussion of whether the content being posted is authentic to the larger story being narrated by the digital individual, a story told through the publication of discourse. While I have mentioned the notion of these digital selves acquiring agency, it is important not to conflate this with acquiring autonomy. This discourse still needs to be created and published by a terrestrial self; however, I do not contend that the digital self needs to be true to the terrestrial self. Indeed, they can be quite separate and differ wildly, but if the content is true to the narrative being told, the digital self may still be said to be authentic to its self, as an individual account. In a case such as this we need not question the authenticity of the digital self, but rather the authenticity of the terrestrial self if they are actively representing themselves in the digital world with a radically different self. It may be better to think not of actors in these relationships, but 'operators', as Baudrillard does (2003: 42). The operator is removed from the need to represent their terrestrial self accurately by the hyperreal nature of the digital world and as such they are at liberty to create a new kind of truth. The crucial part of this is not who the terrestrial operator is, but rather that the digital self can display and appreciate the taste of other members of its network. It is this notion of taste, as highlighted by Bourdieu (1996: 6), which binds disparate individuals together and helps them to identify each other as individual.

The real question here is, of course, what does the term individual really mean, and is there any such thing as an 'individual' in these representations? I suggest that the very fact that a digital network of self-identified individuals has developed using Instagram undermines a definition of the individual as conceived by my informants. These users are not different enough from each other; indeed, they do not wish to be for there is a joy in the shared knowledge, pastimes and aesthetic which all members of this network subscribe to. It seems that the very point of pursuing these notions of individuality and authenticity is to find a group to fit in to, rather than to remain a perennial outcast. The term individual then is not a term to define that which is different, but rather a moniker bestowed on those who fit into a club with a shared level of knowledge and appreciation. These 'clubs' also seem to hold a general consensus that the majority of the society in which they live does not share their particular appreciation for whatever their specific object of desire is.

This is not as simple as having the financial capability and the desire to display one's self enrobed in natively authentic artefacts, garments and accessories. There is an additional layer of performance. One must demonstrate that one has certain aesthetic sensibilities required to pair clothing and accessories together attractively to create a pleasing ensemble as well as a certain emotional investment in the connoisseurship of these objects.

The notion of the individual as a unique autonomous personality, devoid from association with those around them, does not hold true in this study. Indeed, my informants, though all self-styled individuals, belong very much to a club or network of similar selves. Therefore, it is best to think of the term individual, like authentic, as a native term, best described as a collective term for members of a network whose interests are beyond the remit of the majority in the societies where they live. Despite this they still hold a shared set of interests with a small network of others to whom such individuals gravitate, notably in the case of my fieldwork, into the digital world.

Finally, I must consider what this means for notions of masculinity, as this is a book concerned primarily with men. We live in a time of uncertain masculinities. This book has dealt with primarily one form of masculinity, typified by the members of my Instagram network, although there are other forms of masculinity represented less prominently on the fringes of this network, typically by those who sit in overlapping networks. There is no single form of masculinity, and my digital research has promoted the view that we are currently engaging in a post-particular climate of infinite varieties of masculinity, all residing in their own porous and amorphous digital and terrestrial networks. The phenomenon I have described, the bleeding of the digital and terrestrial landscapes into one another, facilitates networks to consider masculinity as any one (or more than one) form of multiple potential versions of masculinity. The digital landscape allows a wide variety of microcosms to develop, each with specific views that are supported by the members which gravitate towards them, allowing alternative masculinities to thrive. As in the world of the sartorial individual which I have been discussing, where prior to a digital landscape one might have had access to a small number of like-minded acquaintances, now there is a potential for far more access, and far more intimate access, to others all across the world with shared ideas. The problem with this is the overload of images and the potentially problematic notion of contradiction that this entails. Ideas of the individual and ideas of authenticity are now so deeply enmeshed that it becomes increasingly difficult to tell them apart. This may lead to a circularity, where notions of individuality are simply equated with being thought of as authentic, despite the crucial yet subtle difference between the two.

What Is the Nature of the Digital Self?

Throughout this book I have postulated the existence of multiple selves (following Kondo 2009: 230–31). This axiom is the starting point for a discussion regarding the nature of a digital self: an additional self to one's terrestrial self. A digital self is a creation, enabled by the publication of content, in one form or another, by the terrestrial self, in a digital landscape. Whilst at first this action may feel like a direct representation of one's terrestrial self (or it may begin as a conscious construction of an alternative self), soon the digital self has sufficient content to take on a presence of its own. At this point, the digital self may start to develop an agency of its own. Furthermore, with time, the terrestrial self may lose agency over the digital self, and the digital self may begin to exert agency over the terrestrial self.

A major factor in this shift is the amount of time involved in shaping and fuelling one's digital self, particularly in an image hungry medium such as Instagram. Crafting scenes, taking digital images, editing them, and uploading them with accompanying text at an apposite moment is hugely time consuming, especially if the network that your digital self belongs to encourages the publication of multiple images every day. After a substantial period of engagement, the impact of altering one's terrestrial life to provide images to grace one's digital self begins to tell. A large proportion of one's everyday thought is taken up conceiving of or producing images and one's finances are adversely affected by the desire to keep acquiring new costumes for your digital self, almost as one might clothe a doll. At this point, one could argue that the digital self has begun to exert its agency over the terrestrial.

The question which must be asked at this point is what is the end point of this decline in terrestrial agency? Are those heavily involved digital users to find themselves marooned in their homes, spending all their time ordering new outfits and taking pictures of themselves to give their digital selves more 'life'? This is of course a case of reductio ad absurdum, and for most this is not a reality; however, there is mention in my network of people staying up through the night working on their Instagram account, having to take breaks for their mental health or furiously working out in the gym to maintain their account followers. Naturally, there are those who appear to use their social media without any obvious negative issues, but the danger of a platform such as Instagram is that one is only privy to the content being posted by another user, which could be a clever masking of that user's actual terrestrial life. In any case, for many users Instagram can be a hugely positive and joyful media, allowing them to share their life with other like-minded individuals; but for others it can be a self-styled digital prison, a Foucauldian Panoptism, where they are imprisoned by the potential gaze of invisible digital others (Foucault 1995: 195–228).

There is another level to the notion of agency, however. What happens when the digital self loses agency? This can happen when images posted to one's Instagram account are reposted by another, as I described happening to one of my images by Mark Powell. I experienced this phenomenon as a strange mix of emotions; I was flattered and yet mildly irritated. I was pleased to be promoted, and that Mark had deemed my image worthy to be posted to his page, but no permission had been given, and it was as though the fact that I was wearing one of his suits gave him permission to repost it. Whatever the reason, I reflected that a sense of my own digital agency was being diluted. There is a crucial link back to Debord (2012) here, and his definition of the society of the spectacle, one where images are a means for mediating social relations. One could argue that Mark Powell is indeed using an image to mediate a complex series of social relationships. However, when the image in question is a part of a digitally constructed self, there is an added level of complexity, and one could even question whether it contributes to a form of digital alienation to use someone else's digital self as a currency to mediate your social relationship with others. This seems to be a little extreme, and therefore draws into question how fully Debord's ideas can be used in an increasingly digitised world. Despite this, the question still remains as to how this loss of agency effects the digital self. This could usefully form the basis of a future study.

Inevitably for images which are open access, pictures are copied and reposted frequently, often leading to terse comments from the original owner asking for acknowledgment. The rules around notions of intellectual copyright, data protection and the theft of these images seem to be very loose on Instagram; however, it appears that while the images are open access it is polite to ask before reposting and to always say where the image came from originally. For those who are reposted a lot, I can only hypothesise that there would be a depletion of one's sense of digital self-agency, with the images one creates to define and fuel one's digital self being manipulated and reinterpreted in a wide variety of alternative circumstances, perhaps even leading to a sense that one's digital self is being stolen (this is a question of image rights, which celebrities are good at securing). With agency being lost from one's digital self, there is a potential for these highly copied digital selves to stray into the realm of hyperreality, where another layer is imposed, bringing the hyperreal digital self yet another step further away from the terrestrial self it originally functioned to represent.

Can You Study a Western-Centric Fieldsite Without Digital Anthropology?

Single, geographically bounded fieldsites are central to a traditional ethnographic method. However, my fieldwork has led me to the conclusion that we must now rewrite this notion of the field to encompass both the terrestrial fieldsite and the digital world occurring in parallel to it. Such an approach will not be appropriate in all circumstances, but for the majority of western-centric research (and much besides) I suggest that digital communication and social media are too deeply entrenched in potential informants' day-to-day lives to be ignored. Therefore, I suggest that future research in fieldsites with a prominent digital landscape should employ an enmeshed form of digital and terrestrial research, where these two facets of the field are not dealt with independently, but rather as an amalgam.

How Does One Conduct Digital Anthropology?

Methodologically much has already been written regarding how to conduct digital anthropology, from those such as Garsten and Wulff (2003), Miller (2011, 2012), Boellstorff (2012), Horst and Miller (2012) and Hine (2000, 2015). However, in line with the work of Holy (1988), Bourdieu and Wacquant (1992), and Wacquant (2004), I want to suggest a radical new approach to the gathering of digital ethnographic data, a kind of 'observing participation' in the digital, to use Holy's words. Far from merely observing one's informants using their digital devices to access the digital world, as Miller (2011) does, I stress the need for the ethnographer to follow their informants into the digital world and employ a methodology of immersive cohabitation

(Bluteau 2019; Bluteau and Bluteau 2020). Horst and Miller's (2006) work on the cell phone which analyses the use of the object itself, rather than the digital world it allows access to, is a prime example of this earlier form of digital anthropology. However, it is understandable in their case, as they are dealing primarily with a pre-smartphone era. It is vital that such a method be reassessed for new anthropological research dealing with modern hand-held smartphones which allow instant access to an infinite digital landscape. Following informants into the digital world as a form of ethnography has been completed by a number of researchers, including Slater (2000); however, it has almost always been completed as a strict form of participant observation, with the anthropologist merely watching from the digital shadows. There have been ethnographers who have engaged more thoroughly with the digital fieldsite, but this is the exception rather than the rule. These include Boellstorff's (2012) work in second life, but this, like much other pioneering digital anthropology, suffers from the phenomenon of treating the digital domain as a new area for experimental ethnography, rather than acknowledging it as an embedded part of the lives of many people.

Methodologically my digital research has been distinct from these other digital anthropological endeavours, and more in line with the work of Luvaas (2016). Contrasting with Burrell (2009: 193), I suggest that a digital fieldsite is habitable, and that the digital field must be inhabited in order to conduct the best possible research. Whereas in a terrestrial fieldsite one can gain huge insight from participant observation, the possibilities for observation are far more limited in the digital world, with typically only a single form of discourse being employed at any one time, and in a far more detached manner than one would find occurring through terrestrial interactions. Therefore, an active engagement in the processes of the platform one is working with is a vital methodological tool for understanding not only how the processes are conducted and enacted by one's informants, but also to gain acceptance and visibility in the digital space. In the case of Instagram this means creating content, posting, commenting, following and liking. Without this active approach it is impossible to fully integrate into a digital network or understand the impact of heavy use on the terrestrial selves of other members of a network.

The Last Post(?)

In the previous chapter I discussed the decision making process surrounding when to make my last Instagram post, where two years to the day from my first Instagram post I made a conscious decision to draw a line in the digital sand and take the previous two years' digital work as a succinct period of fieldwork. I am reminded of the last line of *To the Lighthouse* by Virginia Woolf (1927: 310) – 'yes, she thought, laying down her brush in extreme fatigue, I have had my vision'.

Well, as I laid down my phone in extreme fatigue I believed that there would be some form of closure. Yes, I had made the conscious decision to leave my account live. This was a fieldsite, and much like the doyens of anthropology I had studied under as an undergraduate who returned repeatedly to the same indigenous communities over many decades, it seemed prudent to keep the pathway to my interlocuters open. To this end I continued to post images to Instagram under the name @anthrodandy past the point where analysis for this book ends. Furthermore, the images that constitute the digital arm of this research have not been archived and are still live within Instagram for anyone to view. The decision to continue posting, and to keep past images accessible, was a careful choice and one I feel is still necessary to afford future access to this research space. However, the result of this is that @anthrodandy, my digital self, is very much alive and able to continue interacting and exerting agency even in my terrestrial absence.

My posting has grown sporadic since the official end of my research in October 2017, yet there are now in excess of 1100 posts by @anthrodandy and they will continue to accumulate over time. The longest period of absence thus far has been from February 2020, where for almost twelve months, @anthrodandy remained silent. A global pandemic seemed, to me, a strange time to publicise what one was wearing (though many I followed thought differently), so @anthrodandy made the decision to isolate at home and not post. Despite this, images were taken by your terrestrial author in that time that were later posted to Instagram once @anthrodandy had re-emerged.

Despite this distance, my assertion holds that the digital self can acquire its own agency and I also suggest that a curious relationship can develop, with one's digital self ultimately coming to represent that person's terrestrial self with greater clarity than the actions of their own terrestrial self. This is due to the digital self becoming more real, indeed hyperreal, than the terrestrial. This occurs when people have greater access to one's digital self than their terrestrial one, access which is not only temporal but includes both images and intimacy, though the ever-present nature of a digital self also contributes to this. This end result is that one can feel better informed, more intimate with, and closer in time (both in terms of what the self is doing right now and how much time it takes to access a self) to a digital self than a terrestrial self. Yet when posts stop, the familiarity becomes disjointed from the temporal reality in which the terrestrial self lives. Multiple selves can be created to inhabit a digital world but fundamentally, even if these selves acquire agency in their own right, they still require a terrestrial self to fuel them. In this sense the notion of autonomous digital selves is currently an illusion, albeit one which appears to be tantalisingly genuine.

Digital researchers need to be mindful of this: the digital landscape is a potentially treacherous place; addiction, obsessive consumption and hyper-reality lurk in the corners, ready to pounce, while the potential to gain and lose agency at a moment's notice is an ever-present malady for the digital self. Furthermore, the illusionary nature of these crafted selves, so much a part of our lives yet ultimately intangible, makes for a landscape which will wrong-foot the unwary and consume the vulnerable. Time feels different when you are engrossed in a screen, and this phenomenological finding is yet another vice encountered in this field. Such findings are not meant to dissuade the prospective researcher: the digital landscape is not going away and only through a cartographical and intellectual rendering of this brave new world can policy makers, individuals and academics alike pass judgement with any vestige of coherent understanding. This book paves the way, and this conclusion aims to pose new questions and arm researchers with new knowledge. Yet for all of this, there is still much to do, and this landscape will not stand still.

Finally, before I end, let me return to a question that inspired this book: why do some men choose to spend large sums of money to have clothes made for them? Well, as you may have gathered, there is no single answer. It would be easy to be trite here, and offer a single catch-all response – the Everest solution if you will: for some they buy these clothes because they can. This is glib and not the whole true, as the act of purchasing expensive and bespoke clothing is an act of titillation for some, an auto-erotic encounter with a copious display of wealth. For others, the experience of visiting the tailor is a luxurious and comforting shopping experience. The act of being crafted into a clothed body – which though it may appear dull to onlookers has the tailor's seal of approval – is validating and provides the confidence to access certain spaces or perform certain characters. Still, for others there is a deep appreciation for the artistry of production and the expression of their place within a historic narrative of clothed men. There are some for whom getting dressed is a performance, one that can be played out online or that totally defines their identity, others who purchase garments because they believe them to be beautiful, and those who might have idiosyncratically long arms that only a tailor's expertise can account for. This is not an exhaustive list, but nor is it really the point. Why men dress and how they dress is hugely important, vital to identity and crucial to an understanding of the intersection of masculinity, fashion and studies of culture. So, tell me . . . why do you get dressed . . . and why do you get dressed up?

REFERENCES

Adams, Tony E., Stacy Holman Jones and Carolyn Ellis. 2015. *Autoethnography: Understanding Qualitative Research*. New York: Oxford University Press.

Anu. 2015. 'Profile: Dan Newman, The Big Sartorialist', *The Vestiary*, 15 July. Retrieved August 2016 from https://www.thevestiary.com/single-post/2015/07/15/Profile-Dan-Newman-The.

Archambault, Julie Soleil. 2012. '"Travelling While Sitting Down": Mobile Phones, Mobility and the Communication Landscape in Inhambane, Mozambique', *Africa: Journal of the International African Institute* 82(3): 393–412.

Barry, Ben. 2017. 'What Happens When Men Don't Conform to Masculine Clothing Norms at Work?', *Harvard Business Review Online*, 31 August. Retrieved September 2017 from https://hbr.org/2017/08/what-happens-when-men-dont-conform-to-masculine-clothing-norms-at-work.

Battaglia, Debbora. 1995. 'Problematizing the Self: A Thematic Introduction', in Debbora Battaglia (ed.), *Rhetorics of Self-Making*. Berkeley: University of California Press, pp. 1–15.

Baudrillard, Jean. 1981. *For a Critique of the Political Economy of the Sign*. New York: Telos Press.

———. 1993. *Symbolic Exchange and Death*, trans. I.H. Grant. London: Sage.

———. 1998. *The Consumer Society: Myths and Structures*. London: Sage.

———. 2003. *Passwords*, trans. C. Turner. London: Verso.

Belarde-Lewis, Miranda. 2013. 'No Photography Allowed: Problematic Photographs of Sacred Objects', *Museum Anthropology* 36(2): 104.

Berger, Peter. 1970. 'Identity as a Problem in the Sociology of Knowledge', in James Curtis and John Petras (eds), *The Sociology of Knowledge*. London: Duckworth, pp. 373–84.

Beynon, John. 2002. *Masculinities and Culture*. Buckingham: Open University Press.

Bluteau, Joshua Max. 2018. 'Authenticity, Performance and the Construction of Self: A Journey through the Terrestrial and Digital Landscapes of Men's Tailored Dress'. PhD dissertation. Scotland: University of St Andrews.

———. 2019. 'Legitimising Digital Anthropology through Immersive Cohabitation: Becoming an Observing Participant in a Blended Digital Landscape', *Ethnography*. Online First.

———. 2021. 'The Devil Is in the Detail: Why Men Wear Suits', in Shaun Cole and Miles Lambert (eds), *Dandy Style: 250 Years of British Men's Fashion*. London: Yale University Press, pp. 63–73.

Bluteau, Joshua Max and Patricia Ann Bluteau. 2020. 'Call of Interprofessional Duty: An Ethnographically Informed Discussion on Preparing Students to be Digitally Resilient', *Journal of Interprofessional Care* 34(5): 622–67.

Boellstorff, Tom. 2012. 'Rethinking Digital Anthropology', in Heather Horst and Daniel Miller (eds), *Digital Anthropology*. London: Bloomsbury, pp. 39–60.

Boissevain, Jeremy. 1978. *Friends of Friends: Networks, Manipulations and Coalitions*. Oxford: Blackwell.

Bourdieu, Pierre. 1996. *Distinction: A Social Critique of the Judgement of Taste*, trans. R. Nice. Cambridge, MA: Harvard University Press.

Bourdieu, Pierre and Loïc Wacquant. 1992. *Invitation to a Reflexive Sociology*. Chicago: University of Chicago Press.

Breward, Christopher. 1999. *The Hidden Consumer: Masculinities, Fashion and City Life 1860–1914*. Manchester: Manchester University Press.

———. 2016. *The Suit: Form, Function & Style*. London: Reaktion Books.

Bruna, Denis (ed.). 2015. *Fashioning the Body: An Intimate History of the Silhouette*. London: Yale University Press.

Burrell, Jenna. 2009. 'The Field Site as a Network: A Strategy for Locating Ethnographic Research', *Field Methods* 21(2): 181–99.

Butler, Judith. 1990. *Gender Trouble: Feminism and the Subversion of Identity*. London: Routledge.

———. 1991. 'Imitation and Gender Insubordination', in Diana Fuss (ed.), *Inside/out: Lesbian Theories, Gay Theories*. New York: Routledge, pp. 13–31.

Byström, Arvida and Molly Soda (eds). 2016. *Pics or It Didn't Happen: Images Banned from Instagram*. Munich: Prestel.

Callahan, Rose and Nathaniel Adams. 2016. *We Are Dandy: The Elegant Gentleman Around the World*. Berlin: Gestalten.

Callaway, Helen. 1992. 'Dressing for Dinner in the Bush: Rituals of Self-Definition and British Imperial Authority', in Ruth Barnes and Joanne B. Eicher (eds), *Dress and Gender: Making and Meaning*. Oxford: Berg, pp. 232–47.

Chang, Heewon. 2008. *Autoethnography as Method*. Walnut Creek, CA: Left Coast Press.

———. 2013. 'Individual and Collaborative Autoethnography as Method: A Social Scientist's Perspective', in Stacey Holman Jones, Tony E. Adams and Carolyn Ellis (eds), *Handbook of Autoethnography*. Walnut Creek, CA: Left Coast Press, pp. 107–22.

Clifford, James and George E. Marcus (eds). 1986. *Writing Culture: The Poetics and Politics of Ethnography*. Berkeley: University of California Press.

Coffey, Amanda. 1993. 'Double Entry: The Profession and Organizational Socialization of Graduate Accountants'. PhD dissertation. Cardiff: University of Wales.

———. 1999. *The Ethnographic Self*. London: Sage.

Coffey, Amanda and Paul Atkinson. 1996. *Making Sense of Qualitative Data: Complementary Research Strategies*. Thousand Oaks, CA: Sage.

Cohen, Anthony P. 1992. 'Post-Fieldwork Fieldwork', *Journal of Anthropological Research* 48: 339–54.

Cole, Shaun. 2000. *'Don We Now Our Gay Apparel': Gay Men's Dress in the Twentieth Century*. Oxford: Berg.

———. 2013. 'Queerly Visible: Gay Men, Dress, And Style 1960–2012', in Valerie Steele (ed.), *A Queer History of Fashion: From the Closet to the Catwalk*. Yale: University Press, pp. 135–65.

Cole, Shaun, and Miles Lambert (eds). 2021. *Dandy Style: 250 Years of British Men's Fashion*. London: Yale University Press.

Connell, Raewyn W. 2005. *Masculinities*, 2nd edn. Cambridge: Polity.

Connell, Raewyn W. and James W. Messerschmidt. 2005. 'Hegemonic Masculinity: Rethinking the Concept', *Gender & Society* 19(6): 829–59.

Costa, Elisabetta. 2016. *Social Media in Southeast Turkey: Love, Kinship and Politics*. London: UCL Press.

Crăciun, Magdalena. 2009. 'Trading in Fake Brands, Self-creating as an Individual', in Daniel Miller (ed.), *Anthropology and the Individual: A Material Culture Perspective*. Oxford: Berg, pp. 25–36.

———. 2012. 'Rethinking Fakes, Authenticating Selves', *The Journal of the Royal Anthropological Institute* 18(4): 846–63.

Crompton, Simon. 2015. *The Finest Menswear in the World: The Craftsmanship of Luxury*. London: Thames & Hudson.

———. 2019. 'What Is Authenticity', *Permanent Style Blog*, 24 July. Retrieved August 2019 from https://www.permanentstyle.com/2019/07/what-is-authenticity.html.

Csaba, Fabian F. and Güliz Ger. 2013. 'Patina Meets Fashion: On the Evaluation and Devaluation of Oriental Carpets', in Brian Moeran and Bo T. Christensen (eds), *Exploring Creativity: Evaluative Practices in Innovation, Design and the Arts*. Cambridge: Cambridge University Press, pp. 260–77.

Cummings, Catherine. 2017. 'Queen Victoria's Samoan Bonnet', in Paul Basu (ed.), *The Inbetweenness of Things: Materializing Mediation and Movement between Worlds*. London: Bloomsbury, pp. 191–208.

Debord, Guy. 2012. *The Society of the Spectacle*, trans. D. Nicholson-Smith. New York: Zone Books.

Dilley, Roy. 2004. 'The Visibility and Invisibility of Production Among Senegalese Craftsmen', *Journal of the Royal Anthropological Institute* (N.S.) 10: 797–813.

———. 2013. 'Questions of Authenticity and Legitimacy in the Work of Henri Gaden (1867–1939)', in Thomas Fillitz and A. Jamie Saris (eds), *Debating Authenticity: Concepts of Modernity in Anthropological Perspective*. New York: Berghahn, pp. 175–95.

———. 2014. *Nearly Native, Barely Civilized: Henri Gaden's Journey through Colonial French West Africa (1894–1939)*. Leiden: Brill.

———. 2019. 'Recovering the Absent Presence and the Unseen: Henri Gaden's Photographic Encounters in West Africa, 1894–1907', *Visual Anthropology Review* 35(1): 10–22.

Dumas, Alexander. 1978. *The Three Musketeers*. Norwalk, CT: Easton Press.

Dumont, Louis. 1986. *Essays on Individualism*. Chicago: University of Chicago Press.

Edwards, Elizabeth. 2001. *Raw Histories: Photographs, Anthropology and Museums*. Oxford: Berg.

Edwards, Tim. 1997. *Men in the Mirror: Men's Fashion, Masculinity and Consumer Society*. London: Cassell.

Entwistle, Joanne. 2000. *The Fashioned Body: Fashion, Dress and Modern Social Theory*. Cambridge: Polity.

Entwistle, Joanne and Elizabeth Wissinger. 2006. 'Keeping up Appearances: Aesthetic Labour and Identity in the Fashion Modelling Industries of London and New York', *Sociological Review* 54(4): 774–94.

Entwistle, Joanne and Elizabeth Wissinger. 2012. *Fashioning Models: Image, Text and Industry*. London: Berg.

Evans, Caroline. 2013. *The Mechanical Smile: Modernism and the First Fashion Shows in France and America 1900–1929*. London: Yale University Press.

Evans, Vyvyan. 2017. *The Emoji Code: How Smiley Faces, Love Hearts and Thumbs Up are Changing the Way We Communicate*. London: Michael O'Mara Books Limited.

Fabian, Johannes. 2002. *Time and the Other: How Anthropology Makes Its Object*. New York: Columbia University Press.

Ferguson, James G. 2002. 'Of Mimicry and Membership: African and the "New World Society"', *Cultural Anthropology* 17(4): 551–69.

'Fifty Shades of Grey Christian Grey's Tie'. 2017. *Lovehoney Website*. Retrieved February 2021 from https://www.lovehoney.co.uk/bondage/handcuffs-restraints/wrist-ankle-restraints/p/fifty-shades-of-grey-christian-greys-tie/a28047g44880.html#productReview.

Fillitz, Thomas and A. Jamie Saris (eds). 2013. *Debating Authenticity: Concepts of Modernity in Anthropological Perspective*. New York: Berghahn.

Foucault, Michel. 1980. *Power/Knowledge: Selected Interviews and Other Writings 1972–1977 By Michel Foucault*, ed. C. Gordon. Hemel Hempstead: Harvester Press.

———. 1990. *The History of Sexuality: Volume 1 An Introduction*, trans. R. Hurley. London: Penguin.

———. 1995. *Discipline and Punish: The Birth of the Prison*, trans. A. Sheridan. New York: Vintage Books.

Foulkes, Nick. 2016. 'The Bespoke Experience. *Talk given by Nick Foulkes at Huntsman for The Launch of His Bernard Buffet Biography*', Huntsman Savile Row Website, January. Retrieved 15 March 2018 from https://www.huntsmansavilerow.com/the-bespoke-experience-by-nick-foulkes/#/quicklinks.

Frankland, Stan. 2009. 'The Bulimic Consumption of Pygmies: Regurgitating an Image of Otherness', in Mike Robinson and David Picard (eds), *The Framed World: Tourism, Tourists and Photography*. Farnham, Surrey: Ashgate, pp. 95–116.

Gable, Eric. 2002. 'An Anthropologist's (New?) Dress Code: Some Brief Comments on a Comparative Cosmopolitanism', *Cultural Anthropology* 17(4): 572–79.

Garsten, Christina and David Lerdell. 2003. 'Mainstream Rebels: Informalization and Regulation in a Virtual World', in Christina Garsten and Helena Wulff (eds), *New Technologies at Work: People, Screens and Social Virtuality*. Oxford: Berg, pp. 165–86.

Garsten, Christina and Helena Wulff. 2003. *New Technologies at Work: People, Screens and Social Virtuality*. Oxford: Berg.

Goffman, Erving. 1971. *Relations in Public*. London: Penguin.

———. 1980. *The Presentation of Self in Everyday Life*. London: Pelican.

Gondola, Ch Didier. 1999. 'Dream and Drama: The Search for Elegance Among Congolese Youth', *African Studies Review* 42(1): 23–48.

Griffiths, Mark D. 2012. 'Facebook Addiction: Concerns, Criticisms and Recommendations', *Psychological Reports* 110(2): 518–20.

Hahn, Hans Peter and Ludovic Kibora. 2008. 'The Domestication of the Mobile Phone: Oral Society and New ICT in Burkina Faso', *The Journal of Modern African Studies* 46(1): 87–109.

Hannerz, Ulf. 2010. *Anthropology's World: Life in a Twenty-first Century Discipline*. London: Pluto Press.

Hansen, Karen Tranberg. 2004. 'The World in Dress: Anthropological Perspectives on Clothing, Fashion and Culture', *Annual Review of Anthropology* 33: 369–92.

Haynes, Nell. 2016. *Social Media in Northern Chile: Posting the Extraordinarily Ordinary*. London: UCL Press.

Hine, Christine. 2000. *Virtual Ethnography*. London: Sage.

———. 2015. *Ethnography for the Internet: Embedded, Embodied and Everyday*. London: Bloomsbury.

Hollander, Ann. 1994. *Sex and Suits: The Evolution of Modern Dress*. New York: Kodansha International.

Holman Jones, Stacy, Tony E. Adams and Carolyn Ellis (eds). 2013. *Handbook of Autoethnography*. Walnut Creek, CA: Left Coast Press.

Holy, Ladislav. 1988. 'Theory, Methodology and the Research Process', in Roy Frank Ellen (ed.), *Ethnographic Research: A Guide to General Conduct. ASA Research Methods in Social Anthropology*. London: Academic Press Limited, pp. 13–34.

Horst, Heather A. 2009. 'Aesthetics of the Self: Digital Mediations', in Daniel Miller (ed.), *Anthropology and the Individual: A Material Culture Perspective*. Oxford: Berg, pp. 99–113.

Horst, Heather A. and Daniel Miller. 2006. *The Cell Phone: An Anthropology of Communication*. Oxford: Berg.

Horst, Heather A. and Daniel Miller. 2012. *Digital Anthropology*. London: Bloomsbury.

Hunt, Elle. 2016. 'New Algorithm-Driven Instagram Feed Rolled Out to the Dismay of Users', *Guardian Online*, 7 June. Retrieved July 2016 from https://www.theguardian.com/technology/2016/jun/07/new-algorithm-driven-instagram-feed-rolled-out-to-the-dismay-of-users.

Irving, Andrew. 2010. 'Everyday Adventures in London', in Solrun Williksen and Nigel Rapport (eds), *Reveries of Home: Nostalgia, Authenticity and the Performance of Place*. Newcastle upon Tyne: Cambridge Scholars Publishing, pp. 165–86.

Isherwood, Christopher. 1954. *The World in the Evening*. London: Methuen.

Jeffrey, Robin and Assa Doron. 2012. 'The Mobile Phone in India and Nepal: Political Economy Politics and Society', *Pacific Affairs* 85(3): 469–81.

Johnson, Michelle C. 2013. 'Culture's Calling: Mobile Phones, Gender, and the Making of an African Migrant Village in Lisbon', *Anthropological Quarterly* 86(1): 163–90.

Jouhki, Jukka. 2017. 'The Hyperreal Gambler: On the Visual Construction of Men in Online Poker Ads', *Journal of Extreme Anthropology* 1(3): 83–101.

Kapferer, Bruce. 1969. 'Norms and the Manipulation of Relationships in a Work Context', in J. Clyde Mitchell (ed.), *Social Networks in Urban Situations: Analyses of Personal Relationships in Central African Towns*. Manchester: Manchester University Press, pp. 181–244.

Kawamura, Yuniya. 2016. *Sneakers: Fashion, Gender, and Subculture*. London: Bloomsbury Academic.

Kenaw, Setargew. 2012. 'Cultural Translation of Mobile Telephones: Mediation of Strained Communication Among Ethiopian Married Couples', *The Journal of Modern African Studies* 50(1): 131–55.

Kimmel, Michael. 1996. *Manhood in America: A Cultural History*. New York: Free Press.

Kondo, Dorinne K. 2009. *Crafting Selves: Power, Gender, and Discourses of Identity in a Japanese Workplace*. Chicago: University of Chicago Press.

Krause-Jensen, Jakob. 2013. 'Looking into the Box: Design and Innovation at Bang & Olufsen', in Brian Moeran and Bo T. Christensen (eds), *Exploring Creativity: Evaluative Practices in Innovation, Design and the Arts*. Cambridge: Cambridge University Press, pp. 146–71.

Kulick, Don. 1998. *Travesti: Sex, Gender and Culture among Brazilian Transgendered Prostitutes*. Chicago: University of Chicago Press.

———. 2006. 'Theory in Furs: Masochist Anthropology', *Current Anthropology* 47(6): 933–52.

Lacan, Jacques. 2018. *The Four Fundamental Concepts of Psycho-Analysis*. Abingdon: Routledge.

Laing, Ronald David. 1971. *Self and Others*. London: Pelican.

Lamotte, Sophie. 2015. 'Corsets, Stomach Belts, and Padded Calves: The Masculine Silhouette Reconfigured', in Denis Bruna (ed.), *Fashioning the Body: An Intimate History of the Silhouette*. London: Yale University Press, pp. 199–211.

Larsson, Naomi. 2015. 'Inspiration or Plagiarism? Mexicans Seek Reparations for French Designer's Look-Alike Blouse', *Guardian Online*, 17 June. Retrieved 22 August 2017 from https://www.theguardian.com/global-development-professionals-network/2015/jun/17/mexican-mixe-blouse-isabel-marant.

Latour, Bruno. 2005. *Reassembling the Social: An Introduction to Actor-Network-Theory*. Oxford: Oxford University Press.

Laver, Jean. 1969. *Modesty in Dress: An Inquiry into the Fundamentals of Fashion*. London: Heinemann.

Law, John. 2009. 'Actor Network Theory and Material Semiotics', in Bryan S. Turner (ed.), *The New Blackwell Companion to Social Theory*. Chichester: Wiley-Blackwell, pp. 141–58.

Lee, Jo and Tim Ingold. 2006. 'Fieldwork on Foot: Perceiving, Routing, Socializing', in Simon Coleman and Peter Collins (eds), *Locating the Field: Space, Place and Context in Anthropology*. Oxford: Berg, pp. 67–85.

Lofland, John and Lyn H. Lofland. 1995. *Analyzing Social Settings: A Guide to Qualitative Observation and Analysis*, 3rd edn. Belmont, CA: Wadsworth.

Lua, Alfred. 2018. 'How the Instagram Algorithm Works in 2018: Everything you Need to Know', *Buffer Social*, 14 June. Retrieved 11 November 2018 from https://blog.bufferapp .com/instagram-feed-algorithm.

Luvaas, Brent. 2016. *Street Style: An Ethnography of Fashion Blogging*. London: Bloomsbury Academic.

Luvaas, Brent and Joanne B. Eicher (eds). 2019. *The Anthropology of Dress and Fashion: A Reader*. London: Bloomsbury Visual Arts.

Macdonald, Sharon. 2002. 'On "Old Things": The Fetishization of Past Everyday Life', in Nigel Rapport (ed.), *British Subjects: An Anthropology of Britain*. Oxford: Berg, pp. 89–106.

Madianou, Mirca and Daniel Miller. 2012a. *New Media and Migration*. London: Routledge.

Madianou, Mirca and Daniel Miller. 2012b. 'Polymedia: Towards a New Theory of Digital Media and Interpersonal Communication', *International Journal of Cultural Studies* 16(2): 169–87.

Marcus, George E. 1995. 'On Eccentricity', in Debbora Battaglia (ed.), *Rhetorics of Self-Making*. Berkeley: University of California Press, pp. 43–58.

Marske, Charles E. 1987. 'Durkheim's "Cult of the Individual" and the Moral Reconstitution of Society', *Sociological Theory* 5(1): 1–14.

Mauss, Marcel. 1954. *The Gift: Forms and Functions of Exchange in Archaic Societies*, trans. I. Cunnison. Glencoe, IL: Free Press.

McCracken, Grant. 1998. *Culture and Consumption: New Approaches to the Symbolic Character of Consumer Goods and Activities*. Bloomington and Indianapolis: Indiana University Press.

McIntosh, Janet. 2010. 'Mobile Phones and Mipoho's Prophecy: The Powers and Dangers of Flying Language', *American Ethnologist* 37(2): 337–53.

Mead, Geoff. 2013. 'A Pair of Hockneys', *Geoff Mead Blog*, 13 January. Retrieved 28 April 2018 from https://geoffmead.blog/tag/paul-harnden/.

Miller, Daniel. 1995a. 'Consumption as the Vanguard of History: A Polemic by Way of an Introduction', in Daniel Miller (ed.), *Acknowledging Consumption: A Review of New Studies*. London: Routledge, pp. 1–57.

———. 1995b. 'Consumption Studies as the Transformation of Anthropology', in Daniel Miller (ed.), *Acknowledging Consumption: A Review of New Studies*. London: Routledge, pp. 264–95.

———. 1998. *A Theory of Shopping*. Cambridge: Polity.

———. 2003a. 'Living with New (Ideals of) Technology', in Christina Garsten and Helena Wulff (eds), *New Technologies at Work: People, Screens and Social Virtuality*. Oxford: Berg, pp. 7–23.

———. 2003b. 'Could the Internet De-Fetishise the Commodity?', *Environment and Planning D: Society and Space* 21(3): 359–72.

———. 2010. *Stuff*. Cambridge: Polity.

———. 2011. *Tales from Facebook*. Cambridge: Polity.

———. 2012. 'Social Networking Sites', in Heather A. Horst and Daniel Miller (eds), *Digital Anthropology*. London Bloomsbury, pp. 146–61.

Miller, D. et al. 1998. *Shopping, Place and Identity*. London: Routledge.

Miller, Daniel and Jolynna Sinanan. 2014. *Webcam*. Cambridge: Polity.

Miller, Daniel and Jolynna Sinanan. 2017. *Visualising Facebook*. London: UCL Press.

Miller, Daniel and Don Slater. 2000. *The Internet: An Ethnographic Approach*. Oxford: Berg.

Miller, Daniel and Sophie Woodward. 2007. 'Manifesto for a Study of Denim', *Social Anthropology/Anthropologie Sociale* 15(3): 335–51.

Miller, Daniel and Sophie Woodward. 2010. *Global Denim*. London: Bloomsbury.

Miller, Daniel and Sophie Woodward. 2012. *Blue Jeans: The Art of the Ordinary*. Berkeley: University of California Press.

Moore, Madison. 2018. *Fabulous: The Rise of the Beautiful Eccentric*. London: Yale University Press.

Morris, Brian. 1991. *Western Conceptions of the Individual*. New York: Berg.

Newell, Sasha. 2016. 'Circuitously Parisian: Sapeur Parakinship and the Affective Circuitry of Congolese Style', in Jennifer Cole and Christian Groes (eds), *Affective Circuits: African Migrations to Europe and the Pursuit of Social Regeneration*. Chicago: University of Chicago Press, pp. 269–302.

Nixon, Sean. 1996. *Hard Looks: Masculinities, Spectatorship and Contemporary Consumption*. London: UCL Press.

O'Connor, Kaori. 2005. 'The Other Half: The Material Culture of New Fibres', in Susanne Küchler and Daniel Miller (eds), *Clothing as Material Culture*. Oxford: Berg, pp. 41–61.

O'Flaherty, Mark C. 2012. 'New Aged', *Financial Time Online*, 5 May 2002. Retrieved 3 August 2017 from https://www.ft.com/content/e5108bea-825b-11e1-9242-00144feab49a.

Okely, Judith. 1992. 'Anthropology and Autobiography: Participatory Experience and Embodies Knowledge', in Judith Okely and Helen Callaway (eds), *Anthropology and Autobiography*. London: Routledge, pp. 1–28.

Paoletti, Jo B. 2012. *Pink and Blue: Telling the Boys from the Girls in America*. Bloomington: Indiana University Press.

———. 2016. 'Clothes Make the Boy', *Vestoj* 7: 13–25.

Pipyrou, Stavroula. 2014. 'Cutting Bella Figura: Irony, Crisis and Secondhand Clothes in South Italy', *American Ethnologist* 41(3): 532–46.

Popovac, Masa and Chris Fullwood. 2018. 'The Psychology of Online Lurking', in Alison Attrill-Smith et al. (eds), *The Oxford Handbook of Cyberpsychology*. Retrieved 25 February 2021 from https://www.oxfordhandbooks.com/view/10.1093/oxfordhb/9780198812746.001.0001/oxfordhb-9780198812746-e-18?rskey=82vcNk&result=1.

Rabinow, Paul (ed.). 1991. *The Foucault Reader: An Introduction to Foucault's Thought*. London: Penguin Books.

Rapport, Nigel. 1998. 'Hard Sell: Commercial Performance and the Narration of the Self', in Felicia Hughes-Freeland (ed.), *Ritual, Performance, Media*. London: Routledge, pp. 177–93.

Roberts, Graham H. 2017. 'Angels with Dirty Faces: Gosha Rubchinskiy and the Politics of Style', *Journal of Extreme Anthropology* 1(3): 18–40.

Rocamora, Agnès. 2015. 'Personal Fashion Blogs: Screens and Mirrors in Digital Self-portraits', *Fashion Theory* 15(4): 407–24.

———. 2016. 'Mediatization and Digital Media in the Field of Fashion', *Fashion Theory* 21(5): 502–22.

Rose, Kenneth. 1969. *Superior Person: A Portrait of Curzon and his Circle in Late Victorian England*. London: Weidenfeld & Nicolson.

Rosenblatt, Daniel. 1997. 'The Antisocial Skin: Structure, Resistance, and "Modern Primitive" Adornment in the United States', *Cultural Anthropology* 12(3): 287–334.

Rouche, Jean. 1955. *Les Maîtres Fous*. Retrieved 30 October 2017 from https://www.youtube.com/watch?v=F3nK5KNzZHc&t=686s.

Sartre, Jean-Paul. 1993. *Essays in Existentialism*, ed. W. Baskin. New York: Citadel.

Schiffauer, Leonie. 2013. 'The Mobile Phone in Siberia: The Impact of a New Communication Technology on the Everyday Culture of a Postsocialist Society', *Zeitschrift für Ethnologie* 138(1): 23–35.

Sherwood, James. 2014. *Savile Row: The Master Tailors of British Bespoke*. London: Thames and Hudson.

Simpson, Mark. 1994. *Male Impersonators: Men Performing Masculinity*. New York: Routledge.

———. 2002. 'Meet the Metrosexual', *Salon*, 22 July. Retrieved 30 October 2017 from https://www.salon.com/2002/07/22/metrosexual/.

———. 2014. 'The Metrosexual is Dead: Long Live the Spornosexual', *The Telegraph Online*, 10 June. Retrieved 30 October 2017 from http://www.telegraph.co.uk/men/fashion-and-style/10881682/The-metrosexual-is-dead.-Long-live-the-spornosexual.html.

Sinanan, Jolynna. 2017. *Social Media in Trinidad: Values and Visibility*. London: UCL Press.

Slater, Don. 1997. 'Integrating Consumption and Leisure: "Hobbies" and the Structures of Everyday Life', European Sociological Association subgroup on the Sociology of Consumption Conference, Essex, 27–31 August.

———. 2000. 'Consumption Without Scarcity: Exchange and Normativity in an Internet Setting', in Peter Jackson et al. (eds), *Commercial Cultures: Economies, Practices, Spaces*. Oxford: Berg, pp. 123–42.

Smith, Graham and Chris Sullivan. 2011. *We Can Be Heroes: London Clubland 1976–1984, Punks, Poseurs, Peacocks and People of a Particular Persuasion*. London: Unbound.

Sontag, Susan. 2008. *On Photography*. London: Penguin Books.

Steele, Valerie. 1997. *Fetish: Fashion, Sex & Power*. Oxford: Oxford University Press.

Stevenson, Nick, Peter Jackson and Kate Brooks. 2000. 'Ambivalence in Men's Lifestyle Magazines', in Peter Jackson et al. (eds), *Commercial Cultures: Economies, Practices, Spaces*. Oxford: Berg, pp. 189–212.

Sunderland, P.L. 1999. 'Fieldwork and the Phone', *Anthropological Quarterly* 72(3): 105–17.

Svašek, Maruska. 2007. 'Moving Corpses: Emotions and Subject-Object Ambiguity', in Helena Wulff (ed.), *The Emotions: A Cultural Reader*. Oxford: Berg, pp. 229–48.

Tise-Isoré, Suzanne (ed.). 2014. *One Savile Row: The Invention of the English Gentleman: Gieves & Hawkes*. Paris: Flammarion.

Trepanier, Dan. 2015. 'The Dandiest Tailor in London Feat. Joshua Kane', *Articles of Style*, 20 March. Retrieved 25 February 2021 from https://articlesofstyle.com/blogs/news/the-dandiest-tailor-in-london-feat-joshua-kane?_pos=1&_sid=4a6e2082a&_ss=r._

Turner, Victor. 1979. 'Dramatic Ritual/Ritual Drama: Performative and Reflexive Anthropology', *The Kenyon Review* 1(3): 80–93.

———. 1980. 'Social Dramas and Stories About Them', *Critical Inquiry* 7(1): 141–68.

Uimonen, Paula. 2016. 'Digital Narratives in Anthropology', in Helena Wulff (ed.), *The Anthropologist as Writer: Genres and Contexts in the Twenty-First Century*. New York: Berghahn, pp. 243–53.

Wacquant, Loïc. 2004. *Body & Soul: Notebooks of an Apprentice Boxer*. Oxford: Oxford University Press.

Wagner, Roy. 1995. 'If You Have the Advertisement You Don't Need the Product', in Debbora Battaglia (ed.), *Rhetorics of Self-Making*. Berkeley: University of California Press, pp. 59–76.

Wolfe, Tom. 1968. *The Kandy-Kolored Tangerine-Flake Streamline Baby*. London: Mayflower Books.

Wood, John C. 2011. 'Field Relations, Field Betrayals', in Sarah H. Davis and Melvin Konner (eds), *Being There: Learning to Live Cross-Culturally*. Cambridge, MA: Harvard University Press, pp. 194–207.

Woodward, Sophie. 2005. 'Looking Good: Feeling Right – Aesthetics of the Self', in Susanne Küchler and Daniel Miller (eds), *Clothing as Material Culture*. Oxford: Berg, pp. 21–39.

Woolf, Virginia. 1927. *To the Lighthouse*. New York: Hogarth Press.

Woolgar, Steve (ed.). 2002. *Virtual Society? Technology, Cyberbole, Reality*. Oxford: Oxford University Press.

Wulff, Helena. 1988. *Twenty Girls: Growing Up, Ethnicity and Excitement in a South London Microculture*. Stockholm: Studies in Social Anthropology.

———. 1998. 'Perspectives Towards Ballet Performance: Exploring, Repairing and Maintaining Frames', in Felicia Hughes-Freeland (ed.), *Ritual, Performance, Media*. London: Routledge, pp. 104–20.

———. 2002. 'Aesthetics at the Ballet: Looking at "National" Style, Body and Clothing in the London Dance World', in Nigel Rapport (ed.), *British Subjects: An Anthropology of Britain*. Oxford: Berg, pp. 67–83.

———. 2008. 'Ethereal Expression: Paradoxes of Ballet as a Global Physical Culture', *Special Issue: Ethnography and Physical Culture* 9(4): 518–35.

———. 2012. 'Instances of Inspiration: Interviewing Dancers and Writers', in Jonathan Skinner (ed.), *The Interview: An Ethnographic Approach*. London: Berg, pp. 163–77.

———. 2015a. 'Anthropologist in the Irish Literary World: Reflexivity Through Studying Sideways', in Thomas Hylland Eriksen, Christina Garsten and Shalini Randeria (eds), *Anthropology Now and Next: Essays in Honor of Ulf Hannerz*. New York: Berghahn, pp. 147–61.

———. 2015b. 'In Favour of Flexible Forms: Multi-Sited Fieldwork', in the section 'Forum: Rethinking Euro-Anthropology'. *Social Anthropology* 23(3): 355–57.

Yi'En, Cheng. 2014. 'Telling Stories of the City: Walking Ethnography, Affective Materialities, and Mobile Encounters', *Space and Culture* 17(3): 211–23.

Zenker, Olaf and Karsten Kumoll (eds). 2010. *Beyond Writing Culture: Current Intersections of Epistemologies and Representational Practices*. New York: Berghahn.

Index

Lightning Source UK Ltd.
Milton Keynes UK
UKHW021545280422
402157UK00003B/327